Otto Gierke

Associations and Law

THE CLASSICAL AND EARLY CHRISTIAN STAGES

George Heiman has translated the discussion of classical and early Christian laws of association from the major work by Otto Gierke, *Das deutsche Genossenschaftsrecht*. This work complements F.W. Maitland's translation of a later part under the title, *The Political Theories of the Middle Ages*, and E. Barker's translation of the third part, *Natural Law and the Theory of Society, 1500–1800*. Professor Heiman thus has completed the circle in bringing into English the eminent German jurist's historical analysis of the law.

Professor Heiman furthermore has introduced the work with a substantial, detailed, and scholarly essay on Gierke's work as a whole. He examines and explains Gierke's concept of the group-person and his organic view of the association, society, and the state, and clearly outlines the conflict between individualist Roman and collectivist Germanic law. This introduction provides the first complete analysis in English of the philosophy of a major representative of the school of historical law and a jurist whose thinking is reflected in the general civil code adopted in Germany at the end of the nineteenth century. The book will interest political and social theorists as well as those concerned with jurisprudence and legal philosophy.

GEORGE HEIMAN is a member of the Department of Political Economy at the University of Toronto.

Otto Gierke
Associations and Law

THE CLASSICAL AND EARLY CHRISTIAN STAGES

edited and translated by

GEORGE HEIMAN

with an interpretative introduction to Gierke's thought

UNIVERSITY OF TORONTO PRESS
Toronto and Buffalo

Toronto and Buffalo
Printed in Canada

Library of Congress Cataloging in Publication Data

Gierke, Otto Friedrich von, 1841-1921.
Associations and law.

Translation of sections 3-5 of Die Staats - und Korporationslehre des Altertums und des Mittelalters und ihre Aufnahme in Deutschland, which was originally issued as v. 3 of Das deutsche Genossenschaftsrecht.
Includes bibliographical references and index.
1. Cooperative societies - Germany - Law. I. Heiman, George, 1926-
Title Law 346'.43'0668 76-48741
ISBN 0-8020-5378-5

This book has been published during the
Sesquicentennial year of the University of Toronto

Contents

Acknowledgments

I wish to thank the Canada Council and the Research Administration of the University of Toronto for grants that helped in the preparation of this volume. I am also indebted to Professors W.F. Berns, M. Sage, and E.J. Weinrib for their advice. The book has been published with the help of grants from the Social Science Research Council of Canada, using funds provided by the Canada Council, and from the University of Toronto Press, using funds provided by the Mellon Foundation.

INTRODUCTION

1

The Nature of Associations and Fellowships

In the year 1900 F.W. Maitland published his translation of Otto Gierke's 'Die publicistischen Lehren des Mittelalters' under the title *Political Theories of the Middle Ages.*[1] The work itself represents section eleven of volume three of Gierke's great work, *Das deutsche Genossenschaftsrecht* (*German Law of Fellowships*).[2] As the title indicates, Maitland's work is an attempt to summarize the political thought of the Middle Ages. It is only partially successful in its endeavour for there are many aspects of mediaeval political theory that are not adequately dealt with. Then in 1934 Ernest Barker translated sections fourteen to eighteen inclusive of volume four of Gierke's *Genossenschaftsrecht*, under the title *Natural Law and the Theory of Society, 1500 to 1800*, which carries Gierke's discussion into the modern age. Yet this work, as the translator claims,[3] while being a complement of Maitland's book, is, in all other respects, a separate and independent one.

The present book is an attempt to complete the circle by returning to Gierke's treatment of associations and corporations in classical antiquity and early Christianity. It is also an endeavour to familiarize the English-speaking reader with Gierke's legal philosophy centred on the concept of the group-person, the fellowship (*Genossenschaft*), and the position of the association in a modern 'state of laws' (*Rechtsstaat*). Barker, in his admirable introduction, discusses some of these issues but, possibly owing to the absence of some of Gierke's other publications, never carried the examination to its full conclusion. This work tries to remedy that condition, though without claiming to represent all of Gierke's thought. Thus, for instance, the legal applications of the theory of fellowship in modern German law, as expounded by Gierke in his *Fellowship Theory and the German Adminis-*

1 Cambridge, 1900 (hereafter cited as *Political Theories*).

2 Berlin, 1868, 1873, 1881, 1913 (hereafter *Genossenschaftsrecht*).

3 E. Barker, 'Introduction' to Gierke, *Natural Law and the Theory of Society*, Cambridge, 1934, p. ix (hereafter *Natural Law*).

tration of Justice[4] are utilized only to illustrate his theoretical postulates. The discussion of their application is not entered into, for the simple reason that what was 'modern' law to Gierke has now been transcended by more recent theories and practices.

What will be examined here are some relevant aspects of the *Genossenschaftsrecht* as well as such writings as *The Nature of Human Associations*,[5] *Principles of Constitutional Law*,[6] *Natural Law and German Law*,[7] and *The School of Historical Law and the Germanists*.[8] In these essays and lectures Gierke expounds his views in the most direct and unequivocal fashion, a practice he does not always adhere to in the *Genossenschaftsrecht*. It is in the former writings that Gierke takes his reader most directly into the realm of the group-person – the assumption of its unity of life, the organic view of the association, society, and the state, and his theory of the reality of the group-person. It is noteworthy that the *Genossenschaftsrecht* is written in a manner that assumes that its reader and student is fully conversant and in agreement with the above legal postulates, which are therefore not explained in great detail in all cases.

Yet to appreciate Gierke's exposition of the theory of corporations and associations in classical antiquity and early Christianity, a reader has to keep his specific bias in mind. Thus, if he is critical of Roman corporatism, he bases his attack upon the specific Germanic and German experience. If he finds the Roman associative spirit and practice wanting, then that is due to his own preference for the theory of the living organic group as distinct from the theory of the *persona ficta*, the fictitious personality of Roman law. Despite the bias, however, Gierke's presentation of ancient associative practices is illuminating, for it presents in a concise and comprehensive fashion the major aspects of the subject. If Gierke is critical, then the bases of his criticism have to be made known. If he is concise and comprehensive, then we may profit from Gierke's tremendous talent for synthesis and vast erudition. But, above all, we must remember that Gierke speaks in a legal, philosophic, and historical tradition that is not always and in all instances familiar to the English-speaking reader. For this reason we propose to start the introduction with an examination of Gierke's fundamental work, *The Nature of Human Associations.*

In this work Gierke seeks to find the common denominator that animates all human groups, large or small. The task is not that of sociology alone. Jurisprudence too must concern itself with the problem for it is integral to the commun-

4 *Die Genossenschaftstheorie und die deutsche Rechtssprechung*, Berlin, 1887.

5 *Das Wesen der menschlichen Verbände*, Berlin, 1902 (hereafter *Wesen*).

6 *Die Grundbegriffe des Staatsrechts*, Tübingen, 1915 (hereafter *Grundbegriffe*).

7 *Naturrecht und deutsches Recht*, Frankfurt, 1883 (hereafter *Naturrecht*).

8 *Die historische Rechtsschule und die Germanisten*, Berlin, 1903.

ity. Moreover, jurisprudence must display a degree of historical perceptiveness in its approach to the subject. Only in that manner can it understand the life of the subsidiary groups, fellowships, associations, and corporations and thereby keep in touch with its own true sources. Indeed, legal science is obliged to consider the relationships between the various groups for they constitute the life of the body politic. Thus the legal order does not only regulate the life of individuals but represents the life of the state, church, communities, and various groups.[9] Equally important is the contention that all groups be treated, by positive law, as juristic persons. Like any individual, these group-persons have both rights and duties, and this fact is fundamental to the understanding of the reality that is incorporated in their existence.

In advocating these issues Gierke contradicts the theories of what he calls the individualistic conception of society. This school, predominant in the Age of Enlightenment, viewed society as being based upon a contract between isolated individuals. The trend culminated in Rousseau's thought that divided the social body into a centralized machinery of state and a mass of atomized free and equal human beings. 'The sovereign state and the sovereign individual allied themselves against the corporation,'[10] Gierke claims. No room was left for the organic intermediary bodies that could have served as mediating links between the one and the many. On the legal side, the individualistic theory maintained that the juristic person was no more than a fictitious creation brought forth for certain specific purposes. The act of creation, and particularly its compulsory recognition by the state, conceded an artificial and inorganic existence to its members. This theory is rejected by Gierke.

A person, individual or communal, cannot be a creation out of nothing; it cannot stand for a contrived, artificial unity; nor is it a synthetic being resembling Faust's *homunculus.*[11] Equally fallacious is the idea propounded by the individualistic theory of society that only single individuals but not groups can be endowed with a personality. The assumption that only the isolated single individual is capable of acting and willing in an independent manner robs the group of its juristic personality. But, as Gierke sees it, historical and social reality do not support these views.

He declares that ascribing a fictitious personality to the group leads to the erection of a false and nebulous image. Here the group is viewed as incapable of action and will and placed in the same category as children and the mentally retarded, who require a guardian or a spokesman.[12] When the inadequacies of this

9 *Wesen*, p. 7.
10 *Naturrecht*, pp. 28-9.
11 *Wesen*, p. 9.
12 *Ibid.*

theory became obvious to the school of historical law, there were demands to do away with the concept of the *persona ficta* entirely. What use was there for such a 'bloodless spectre' and 'lifeless scarecrow'? By eliminating these apparitions, social life could be viewed in its true context, solely as a complex of relationships between isolated individuals and inorganic groups. Even the personality of the most pre-eminent association, the state, was denied. It is these views which Gierke most positively rejects.

After many disputes, the teachings of the school of historical law[13] came to be accepted in Germany. This school, and Gierke was one of its foremost protagonists, maintained that the organized group had an independent personality of its own. The state's personality, which had been denied by the proponents of absolutism, whether of monarchical or radical populist hue, was recognized. Similarly, the reality of the personality of the association, large or small, could not be denied any longer. The essence of the individual did not disappear when he entered into an association with other persons. Rather than creating a nebulous, fictitious entity whose existence could be easily denied, the group represented a real living being.[14] Human associations were seen by Gierke, and his followers, as actual organic unities that ultimately received the legal recognition that was their due.

This view was merely the formal acknowledgment of the thesis that human communal existence was a process of a higher order that absorbed but did not eliminate individual life and ambition. True communal existence could not be represented as a haphazard collection of individuals banded together in a mechanistic fashion – an eighteenth-century view which was transcended by the nineteenth-century interest in the community, the *Volk*, the indigenous language and art, and, above all, the native customary law. Thus the essential importance of the concept of the organic community and its articulated subsidiary members and groups was recognized and placed in proper perspective. Fichte[15] and Hegel[16] had led the way in philosophy and the school of historical law added the juristic dimensions, while the emerging 'young science of the history of culture, the psychology of peoples, and comprehensive sociology'[17] added their share to the new trend.

In the late nineteenth century the process resulted in the conviction that a legally ordered whole (*Gesammtheit*) is an entity that possesses a real unity and that this unity has to be accepted and dealt with by jurisprudence. Recognition

13 See below, pp. 56 ff.
14 *Wesen*, p. 12.
15 *Ibid.*, p. 13.
16 *Ibid.*, p. 14.
17 *Ibid.*

has to be accorded to the assumption – indeed the fact, as Gierke sees it – that the association, like an individual, has a material and spiritual unity of life. Law arranges and penetrates this inner unity, and hence the inner structure of the group,[18] but it does not serve as its source. The association, or group, is a living entity characterized by the relationship between the unity of the whole and the multiplicity of its parts. The relationship is guided by the manifestations of the human will. Every group has a real and independent communal life, a conscious will, and an ability to act that are distinct from the lives and wills of its individual members. Thus group-life exists side by side with individual life, not divided into a separate sphere, but inextricably bound to it. An organic tie links the two entities, a tie that is as basic and fundamental as life itself.

The organic theory of state and society reflects these ideas. The organic analogy is tempting and our language abounds in examples of it. Thus we speak of the 'social body,' the corporation (*Körperschaft*), the 'head' and 'members' of an association, its organs, and an 'organic ordering of parts.'[19] The organic theory also borrows heavily from the theological realm. The notion of the church as the mystic body of Christ and the organic interdependence of its parts led to the view of the church as a vast institutionalized organism consisting of a single head and a multitude of related integral members.[20] Leaving the theological realm eventually, the organic theory was transferred by mediaeval thinkers into the political sphere. Not only the religious but the temporal community was analogously compared to a composite body endowed with a ruling member, the head, and a multitude of integral parts that served to make up the body politic. But the analogy is not without its dangers and Gierke is aware of them.

Gierke admits that an analogy is, at best, a comparison that can serve to clarify issues but cannot fully explain them.[21] Thus the organic theory is abused when the state is seen as representing the male sex while the church is envisaged as representing the female sex.[22] Equally fallacious is the tendency to adhere too closely to examples derived from the natural sciences. To view the social body as a purely natural phenomenon and to examine its anatomy and psychology with the methods of the pure natural sciences is a futile enterprise. Such an approach is too mechanistic for it disregards the spiritual and ethical life that is part of human communal existence. The observation of plant and animal life may be valid in itself, but its findings cannot automatically be applied to the social organism

18 *Ibid.*, p. 15.

19 *Ibid.*, p. 16.

20 See below, pp. 145 ff.

21 *Wesen*, p. 16.

22 This theory was advocated by J.K. Bluntschli in his *Lehre vom modernen Staat*, 1876, (*The Theory of the State*, D.G. Ritchie, et al., transl., Oxford, 1892, p. 23).

whose members are free human beings endowed with will.[23] To understand the organic theory correctly, one must realize that the comparison can go no further than to argue that the social body has a living unity of its own and that it is a totality consisting of diverse living parts. But it must be realized that the inner structure of the whole consists of human beings who are linked by spiritual and not merely by physical and natural bonds. It is precisely at this point that the natural sciences cease to have an impact upon social thought and are replaced by the humanities.

Opponents of the organic theory of the state and society deny that a group can have a life of its own, a life that reaches beyond individual existence. Indeed, they charge the organicists with a form of mysticism. They argue that the physical senses can recognize only individual human beings and whoever ascribes life to the group endows it with transcendental characteristics. But as far as Gierke is concerned, this criticism is not valid. The state, the highest association, as well as the lesser groups that it contains, is endowed with a life arising out of an invisible spiritual bond. This invisibility does not make its life any less real, and there is truly no need to resort to such allegorical figures as Germania[24] or Britannia to verify the state's organic nature. Transcendental, spiritual ties are transformed into legal reality whenever or wherever the assumption is accepted that there is a living whole that is endowed with a unity distinct from the sum total will of its members.

Admittedly, such a distinction transposes the argument into an invisible world, but this world is not necessarily without its own reality.[25] Reality, Gierke maintains, is not limited to material manifestations. Indeed, life, the most basic material manifestation, remains ultimately unexplained and inexplicable, but that does not detract from its reality. The secret of the organism is the secret of life. We may not fully comprehend its origins, but we cannot for this reason deny its existence. Similarly, the actual nature of the concept of unity within a multiplicity remains, ultimately, a secret.[26] Nevertheless, this unity is a social reality that has to be taken into account by jurisprudence. The legitimacy of the organic theory of state and society does not rest upon the ability to explain life and organism in scientific terms but must be accepted simply because they exist and are active in the communal sphere.

In order to support his thesis, Gierke turns to historical precedents. History is a record of the relationships between communities that exert power to attain certain desired aims. Communities consist of individuals but their effectiveness is

23 *Wesen*, p. 18.
24 *Ibid.*, p. 20.
25 *Ibid.*, p. 21.
26 *Ibid.*, p. 22.

based upon the fact that they act in concert in certain given circumstances. In other words, man is influential primarily through his social tendencies and not as an isolated human being. History has known some individuals who changed circumstances on their own volition. Yet even the most eminent of these men were dependent upon a measure of co-operation from their community. Their society had to be receptive to their ideas and leadership, and even the most pronounced cult of the hero has to admit that there exists a mutual interdependence between the hero and his community.[27]

Nor are the achievements of a community the result of the sum total of individual attainments. There are such supra-individual manifestations as law, customs, and language. They are not and never were the products of a group of isolated individuals but they are the accomplishments derived from a 'supra-individual unity of life.'[28] This concept is not an absolute existing in isolation. It requires a community, a group, an association, and these, in turn, require constituent individuals. The reality of the community with its supra-individual life is derived from man's consciousness and his associative urge. Thus individuality is never lost but rather re-inforced by its creative associative tendencies. The individual is conscious of his self but he is also aware of the fact that part of his self is transferred to a supra-individual unity of life. It is only through that process that he becomes aware of himself as being part of a greater, living, actual whole.

Man, Gierke argues,[29] would be unrecognizable without his membership in the state, and the *Volk*, his religious affiliations, his vocational groupings, and his other innumerable associations. These ties do not represent mere external links of convenience but relate to man's inner self and stand for the integrative part of man's spiritual essence.[30] No individual, however, can fully encompass the supra-individual unity of life. Yet though he can be only part of the entire unity, he can certainly incorporate part of his self in the social whole. It is this process of integration that produces such communal phenomena as the 'soul of a people' (*Volksseele*), the 'sentiment of a people' (*Volksempfindung*), the 'will of a people' (*Volkswille*), class-consciousness (*Standesgeist*), and family spirit.[31] These living psychological forces contribute to rather than detract from the individual's private essence.

The realm and spiritual content of the group are verified by observing its manifestations. They exert power and influence, play a tangible part in communal life,

27 *Ibid.*, p. 23.
28 *Ibid.*, p. 24.
29 *Ibid.*
30 *Ibid.*, p. 25.
31 *Ibid.*

and thrive whenever they are given the opportunity. But this remains an observation of existing, tangible forces and is not a verification of a scientific fact. Ultimately, Gierke admits, 'The mystery of the real nature of this unity of life (*Lebenseinheit*) remains undiscovered.'[32] Fantasy plays a role and, in the final analysis, faith in the supra-individual unity of life is required. There are demands for metaphysical explanations that do not disappear in the light of natural and empirical sciences; and faith, bolstered by metaphysical speculations, accounts for the inner life and unity of the group. The task of jurisprudence is, so far as Gierke is concerned, to translate this faith into legal practice. It must ascribe to the concept of the group-person attributes which are not immediately discernible and visible yet whose existence is an undisputed fact. Whenever an association appears as a legally ordered whole and is accepted as a juristic person, legal science must consider the social, real, supra-individual unity contained in that body. Thus the problem raised by the concept of a juristic person is not a moot one and is not really confined to jurisprudence alone. Its implications are wider.

'The systematic foundation of law, the form and content of its most important ideas, and the resolution of numerous very practical questions are dependent upon the construction of the personality of association.'[33] The organic approach is the most appropriate method through which an understanding of the reality of the associative person can be arrived at. Despite some of its obvious fallacies, recognized by Gierke himself, he clings to the organic analogy as the most useful and penetrating one. Law has to accept the existence of a force, an urge, a stream of consciousness that has to be placed into a legal context. But the implications of this associative urge go beyond the law and indeed precede its appearance. Moreover, the observable manifestations are but one side of the coin. Faith, as he himself said, is required to appreciate the forces of the supra-individual unity of life that animates the group.

It follows that associative law touches upon both the inner core of the individual and the life of the group-person. Both are living entities that must be recognized as subjects of law, capable of holding and manipulating rights. Law, moreover, must recognize a fundamental duality in human nature: an autonomous self and, simultaneously, part of a higher whole. This dual nature is reflected in the existence of law as it pertains strictly to the individual and a body of law that Gierke calls 'social law' (*Sozialrecht*).[34] There are concepts in this social law that have no counterpart in the law concerned with individuals. Social law is divided into public and constitutional law, and these categories concern themselves with

32 *Ibid*., p. 26.
33 *Ibid*., p. 28.
34 *Ibid*.

the composition of the entire social body and the group-persons that belong to it.[35] The legal pronouncements of social law focus upon the links between the constituent groups, their mutual relationships among themselves, as well as their ties to the highest association, the state. Above all, social law verifies and declares the real unity of life contained in the groups and determines the conditions according to which the members of the groups and the groups themselves become organic parts of the whole. Care must be taken that this unification not be looked upon as a process of concession in the manner of the theory of the *persona ficta*. The life of the groups and their inner unity is not derived from the law. The latter, as said, merely acts in a declamatory fashion even though it does have a supervisory role. Social law does not, in other words, promulgate but merely verifies and guards the life of the groups.

Because of the complexity of modern society, a variety of different and complex norms serve to determine the legal nature and number of the multitudinous organs. The limits of their competence have to be established and their relationships to the higher organs have to be regulated. Social law also assists in the formation of associations, encourages them in their process of organizing and observes the relationships between the individual members and their group. But social law is based upon the premise of organicism, and the 'legal concepts that pertain to the organism are of a specific nature and may not be equated with the idea of representation derived from individualistic law.'[36] Social law is not interested in the representation of the single isolated person. Rather, it concerns itself with the manifestation of the living unity of the whole, an organic entity that speaks for the invisible but nevertheless real personality of the group.

Indubitably, the individual is the basic element of the group. But he is already well represented by a core of law that deals with the relationships between individuals. Social law concerns itself with the real personality of groups which have an actual essence like any individual. Being an organic and integral, willing and acting subject under the law, the juristic person does not require a legal guardian to make itself heard in the realm of social law. According to the latter, the group acts independently and is endowed with its own body of rights. Consequently it is also capable of committing offences and is therefore liable to be held responsible for them. Regardless of the size of its membership, the group, under social law, is held collectively responsible and is treated as a legal adult in every respect.

Moreover, it is important not to consider the group as being based upon a contract between solitary individuals. Rather, social law envisages the formation of

35 *Ibid.*, p. 29.
36 *Ibid.*, p. 30.

a common will and a 'common hand' springing from the relevant, that is the associative, parts of the human will.[37] All associations are derived from and lead to the formation of an independent living unity that is not contractual but organic. The common will to form and enter into a group is not the result of linking external individual wills into a social body but is the expression of an inner unity contained in human nature as well as in the nature of the organic group. The resulting association, then, is not a mere legal agglomeration of delegated and represented wills. Rather, it is the sum total of associative tendencies in man that lead to a more comprehensive and real unity than any attainable by a mere contract. Thus, 'the free act of wills that produces an associative person is not a contract but a creative communal act.'[38]

Based upon these premises, social law can organize the relationships between members of groups and between groups. Hence there are legal provisions for persons who are members of groups, laws that regulate the property of the groups, laws referring to the election practices within the groups, and even laws pertaining to the hereditary monarch, the head of the most pre-eminent association, the state. One of the most important tasks of social law is the incorporation of the lower groups into this 'sovereign communal being.'[39] But 'incorporation' is not to be understood as total absorption but rather as a legal ordering of the organic members of the body politic. Indeed, the inner life of the member-groups gain additional dimensions and legal significance in that they can exert their influence upon the sovereign entity.

The state represents the 'sovereign plenitude of powers' (*souveräne Machtvollkommenheit*)[40] and is subject to a law of a higher order. But the state does not exist in isolation from social law either.[41] Certain groups of paramount public importance, such as the judiciary and the legislative bodies for instance, are admitted to the realm of the state's law, that is to the realm of constitutional law. And besides the state's law there is the law of associations, or social law, that pertains to such huge groups as the church and local communities. Every single social being, whether it is the sovereign state or a local group of vocationally linked men, has its own concrete legal individuality and a corresponding body of special privileges (*Sonderrechte*). The groups are so numerous that an enumeration of their privileges could lead one to the conclusion that they lack a common denominator. Yet social law does have a common principle, and that is the organic conception of the groups and the conviction that all these groups have a real

37 *Ibid.*, p. 31.
38 *Ibid.*, pp. 32-3.
39 *Ibid.*
40 *Ibid.*, p. 33.
41 See below, pp. 42 ff.

inner unity of life of their own. Viewed in this light, then, law can be seen as but one, and not necessarily the most important, manifestation of communal life.[42] Since it expresses only one side of this life, law must therefore remember its limitations. These limitations become evident upon observation of the action of social organisms. Such organisms exert power and represent cultural factors that are extra-legal if not illegal. They emerge independent of law and indeed sometimes in contradiction to law.[43] Group-formation and group-activity then are basic and elemental forces that law, whether it be social or constitutional, has to learn to accommodate.

Jurisprudence has to accept two major assumptions. One, the real unity of the community is of ethical significance that transcends if not obliterates individualistic enterprise. Second, the community, the association, the group, has a value of its own.[44] Man's ethical duty is therefore derived from two sources. He acts and wills as a free moral agent partially in isolation but also partially in conjunction with a group. In the case of the highest association, the state, it is his duty to devote part or even his entire life to it if conditions so require. The tenet 'love thy neighbour as thyself' is the most appropriate guideline for relations between individuals. On a communal level, however, Gierke argues,[45] the command ought to be, 'love the whole more than thyself.' But this idea is valid only if the whole, the community, is indeed a higher and ethically more valuable entity than a mere sum of haphazardly aggregated individuals. The nature of the human association, the proper human association, Gierke concludes, is that it can be an ethical whole, carefully articulated into an organic order with a legal system that allows for and encourages the associative tendencies of man. Above all, it recognizes the supra-individual unity of life inherent in the group.

In the light of Gierke's exposition of the nature of the human associations it comes as no surprise that he declares, 'Whatever man has accomplished is due to his association with other men.'[46] It is obvious from the foregoing examination that nothing is as important to Gierke than the recognition of the impact of man's group-activities. Indeed, is has been argued that in order to support his thesis, Gierke interposes a third realm of law between private and constitutional law; this third realm he calls social law and he sees it as completing and furthering the juridical and social image of the political community.[47] There may be consider-

42 *Wesen*, p. 34.
43 *Ibid.*
44 *Ibid.*, p. 35.
45 *Ibid.*, pp. 35-6.
46 *Genossenschaftsrecht.* I, p. 1.
47 G. Jellinek, *Allgemeine Staatslehre*, Bad Homburg, 3rd ed., 1928, p. 106.

able truth to this observation. As Gierke's discussion of social law indicates, law is not and cannot be the creation of a single will, that of a monarch or of a collective group of haphazardly contracted individuals, but is the result of man's natural associative tendencies and the relationships between the groups that make up the body politic. Law is thus not external to the social process but becomes its creature and even its servant. Law may be supreme in the type of 'state of laws' (*Rechtsstaat*) that Gierke wishes to attain but it is not imposed upon social reality. The modern state, particularly if it permits the unhindered formation of groups, becomes a complex and, at times, bewildering composite of contending factions and interests.

Given this reality, it is not impossible to envisage the origins and existence of a law derived from and concerned with the interaction between the various groups. The source of the law is the individual will but also the distinctive will of the group. Gierke does not disagree with the conception of the distinctness and supremacy of the individual will in a specific realm of the law. He goes further and proceeds from the strictly individualistic to the social origins of law. He never denies that law is, in parts at least, the result of individual wills; but no will, he contends, can remain in isolation if it is going to exert itself effectually. The will of a person, understood in this instance in both the psychological and legal senses, needs an object upon which it can impose itself. If nothing else, it needs verification of its existence by other wills. To put it bluntly, a will in the absence of other wills is not a will at all. Legal and social verification and even legitimization are required before circumstances can reflect the urges and wishes of the will.

It is, moreover, unlikely that the individual will can have a measurable impact upon modern society and state under normal circumstances. The odds against the single, unassociated will making itself felt are too great. Therefore the possessor of the individual will is obliged, partly through necessity and partly by his inclinations, to seek some group or another. Whether this group is the imposing association of the state or a lesser group such as a trade union is not important. What matters, according to Gierke, is the satisfaction of man's associative instinct and the rational advantages gained by joining an association. This would be nothing more than a mere acknowledgment of an existing condition if it were not for the fact that Gierke derives his concept of social law from this process. It can be argued, of course, that ultimately all law is social and that generally speaking laws are made not for individuals but for society and its constituent groups. But Gierke's theory is that the process points to two legal centres of legal existence, the individual and the associated sides of human personality. These two elements, moreover, serve to produce a third centre of social power, the will of the association or group.

It is very significant that Gierke does not claim that social law can and will resolve all the difficulties inherent in individual as well as communal existence. There is a sphere where no group, be it the state or any lesser association, can intrude. This is the sphere of inner, private man which is confirmed rather than threatened by social law. On the other hand, the demands of social law are more exhaustive than those of a private or even constitutional law. In joining a group – that is a proper group with its own supra-individual unity of life – the individual transfers part of his living inner self to the group. Only in that manner can the group attain a real life of its own. This is a much more severe demand and also a thesis that is ultimately based upon an act of faith. In discussing this issue, Gierke admits that the organic tie which is supposed to link the members of the appropriate group cannot be derived from the natural sciences. Nor can it be logically deduced as being the sum total of individual wills, banded together for a specific purpose in the manner of the Roman *universitas*. The narrow interpretation of the group is not accepted by Gierke for it rejects the reality and the life inherent in the group. This life cannot be denied, for it is a segment of an organic personality that transferred part of itself to the group. The process is a transference of a real manifestation and the result is a real living entity. It is not a fictitious spectre nor is its essence merely conceded to it. Social law is exclusively concerned with the real inner unity of the groups and their relationships and in this aspect it differs from other bodies of law. There are, however, some difficulties inherent in this theory.

The existence of groups, whether they are called fellowships, associations, or corporations in the Italo-Roman sense of the word, cannot be denied. It is, however, not necessary to share Gierke's act of faith that ascribes a real organic life to the groups. It is indubitably true that in joining a group the individual sacrifices a portion of his freedom in order to attain certain ends. In this respect, and in this respect only, Gierke's scheme resembles Rousseau's speculation about the contractual relationship between individual and state. Rousseau argues that 'What man loses by the social contract is his natural liberty and an unlimited right to everything ... what he gains is civil liberty and the proprietorship of all he possesses.'[48] While Gierke most definitely rejects the contract theory as the basis for his associations, large or small, he too has to come to terms with the loss of freedom that is the price an individual pays for joining a group. Gierke resolves the issue by establishing the two realms of legal existence, individual and associative, and endowing the latter with an independent life of its own. In view of the assumption that the group is the creation of the associative part of human nature, it cannot detract from but indeed adds to its dimension of individual freedom.

48 J.-J. Rousseau, *The Social Contract*, G.D.H. Cole, transl., London, 1913, Bk. I, chap. 8.

To Gierke, men's will and right to associate are so fundamental that they appear almost as a natural law,[49] a basic human attribute and a fundamental expression of individuality. The historical verification of his thesis in the four volumes of the *Genossenschaftsrecht* is impressive indeed and at times overwhelming, for he sees every appropriate human agglomeration as an example of the natural spirit of associative tendency. His concept of freedom, then, is bound to the free expression of the associative instinct and a careful balance between individualistic aims and the goals of the whole. Freedom is primarily a harmony between the contending forces of individualism and group-life, guarded by the positive laws of the *Rechtsstaat*. This community is the result of organic and historic forces that lead towards Gierke's conception of freedom. Essentially it is a freedom under the law, but its specific nature consists of the assumption that part of this law is produced by group-entities which have a life of their own. It is significant that the notion of the supra-individual unity of life is ultimately based on faith, for therein may lie the weakest link of Gierke's theory.

Gierke may be on firm ground when he perceives and argues for the reality of the associative urge and its historical importance. The premise that man is a social and political animal and that it is natural for him to live in association with his fellow men has, despite Hobbes, never been seriously refuted. Moreover, the complexities of the modern state can naturally lead to the formation of groups, provided that the political climate is sympathetic to such an evolution. But not even Aristotle, with his deep involvement in the natural teleological process of life, suggested that his most pre-eminent association, the *polis*, had or could have a supra-individual unity of life of its own. Both ancient and modern juristic and political thought lack Gierke's faith, and therefore it becomes a matter of either sharing his faith or rejecting it. Indubitably, most men are of an associative nature. Undeniably, modern society is divided into sociological, economic, and legal groups. But it is hard to accept, as an act of faith, that these groups have a reality, a life, a will, and a capacity to act in the manner of living, rational beings.

The question of reality, Gierke's reality, is of paramount importance. If reality consists only of those facts and ideas that can be empirically verified, then the independent life of the associations is as fictitious as the *persona ficta* of Italo-Roman law. Gierke's conception of reality, however, includes the transcendental realm where empirical speculation yields to Hegelian idealism. In making references to such notions as the 'soul of a people' (*Volksseele*) and 'conviction of a people' (*Volksüberzeugung*) and in classifying them as living social forces, Gierke places himself in the ranks of those idealists who had accepted these romantic notions. It is also a clear indication that Gierke belongs to the school of historical

49 *Naturrecht*, p. 29.

law that encompassed a good many of the idealist and romantic concepts of their predecessors. Thus Gierke's reality is derived from historical and idealist rather than rationalist roots.

The question then arises whether Gierke's understanding of reality provides an adequate and acceptable source of law, or, in other words, can faith in somewhat nebulous concepts provide the basis for social law? The answer can only be a qualified 'yes.' The qualification demands recognition of Gierke's tradition and school of thought which are distinct from the rationalist and empiricist schools. He thought that he found reality in such concepts as *Volk, Volksgeist* ('spirit of a people'), and an idealized version of the *Gemeinschaft* ('community'). He utilized them to refer to, if not empirically prove, the supra-individual unity of life inherent in the groups. So long as Gierke is not removed from his realm and quoted out of context, his position is secure. Moreover, the romantic and idealist approach to law had a very real and tangible influence upon the followers of the school of historical law who, in turn, contributed to the establishment of the general civil code in Germany.

It must also be noted that Gierke's conception of reality is supported by a very substantial dose of juristic sobriety. It is not idealistic to apportion powers to the groups of which the body politic is composed. To envisage the forces exerted by the groups in an appropriately organized *Rechtsstaat*, where every segment is assigned its own sphere of rights and duties on a constitutional basis, is not blind idealism. Above all, to advocate the thesis that law is the result of social relationships as they develop over history is far from being a fantasy. Finally, it is a realistic expectation that such a body of social law will not be inimical to the interest and ambitions of the individuals and the groups that make up the totality. Coercion alone cannot be the basis of law, for, as it has been argued, 'Law presupposes ideas, however rudimentary, of justice.'[50] But justice, the concept presumably animating the institution and administration of law, is in itself a contentious principle when viewed in a strictly empiricist light. It is not a tangible and observable scientific fact but is derived from the realm of ideas. Nevertheless, a certain confidence, if not necessarily faith, in this concept serves to elicit the voluntary co-operation of citizens. There may be innumerable interpretations of the concept of justice starting with the first book of Plato's *Republic* and ending with the positivist school of jurisprudence. But if society is to function on at least a partially voluntary basis, there must be present a measure of conviction, however remote and ill-defined, that justice is the measure of the law. Such a view may again approach the realm of faith, yet a conviction, some form of consensus, or a generally held opinion are tangible factors of political existence. Thus

50 Sir F. Pollock, *Jurisprudence and Legal Essays*, London, 1961, p. 17.

Gierke's attempt to make his readers share his faith in the living unity of the organic group may be no more unrealistic than the expectation that every proper state lives according to some principles of justice, however nebulous that concept may be.

As for Gierke's organicism. He himself has indicated the fallacies in which theory can culminate. Yet he remains a firm follower of the theory, and one can argue that whether we call them 'organic bonds' or the 'interaction of social groups' within the body politic, there are some psychological, non-material forces that contribute to the cohesion of the legally constituted whole. Perhaps he expresses too much confidence in the social, associative tendencies of man and neglects the asocial sides of human nature. But as the spokesman for the importance, indeed paramount importance, of the association Gierke cannot be expected to place too much emphasis on the first part of what has been called man's 'asocial sociability.'[51] His major interest centres upon the legal ramifications of the association and its real living unity. Among all the associations or groups that he examines, there is one that stands out, and that is the Germanic and German fellowship.

In keeping with his vocation, that of a protagonist of the Germanist wing of the school of historical law,[52] Gierke wants to establish a whole new system of law that takes into account the importance of the subsidiary groups within society. This 'new theory was to be philosophically true, morally righteous, legally implicit in codes and decisions, practically convenient, historically destined, genuinely German, and perhaps exclusively Germanistic.'[53] The core of the new doctrine revolves around the contention of the real unity of life inherent in the group as exemplified by the fellowship but also by the appropriate corporation and association. Indeed, Gierke uses the terms almost interchangeably, although 'corporation' (*Körperschaft*) is usually reserved for the collective bodies within Roman and Italo-Roman law. The term *Verband*, or association, is used in the widest sense of that term. The fellowship is an association also but it has some special connotations. It has been described, perhaps somewhat poetically, as 'the company of brothers, linked by the right hand of fellowship, and knit together by a spirit of fraternity, who pursued the common interest of the group (whether based on profession, or occupation, or the simple foundation of voluntary association), and vindicated its common honour with a common ardour.'[54] It is so

51 I. Kant, 'Idee zu einer allgemeinen Geschichte in weltbürgerlicher Absicht,' *Kleinere Schriften*, Hamburg, 1959, p. 9.

52 See below, pp. 56 ff.

53 Maitland, 'Introduction,' *Political Theories*, p. xxv.

54 Barker, 'Introduction,' *Natural Law*, p. lviii.

fundamentally Germanic that Barker is prepared to trace its origin back into the Hercynian forest, to Tacitus and the appearance of the tribal kin-group.[55] Indubitably Gierke is thinking of the fellowship as something fundamental to the Germanic development, as something produced specifically by his early antecedents. Yet when it comes to the definition of the fellowship, juristic thought prevails over romantic and historic imagination. He says, 'A fellowship is a German legal corporation [*Körperschaft*] founded upon [the idea] of free association; that is [it is] an association endowed with an autonomous legal personality.'[56]

The definition exemplifies Gierke's challenge to the Roman system. It contains the demand for the free right to associate without help or hindrance from the state. It further indicates that the concession theory according to which the associations or groups were brought into being and existed at the sufferance of the state is valid no longer. The fellowship and every other appropriate association in accord with his definition is not the result of a unilateral legislative act but a natural phenomenon rooted in the associative or 'fellowship-instincts' of a generic group or a people. These instincts express themselves in social forces that lead to the establishment of social law. Thus, *Genossenschaftsrecht*, or the law of fellowships, is the law that originates in these associative tendencies of man. It rejects the Roman corpus of law which clung to the assumption of the *persona ficta*, the concession theory, and the separation of the individual from public law and which above all denied the organic nature of associations and with it that of fellowships.

The basis of the German fellowship's existence lies in itself. It has its own *raison d'être*, its own independence, and its own will. Like any individual it enters law as an ethical and free being that exists and wills for itself and is recognized as such by the law.[57] The notions of an artificial personality and the concessive legitimization of the association were, originally, entirely alien to Germanic law. Only when Roman law was imposed upon the native law did these notions take hold. The essence of the fellowship, however, was not lost, though it did suffer at the hands of Roman jurisprudence. But the free right to associate and the reality of the group-person and its supra-individual unity of life were not forgotten. Indeed it was resurrected by Gierke and his collaborators. What could not be disregarded was the contention that the formation of fellowships preceded the formation of the state. Its roots actually reached back into the distant past when the idea of the German state was simply non-existent.

55 *Ibid.*
56 *Genossenschaftsrecht*, I, p. 5.
57 *Ibid.*, II, p. 867.

Nor is the fellowship a creation of the law. The latter merely confirms what was spontaneously and perhaps unconsciously created by historical forces and circumstances. For this reason, the fellowship can look to the law for confirmation but not for legitimization. It has, as Gierke argued, its own *raison d'être* and, theoretically, does not require a *lex specialis* issued by the state. At best, the state enters in a supervisory capacity,[58] but it cannot create what existed before its own inception. The state has to recognize the fellowship's ability to act and to will of its own volition[59] and the fact, or the assumption, that the fellowship is the creation of independent individual wills whose existence precedes the appearance of the state.

Yet under more advanced social conditions, it is necessary that a process of recognition, if not legitimization, be extended to fellowships.[60] No modern society can have its subsidiary groups functioning in a haphazard manner that disregards the legal implications of their existence. Fellowships, like any other legal associations, enter into legal relationships, they own and manipulate property, enter law suits, contracts, and accompanying obligations, and these issues are subject to legal supervision. But it is more important to realize that the fellowship is a 'united multiplicity of persons that can be envisaged as a united whole and a collective unity.'[61]

The explanation for this somewhat convoluted formula is relatively simple. Gierke, as we have said, rejects the contract theory. His fellowship and appropriate association are based upon the transference of part of an individual's essence to the group. However, the individual is not obliterated in this process but remains a rightbearing (*rechtsfähig*) person despite the transference. Thus the fellowship is a multiplicity of persons. But it is also more than that. It is a thoroughly integrated body, a group much more intimately linked than any aggregation based upon a mere contract. For the act of unification produces a communal unity whose strength rests in its organic nature as well as in the fact that it is diverse while still united. Its diversity emanates from the multiplicity of the human natures it encompasses. Its unity rests upon the fact, or assumption, that the act of union creates an independent personality, that of the group itself.

The origin of the fellowships can be divided into two related categories. First, there was the fellowship as a naturally and historically produced fact. The free will of its members did not create but rather imparted a form to their fellowship, whether it was an ancient independent rural fellowship (*Markgenossenschaft*), a

58 Gierke, *Die Genossenschaftstheorie und die deutsche Rechtssprechung*, Berlin, 1887, p. 652 (hereafter *Genossenschaftstheorie*).

59 *Ibid.*, p. 9.

60 *Ibid.*, p. 18.

61 *Ibid.*, p. 343.

dike-association, or a fellowship centred on a common pastorage.[62] Reacting to certain exigencies, these groups formulated the nature and character of their fellowship. Their members were not concerned with the question *whether* they should organize themselves into a group but rather *how* they were going to obtain their desired aims. One could call these groups naturally derived and spontaneous manifestations whose roots reach far back into history. The second type of fellowship recognized by Gierke is the group that is based upon the arbitrary will (*Willkür*) of its members. Through a conscious and creative act the will of its members brought into existence such groups as the guilds and the trade unions.[63] The distinction between the two forms of fellowships is certainly not absolute. Arbitrarily willed fellowships can call upon natural and historical precedents, while fellowships that are the result of spontaneous, natural factors have their share of conscious free will that transcends their original purpose of only imparting form to a given reality. Thus, for instance, a fellowship concerned with the construction and maintenance of communal dikes could very easily co-opt members in an arbitrary manner. Natural and historical factors combine with the impetus of the free creative will to bring about certain fellowships. But whatever their origin, fellowships share some common characteristics.

Regardless of their inception, the fellowships are not merely a sum of individuals but a universality and 'hence not only a carrier of communal individual rights but also a carrier of communal fellowship rights.'[64] That is to say that a fellowship is not an aggregate of individual wills but only the sum total of the associative side of individual volitions. It encompasses and expresses the social urges within man but still leaves his private individuality untouched.

The fellowship represents the unhindered right to associate for certain specific purposes. This right is so fundamental to Germanic legal practices that it appears to have the force of natural law. Nothing can prevent the formation of a fellowship as long as it does not go against the religious, social, and then eventually the legal injunctions of society. But since fellowships, expressing man's associative instincts, existed before the advent of the state, theirs is a prior claim. Moreover, the fellowship is assumed to have a personality of its own and to be able to express its own will and to act in an unhindered fashion without the services of a guardian or spokesman. Being persons in their own right, fellowships can hold and dispose of property in the manner of legal adults.

So far as property relationships are concerned, fellowship right was originally most clearly expressed in such communal holdings and collectively utilized areas

62 *Genossenschaftsrecht*, II, p. 867.
63 *Ibid.*, p. 868.
64 *Ibid.*, p. 38.

as common lands[65] pastures, forests, vineyards[66] and bodies of water subject to communal riparian rights. Paramount to the consideration of the property of the fellowship is the principle of the 'common hand' (*gesammte Hand*). This principle is based upon the special bond that links the members of the group. Without this bond there can be no special fellowship right nor can there be a special property. But just as Gierke discerns the existence of a special link between members, he also finds a special type of property ownership. The fellowship has a 'common hand' in so far as its property is not the accumulation of individual pieces of property donated to or instituted for a common purpose. The fellowship, being a person in its own right, has property distinct from that of its members. By its very nature it cannot disregard the wishes and disposition of its constituent parts,[67] for its existence is dependent upon the unity that prevails within the fellowship. Moreover, it is essential that the principle of the 'common hand' be understood as the 'effectiveness of a legal property of an association that has been recognized as a person.'[68] This person is concerned with the manipulation not of individual pieces of property produced in order to found a trading company but with the special property that is at the disposal of the organic group. Like the fellowship itself, the 'common hand' becomes a supra-individual unity or at least the tool of a supra-individual unity that, while bound to the life of its constituent members, has a sphere of activity of its own.

In keeping with his general view of the nature of human associations, Gierke also argues that the fellowship is brought about by the transference of the associative segment of the single individual. Although this segment becomes part of a communal organism, the process does not eliminate the entire personality of the individual. In matters that are of no concern to the fellowship, the individual retains his essence and full autonomy.[69] There are therefore three categories involved in the fellowship-process. There is the fellowship itself endowed with a living, organic, legal personality of its own; there is the 'fellow,' the associated member of the group or, more precisely, that portion of an individual that has been transferred to the group; finally there is the unassociated part of the original personality, that is that portion of the individual's life and ambitions that relate only to his private existence. Whether membership in a fellowship is compulsory or not, one fundamental fact remains. No individuality is fully exhausted by its membership in a fellowship. Regardless of how strong and important the associative urge that culminates in the fellowship is, there remains at every man's dis-

65 *Ibid.*, p. 134.
66 *Ibid.*, p. 873.
67 *Genossenschaftstheorie*, pp. 344-5.
68 *Ibid.*, p. 353.
69 *Genossenschaftsrecht*, II, p. 874.

posal a realm in which his private will is supreme. He is free to join one or more fellowships simultaneously, but no amount of associative activity will fully occupy his time or satisfy all his individual needs and ambitions.

The law of fellowships is relevant to both private and public law. Ultimately however, all fellowships and other associations are touched upon by the positive law of the state. Minor associations and, above all, commercial societies or companies originate in private law.[70] Joint stock-companies and registered fellowships such as credit unions and labour unions come under the former category. Public law concerns itself primarily with such fellowships as local communities and the fellowships of state officials, in other words with those associations that are most intimately linked with the governance of the state.[71]

Finally, the fellowship-principle is territorially limited.[72] Being the product of Germanic and German law, its life is demarcated by the limits of those bodies of law that derived their existence from the German experience. And therein, one may add, lies really one of the predominant characteristics of the fellowship. For on closer observation it becomes evident that many features of the fellowship are shared by corporations and associations of other origin. Thus, for instance, Gierke argues[73] that a proper fellowship requires an internal constitution that regulates the affairs of the group. But the same requirement also applies to joint stock companies, commercial societies, religious foundations and other groups not exclusively within the realm of German fellowship law.

Gierke's argument for the real living unity of the fellowship is more original. Certainly the notion that the group can have a life of its own, partially independent of its members, is rooted in his organic conception of the group. But again it can be noted that such an 'inorganic' group as a modern stock company is an entity distinct from the individuality of its members. It may not be a juristic person in Gierke's sense but it can be treated as such by the law. Certainly the modern stock company can speak and act for itself and hold and manipulate property. True, no transference of an individual's legal personality takes place when he buys shares in or joins a company. In this respect Gierke's exposition of the transference of a part of an individual's essence to the group is something that belongs specifically to the concept of the fellowship. But stock companies or indeed all joint commercial undertakings may subscribe to the principle of the 'common hand,' at least in so far as the property of the company is clearly distinguishable from that of its individual members.

70 *Genossenschaftstheorie*, p. 162.
71 *Ibid.*, p. 166.
72 *Genossenschaftsrecht*, II, p. 870.
73 *Ibid.*, p. 880.

Ultimately, the understanding of the concept of fellowship must return to Gierke's own definition that envisages the fellowship as a legal association within German law that is endowed with an autonomous legal personality. Or as he puts it, 'the core of the theory of the fellowship is the recognition of the corporation (*Körperschaft*) as a real group-person (*Gesammtperson*) that stands in strict contradiction to the phantom-theory of the *persona ficta*.'[74]

74 *Genossenschaftstheorie*, p. 5.

2

Person – Fictitious and Real

The term *persona* is derived from Roman jurisprudence. Originally the word denoted the mask that an actor wore during his performance on the stage. This use imparted a subtle and attractive significance to the term. The actor's natural identity was hidden behind a device in order that he could play a certain role for a specific purpose. Transposed into the legal realm, natural man was endowed with a 'mask,' in order that he could be effective in the eyes of the law. There are many experiences and manifestations in an individual's life. He is, more often than not, a member or a head of a family, he is a provider, he acquires, holds, and disposes of property, he may be a member of a religious group. He is political in some of his manifestations but, above all, he is a conscious and willing entity.

If he lives in a civilized community, he is subject to the law of that community. But his contacts with the law are usually limited to special circumstances. It is when he confronts the law that the individual wears the mask of the *persona*. He acts out a certain role in some juristic process, be it as a plaintiff, a litigant, a party to a contract, or a testator, to mention just a few instances. In such and similar cases the individual as a legal person is party to what may be called a juristic drama where the individual, for the sake of that drama, assumes a legal mask. In doing so, he forsakes, momentarily, his natural personality and becomes, in the eyes of the law, a person. As such he is assumed to have a will and a purpose of his own, a strictly individual status that is confirmed by the law. At this point the uniqueness of every individuality collides with the law that is the expression and the creation of society. In order to meet society's legal demands, then, man has to wear a mask and thereby subordinate his natural personality to a legal one. In fact, the process of wearing the mask of the legal personality is not a sporadic occurrence. As far as the law is concerned, it must be a permanent condition. That is not to say that the law is intent upon or even interested in the total suppression of the manifestations of the natural personality. It is, however, concerned with the limitations upon those natural impulses that may prove to be socially and hence legally harmful.

Law also requires that a certain uniformity exist among the subjects it deals with. It cannot cater to all the vagaries, idiosyncracies, and moods of the multitude of natural persons that it encounters. Therefore, for legal purposes, the mask of the *persona* has to be assumed, for ultimately 'Natural persons alone cannot satisfy the needs of human society: it is in juristic persons that they find their necessary complement.'[1] Or, in other words, the 'noble savage,' if there ever was one, has to mask part of his natural vagaries in order to be accepted as a legal entity. That is no more than saying that the individual, even if he is assumed to be rational and ethical, has to subordinate some of his impulses and desires to the order of the social whole. Whatever he may lose in the process of becoming a legal person, however, he regains in status. Thus the former mask of the actor, transposed into the legal realm, serves two purposes. First, it disguises the natural face of its bearer. Second, the mask signifies legal personality leading to a recognition of the importance of the role played by the actor in the legal drama. This recognition is of paramount importance because, in the legal realm, it attests to the attainment of a status. Without this recognition no one can participate in legal proceedings. Indeed it can be argued that the attainment of the status of person is the precondition of orderly legal and social existence. Law concerns itself only with persons, whether they be individual or corporate actors. Or, as it has been said, 'Law necessarily deals with duties and rights of persons.'[2]

Status signifies a person's rightful ability to participate in the legal drama and the recognition that he is entitled to do so. In Roman and German jurisprudence, and not in that realm alone,[3] this is an issue of paramount importance. German legal thought, moreover, carries the issue further. It divides the juristic realm into two spheres, the objective and the subjective. In its special manifestations, objective law is the sum of legal norms as they pertain to the whole community. It is the positive law of the state as applied by its courts. In its subjective aspect, law signifies the sum total of rights and duties of persons, whether they are indivi-

1 R. Sohm, *The Institutes*, J.C. Ledlie transl., Oxford, 1907, p. 163.

2 F. Pollock, *Jurisprudence and Legal Essays*, p. 60.

3 Cp. Edwards v. Attorney General of Canada, 1930, A.C. 124. This case considered the eligibility of women for a seat in the Senate under Section 24 of the British North America Act and, correlatively, whether women were 'persons' in the eyes of the law. The Supreme Court of Canada had unanimously answered the question in the negative, arguing that, according to common law, women were not entitled to hold public office for they were not 'persons.' The Judicial Committee of the Privy Council of the House of Lords reversed the decision. Lord Sankey in his summary submitted that 'The exclusion of women from all public offices is a relic of days more barbarous than ours. ... Such exclusion is probably due to the fact that the deliberative assemblies of

duals or group-persons according to Gierke's understanding of that term.[4] But subjectivity denotes not only that a person is subject to law but also that he is a legally enabled (*rechtsfähig*) entity prepared to hold, wield, and manipulate rights; that he is, in short, a possessor of rights.[5] German jurisprudence has expended a tremendous amount of energy trying to ascertain what the preconditions of this subjective legal ability (*Rechtsfähigkeit*) are, how they are derived, and of what the resulting series of obligations and rights consist. There is, however, no doubt that as far as Gierke is concerned, the legal person is not only an individual but can also be a group. This group, under both objective and subjective law, is legally enabled. This contention is central to his examination of the Roman association and corporation.

As will be seen,[6] the development of institutionalized persons and their legal enablement was a tardy process in classical and in Justinian jurisprudence and this is, according to Gierke, the weakness of Roman legal thought. He contends that the group-person, be it fellowship, association or corporation, has the same attributes as the personality derived from the individual. It is of paramount importance to ascertain that the group-personality be considered legally enabled (*rechtsfähig*) and that it be given the same status as the personality derived from a single individual. In considering these issues, Gierke has to take into account not only the Roman *corpus* of thought as derived from the classical and Justinian lawyers but also the work of Friedrich Carl von Savigny, his great predecessor in German legal science. Without Savigny no German jurist could meaningfully discuss Roman and German law, for his *System des heutigen römischen Rechts*[7] is a milestone in nineteenth-century continental jurisprudence.

In his methodical exposition Savigny does attain a logical and unified theory based upon the principles of Roman law, a logical unity and coherence of thought

the early tribes were attended by men under arms, and women did not bear arms.' In support of his contention, Lord Sankey turned to Tacitus, *Germania*. While noting that the men of the Germanic tribes assembled under arms (Tacitus, *Germania*, c. 13), he pointed out that 'they did believe that women had a certain sanctity and foresight and [therefore] they heeded their advice and did not neglect their counsels.' (*Ibid*., c. 8). Then, after citing various legal precedents, Lord Sankey noted that the word 'person' even though ambiguous undoubtedly referred to members of either sex. Therefore the question of whether women are persons 'should be answered in the affirmative and ... women are eligible to be summoned to and become members of the Senate of Canada.' The Judicial Committee so ruled.

4 Gierke, *Grundbegriffe*, p. 102.

5 H.J. Wolff, *Organschaft und juristische Person*, Berlin, 1934, I, p. 128.

6 See below, pp. 127 ff.

7 Berlin, 1840 (hereafter *System*).

that is, in fact, absent from the original sources.[8] He disregards the changes brought about in Roman jurisprudence by the growth of canon law, the influence of non-Roman, primarily Germanic ideas, and the major revision of the original *corpus* at the hands of the Italo-Roman school in Bologna in the thirteenth and fourteenth centuries. Savigny's *System* represents a purified reconstruction of classical Roman law as expounded by Papinian, Ulpian,[9] and Paulus.[10] The major function and merit of the Justinian compilation are seen by Savigny as preserving and transmitting the spirit of Roman law to successive ages.[11]

In establishing the fundamentals of 'contemporary' (*heutiges*) Roman law, Savigny returns to those aspects of jurisprudence that take, as their example, the strictly individualistic conception of the person. As he puts it, 'Every legal relationship consists of the connection of one person to another person.'[12] The human ingredient behind the concept of the juristic person is not neglected either, for Savigny adds that 'All law exists for the sake of that ethical freedom that is innate to every man. Hence the original concept of the person, or of the subject of rights, must coincide with the concept of man. The original identity of both concepts may be expressed in the following manner: every individual man, and only the individual man, is legally enabled [*rechtsfähig*].'[13] This strictly individualistic interpretation of the concept of person is a distinct challenge to Gierke's conception of the group-personality and its autonomous life.

Moreover, Savigny is a firm believer in the theory of the *persona ficta* that denies the group any independent personality of its own. This is the aspect of Savigny that Gierke feels called upon to contest. It is not that Savigny denies the existence of numerous associations, corporations, and other groups within the Roman system. To do so would be a denial of ample existing evidence. Indeed, Savigny is prepared to recognize these groups as juristic persons, maintaining that this is in harmony with the spirit of Roman law. He distinguishes between juristic persons of natural descent and arbitrarily formed juristic persons, a distinction accepted by Gierke. Among the naturally formed juristic persons, Savigny lists communities, cities, and villages that preceded the appearance of the state.[14] The

8 F. Hallis, *Corporate Personality*, Oxford, 1930, p. 4.

9 F.C. von Savigny, *Vom Beruf unserer Zeit für Gesetzgebung und Rechtswissenschaft*, Heidelberg, 1840, 2nd ed., p. 33 (hereafter *Vom Beruf*).

10 *Ibid*., p. 34.

11 *Ibid*., p. 35.

12 *System*, II, p. 1.

13 *Ibid*., p. 2.

14 *Ibid*., p. 242.

arbitrarily formed juristic persons are those that originated in the will of some individual persons banded together for specific purposes.[15] These groups, according to Savigny, can be referred to by the generic term of 'corporations.' They were represented by such organizations as trade guilds,[16] religious associations such as the college of priests and the association of such state-officials as the *librarii, fiscales, censuales*, known by the general term *scribae*.[17] Perhaps the most ancient of all arbitrarily formed associations were the *collegia tenuiorum*, the burial societies whose purpose was the securing of proper funeral services and burial grounds for their impecunious members. Finally, there existed such groups as the *sodalitates*, originally religious associations that, over time, assumed the role of social and political clubs. Being partially of political nature they served, at times, as centres for political agitation.[18] The most common term for all groups, natural or arbitrarily formed, was *universitas*,[19] and it represented, to Savigny, the conceptual and institutional opposite of the single, unassociated individual.

A number of pertinent facts emerge from Savigny's observations that have a direct bearing on Gierke's treatment of the Roman association. First, republican Rome had a rich associative life where groups of various colours and hues flourished. Indeed the recognition of the association can be traced to the Twelve Tables where it is stated in Table VIII that 'guild members shall have the power ... to make for themselves any rule they may wish provided that they impair no part of the public law. ... '[20] Second, it becomes clear that, according to Savigny, juristic personality was accorded to groups as well as to individuals. Thus the concept of the juristic person derived from the common will of an aggregation of men became a historical and social reality. This meant that the notion of the juristic person originally derived from and relegated to the realm of the *singuli*, the isolated individual person, was transposed into the realm of the composite group-personality. Third, in the course of this process the juristic person was, by necessity rather than by design, carried from the sphere of private into that of public law.

This process was contrary to the original division between the two realms for it had been stated early on that 'Public law is that which regards the government of the Roman Empire; private law that which concerns the interests of indivi-

15 *Ibid.*, p. 243.
16 *Ibid.*, p. 245.
17 *Ibid.*, p. 253.
18 *Ibid.*, pp. 255-6.
19 *Ibid.*, pp. 261-2.
20 'The Twelve Tables,' *Ancient Roman Statutes*, A.C. Johnson et al. transl. and ed., Austin, 1961, p. 12.

duals.'[21] Gierke argues[22] that in the course of events the *fiscus* or imperial state treasury came under the jurisdiction of private law and the barrier between public and private law was thereby surmounted. On the other hand it can also be noted that the distinction between the *jus publicum* and the *jus privatum* became unclear as soon as the state intervened in the most fundamental aspect of the associative person. According to Roman law, the multiple person's right to exist was based upon an act of concession emanating from the state. No association could function without the specific permission of the state, a clear intervention of public into private law.

In its legal-political attitude the Roman Republic was more generous towards the associations than the Roman Empire. It appeared to adhere to the principle of Table VIII that extended to guild-members the right to associate. A strong tendency to prohibit the formation of associations emerged already under the *principate* and was intensified during the Dominate. The *Lex Julia* became the fundamental law regulating the associations and it maintained that no group could exist without the express consent of the state. Furthermore, no association was tolerated unless it was of direct benefit to the state. Ever jealous of its *potestas* and *auctoritas*, the Roman imperial state viewed all associations with marked suspicion. Typical of this attitude towards subsidiary groups within the state was Emperor Trajan's refusal to permit Pliny, governor of the province of Bithynia, to authorize the formation of a fire-brigade. It was feared that such a corporate organization would become the centre of political agitation.[23]

Under these conditions, the concession theory ruled supreme and Savigny gives no indication of yielding from that position. A strong proponent of the fiction theory, which is the inevitable corollary of the concession theory, he claims that a juristic person is 'an artificially conceived subject that is capable of holding property.'[24] Thus despite the individualistic nature of Roman law and its acknowledgment, albeit reluctant, of the group-personality, pure Roman law, as perceived by Savigny, refuses to ascribe an independent life to the association. His definition of a person as an artificially conceived subject has further implications. The sentence appears politically and juridically harmless unless one remembers that the process of concession, according to the theory of the *persona ficta*, can emanate only from the state. Thus the assumption that the person is an artificially conceived fictitious being denies two major premises. First, man as a rational and ethical being has the natural and fundamental right to associate without any

21 *The Institutes of Justinian*, T.C. Sandars, transl., London, 1956, 1.1.4 (hereafter *Institutes*).

22 See below, pp. 112, 133.

23 E. Barker, *From Alexander to Constantine*, Oxford, 1956, p. 252.

24 Savigny, *System*, II, p. 239.

previous consent or concession. Second, the fiction theory, so elaborately maintained by Savigny, denies the existence of those psychological social forces that endow the group with its cohesion, or as Gierke would have it, its real inner unity of life.

In the case of the theory of the *persona ficta*, a natural process is replaced by a strictly juristic one. This process consists of transferring the natural legal ability of man *qua* man to an 'ideal,' that is to an imaginary subject.[25] This subject has no life, no will, and no consciousness of its own unless the state imparts these qualities to it. The reason for Savigny's approach is simple. If it is not the state that creates the juristic person then it must be the private will that does so. But the private will is arbitrary and also capricious and can therefore lead to 'the greatest uncertainties in legal conditions.'[26] For this reason the individual and his association must become subject to the state's sovereign powers without any further proviso. Their legal subjectivity, their legal enablement (*Rechtsfähigkeit*) are thereby severely curtailed. In political rather than strictly juridical terms, the fiction theory can lead in only one direction, towards the absolutistic state.

Savigny fails to note that this state can be quite as arbitrary and capricious as the single individual. Writing at a time when the geographic entity usually referred to as 'Germany' was still divided into numerous principalities, Savigny wanted to see the emergence of a strong central authority. Hence his advocacy of the fiction theory. Gierke, writing mostly after the unification of the German lands had become a fact, was intent upon guarding against a degree of centralization that would deny the importance and influence of the component elements of the body politic.

It should be noted that a cohesive theory of the *persona ficta* and the concession theory were not developed in any clear and concise manner by either the jurists of classical Roman law or the compilers of Justinian's Code.[27] While practising absolutism, the imperial Roman state paid at least lip-service to the power of the people if not to those organizations that it tolerated. In the Code the declaration, 'That which seems good to the emperor has also the force of law,' was tempered by the addition: 'for the people by the *lex regia*, which is passed to confer on him his power, make over to him their whole power and authority.'[28] Indubitably, this delegation of popular sovereignty to the emperor was a piece of legal fiction no less artificial than the whole theory of the *persona ficta*. But at least it retained, if only in theory, the notion that the will of the people represented one of the sources of the law.

25 *Ibid.*, p. 278.
26 *Ibid.*
27 *Genossenschaftsrecht*, III, p. 129.
28 *Institutes*, 1.2.6.

As for the fiction theory itself, it received its strongest and clearest expression in the Middle Ages and at a time when its absolutistic characteristics served the purpose of its enunciator. It was Pope Innocent IV (Sinibaldo Fiesco) who spoke of the 'fiction of the undivided person' and proposed that a *collegium* could act as a person only on fictitious grounds.[29] It was no coincidence that the statement came from Innocent IV. He was the protagonist of the doctrine of the plenitude of powers (*plenitudo potestatis*) that sought to bring all powers, secular and spiritual, under the pope's jurisdiction. The doctrine represented a strong drive toward centralization within the church. Simultaneously, it also claimed the church's supremacy in secular affairs.[30]

The utility of the concession theory for this papal policy was clearly evident. In matters of both church and state all powers flowed from the head of the church who, at his discretion, could concede a fictitious personality to associations and groups. Thus the group's 'real' life was dependent upon an act of papal concession without which it could not exist. If a group or even an individual aroused the pope's displeasure, he could, in theory, withdraw his concession to the group or excommunicate the individual. He thereby divested the person of his juristic, rightful status. The process could, in other words, turn a person into a 'nonperson,' thereby removing this entity from the community of rightful beings and banishing it beyond the realm of the law. As it turned out, however, the theory of the papal plenitude of power did not emerge victorious. The claims of the *sacerdotium* were strongly contested by the newly emerging secular powers of the state.

The potential of the concession theory did not escape the attention of the absolutistic rulers of post-mediaeval Europe. The rich corporative life of the Middle Ages with its profusion of organically articulated groups was subjected to a strict application of the concession theory. In Germany, as of the sixteenth century, the organization of associations was prohibited, unless they had the express consent of the ruler. Severe limitations were imposed upon the right of assembly and the right to associate.[31] The threat of depriving a group of its legal status was a potent weapon in the hands of the absolutistic ruler. The individual's or the group's dependence upon the will or whim of the state that could create as well as destroy the fictitious personality had the characteristics of an ultimate coercive sanction. It was no coincidence that the absolutism that followed in the seventeenth and eighteenth centuries showed little tolerance for associations that could have acted as intermediaries between the individual and the state. The lat-

29 *Genossenschaftsrecht*, III, p. 279 and n. 102.

30 E. Lewis, *Medieval Political Ideas*, New York, 1954, II, p. 359.

31 *Genossenschaftsrecht*, III, p. 769.

ter insisted upon wielding a strong central authority and was unwilling to share its prerogatives, even lesser prerogatives, with any other association. As noted, Savigny, writing in a period when Germany was still fragmented into numerous principalities, obviously opted for a strong central authority. Thus, his theory of 'pure' Roman law, or at least what he took to be such, shifted from the juristic to the political realm.[32] Gierke, though respectful towards Savigny, makes it his task to combat the implications of the theory of the *persona ficta* that denied, in his eyes, the reality of the group-person and the decentralization that concept stands for. To carry out his aim he had to examine the Roman concept of the juristic person in detail, expose its fallacies, and compare the Roman to the German understanding of that concept. To that subject we shall now turn.

Since Savigny, Gierke argues,[33] it has become customary to expound the theory of the juristic person in the following manner. Originally, the concept of the juristic subject coincided with the concept of man. Every individual and only the individual is legally enabled (*rechtsfähig*). Positive law both limits and expands upon this point. It can, in the first instance, delimit or entirely negate a man's legal subjectivity and it can deny his status and his rights. But positive law can also transpose legal ability to an entity that is external to the individual, that is, it can artificially create a juristic person. It is Gierke's contention that, first, man's claim to personality is a philosophically accepted principle. Second, the assumption that only the individual human being can be considered a person is not supported by his philosophy of law. The historical development of the concept has shown that the human association is endowed with a personality and a living reality. Indeed it can be argued that history did not start with the individual rights of persons at all but was familiar only with communal held rights and privileges. These communal rights were the 'law of the people' (*Volksrecht*)[34] that set the standards of legal relationships within the community. The individual derived his legal enablement (*Rechtsfähigkeit*) from the fact that he belonged to the group, by being in 'fellowship' with his people. Foreigners and slaves were denied rights since they were alien to the original community. Individual rights, moreover, were valid only through their relationship to communal rights, and this situation was reflected in property arrangements also. The property of the community was at least as ancient as private, individual property. Indeed, Gierke argues that in the case of primitive peoples communal property preceded the appearance of

32 Hallis, *Corporate Personality*, p. 13.

33 *Genossenschaftsrecht*, II, p. 25.

34 *Ibid.*, p. 26.

private property. Thus the notion of the isolated individual as the original right-bearing and propertied entity is simply not borne out by history.

In essence, the Roman concept of person closely resembled Savigny's description. The juristic person was not derived from historical observations but was placed into theoretical as well as juristic isolation. As the first people to establish law as an independent sphere of thought and action, the Romans discovered the abstract idea of law. But this discovery concerned itself mainly with private law. As their term *jus publicum* indicates, the Romans did have a conception of a higher unity, but that was the result of their monistic and indivisible theory of the state. Setting the realm of public law aside, they established a separate sphere for private law and therein, according to Gierke,[35] lies the great Roman accomplishment. In this realm of private law, the concept of the person coincided with the idea of private legal enablement (*Privatrechtsfähigkeit*) and concerned itself with the multitude of rights and duties as they pertained to the *singuli*. Roman public law, on the other hand, knew of only one legal subject, the Roman state itself, and it did not concern itself with the private individual. Private law, being centred upon the single individual being, assigned to this entity a specific sphere of will. Unless he was an alien or a slave, the individual human being *qua* human being was considered a person. No total equality, however, existed between the persons in the Roman realm, for the law distinguished between citizens and freedmen,[36] both of whom were persons but did not occupy an identical position. Nevertheless, the practice of ascribing legal personality to certain men did have a levelling effect.[37] By assigning to every individual a special sphere of rights and establishing the distinction between the realms of the one and the many, Roman law consolidated the notion of individualism on a legal plane.

Over the course of Roman history, it became necessary to recognize a person, a legal subject, that was distinct from individual human beings. The communal properties of municipalities, of the colleges of priests, and of the guilds of artisans represented a supra-individual entity that had to be given legal recognition also. By a stretch of the legal imagination even the state treasury, the *fiscus*, could be considered as a subjective person under private law.[38] Moreover, being absolute, the rights of the constituent individuals were not limited by their membership in any group. Their nature, that of *singuli*, was not altered nor did their inner essence touch upon the essence of the group itself. For this reason, an independent personality had to be assigned to the group so that it appeared as an individual among other individuals subordinated to the clauses of private law. In

35 *Ibid.*
36 *Ibid.*, p. 27.
37 *Ibid.*, p. 28.
38 *Ibid.*, p. 29.

the absence of any theoretical organic link, an artificial, fictitious personality had to be ascribed to the groups.[39]

These were the factors responsible, so Gierke argued, for the peculiarities of the Roman understanding of the concept of the person. In the sphere of private law the unlimited will of the individual reigned supreme. The state prevailed in public law. The Roman person was therefore an absolute, untouched by its relationships with other legal subjects. At best, private wills were co-ordinated with similar other wills, but their isolation remained permanent and their position sovereign within their own narrow spheres. Being sovereign, the person was, theoretically at least, indivisible and incapable of transferring or delegating part of itself to such a distinct entity as a group-person. Consequently, the Roman person was denied the opportunity to develop, on theoretical grounds, any meaningful sense of obligation to and active participation in associative life. Owing to these limitations, then, the Roman juristic person had to develop surrogates that could, theoretically, contribute to or exercise leadership in legal communal existence.[40]

The Roman understanding of the concept of person was so indigenous to that system that its transplantation into another legal realm could only lead to absurdities. Such a process did take place with the Reception of Roman law in sixteenth-century Germany. But before that process came about, Germanic and German law had already developed its own theory of the person. Thus, when one turns to the examination of the German understanding of this concept, it becomes apparent that German law did not treat the person as an isolated abstraction. Through custom and practice it developed organic fellowships centred on generic associations, estate communities, community fellowships, groups linked by common bonds of service, and communal properties.[41] All these groups incorporated the person not as an absolutely independent whole but as a portion of a higher unity. Another feature of German law that distinguished it from the Roman system was the practice of incorporating public and private law into one legal realm.[42] Roman jurisprudence excelled in developing private law that assigned to the individual an autonomous sphere of activity but prevented him from participating in public law. The German accomplishment came with the establishment of a body of law that regulated the relationship between citizen and state and the ordering of both private and public law into one uniform realm.

A thousand years passed before the unified German nation-state was formed. While France and England emerged as unified and centralized monarchies displaying the characteristics of independent nation-states, Germany re-

39 *Ibid.*, p. 29.
40 *Ibid.*
41 *Ibid.*, p. 32.
42 *Ibid.*, p. 33.

mained a collection of feudal principalities that could barely cling to a common legal tradition. In the absence of a single, unified body politic, the existence of a uniform German law was actually confined to the cities and to the *Länder* or provinces. Tenaciously these centres clung to their legal tradition including the German conception of the person. Not even the Reception of Roman law in the sixteenth century could successfully eliminate the German tradition of a law that encompassed the public and private legal sector. This tradition was reflected in the German understanding of the concept of person that also withstood the onslaught of Roman law.

Personality, in German law, did not mean legal enablement (*Rechtsfähigkeit*) in the sphere of private law only.[43] Rather, personality signified the ability and the will, on the part of the individual, to act in both the private and the public legal realms. The Roman division of law into the domain of the state on the one hand and of the autonomous isolated individual on the other was rejected. Instead, German legal thought and practice started with the concept of a uniform will, both public and private, that incorporated the idea of individual and communal freedom. One premise was never forgotten. The basis of the German concept of person was individual free will. This will was, however, limited by certain ethical considerations. In other words, personality consisted of the recognition of an ethically delimited but otherwise free being that was a legal subject, a possessor of rights. This idea was retained even as the modern state eventually emerged.

Then, by necessity, private law was separated from public law, but merely for the sake of technical convenience. The unity, the linking of private public aspects of the personality, was never forgotten. Nor were the ethical aspects of a juristic person disregarded. But, above all, the conviction remained that the individual reigned in the realm of private law not as an absolute, unlimited single will but as something that was predetermined and delimited by the ethical order of the whole community and its public law.[44] Thus individual freedom and necessity were resolved in the higher unity of ethical freedom manifesting itself in a national whole. Under these conditions the individual was not a mere object of the law, that is the target of the state's positive legislation. The individual became a subject, a legally enabled (*rechtsfähig*) entity who had both private and public privileges.[45]

It was a fundamental contention of German law that a person's freedom and his status as a right-bearing entity were not derived from the law of the state. At

43 *Ibid.*
44 *Ibid.*
45 *Ibid.*, p. 34.

best, the state and its institutions preserved and vindicated freedom but could never serve as its source. This expansion of the concept of freedom represented an inherent limitation upon positive law, for it contained the idea that every individual had the absolute right to the status of personality. Thus it was not positive law that extended a status to the human being. Instead, the idea prevailed that man entered into the legal realm as a person on an *a priori* basis. There was no need for conceding that which preceded the state and its law, and hence the German concept of person was both natural, fundamental, and essentially free. Law was merely concerned with the establishment of conditions conducive to the pursuance and expression of subjective rights. Law then, according to Gierke's theory, did not create the person, but merely confirmed it.

The will of the person, however, cannot be unlimited. There are ethical boundaries that may not be exceeded. Social conditions add their share of limitations on individual free will. Therefore, German law does not recognize an unlimited absolute personality but only one that is engaged in reciprocal ethical and social relationships. It follows that there is no absolute separation between rights and duties. The will is ethically and socially delimited and the exercise of rights is balanced by a sense of limitations contained in the fulfilment of duties. Under these conditions the will of the person is 'simultaneously a ruler and a condition of being ruled.'[46] It is a ruler while concerning itself with strictly individual matters. It is ruled when it enters into the unavoidable social relationships and when it makes itself part of the group. Thus the German concept of person is far from being indivisible. The person has the option of transferring part of his will to group-persons and thereby creating a distinct and independent new personality in the form of a fellowship, association, corporation, or community. In so doing, the person does not delegate but actually transfers to the group-personality such rights as representation and administration, and transforms part of its individual essence into the will of a new communal person. This new creation, this new communal person, is endowed with rights and duties of its own. It has a sense of individual unity that is equivalent to that of a single person and it confronts the latter under these conditions.[47]

It is mainly through his associations that the individual person reaches the realm of public law. The group-persons enter into that sphere as real individuals, endowed with their share of rights and duties. Moreover, they not only come to represent their own will but they share in the will of the community. From its inception, the German concept of person related not only to itself but also to a

46 *Ibid*. Note the similarity to Aristotle's definition: 'The good citizen must possess the knowledge and the capacity requisite for ruling as well as for being ruled.' *Politics*, E. Barker transl., Oxford, 1946, 1277b.

47 *Ibid*., p. 37.

higher community of which it was a member as well as a representative. A 'mixed' personality emerges from this process.[48] Part of the personality is concerned with its private associative functions and part of it is devoted to the institutions of the higher public person, ultimately to that of the state itself. The latter is a sovereign communal person (*souveräne Gesammtperson*)[49] and like any other person is endowed with its own set of rights and duties. It exists not only for itself but for the sake of its members, creating thereby a close, organic link between the higher and lower associations.

Ultimately, then, the individual person's life is not totally self-centred, indeed it cannot take on that cast. Nor is it relegated and isolated to its own little niche in private law. The individual's life is not wholly devoted to the group either. According to the German understanding of the concept of person, there can be no unlimited egoism nor can there be a total subjugation to the group. Rather, ' ... everyone lives for himself as well as for the whole.'[50] There is no fundamental distinction between the ambitions of individuals and the ambitions of groups, for they absorb one another in certain specific instances and for certain given aims. But this absorption does not signify that the individual becomes a means for the totality, nor is the latter to be thought of as a mere tool for self-aggrandizement. The two entities exist, mutually dependent, separate yet identical in certain instances, and they thrive, preferably in a condition of harmony. In these respects the German concept of the person differs from the Roman understanding of that term, and obviously lies at the root of the theory of the organic individuality of groups that contributes to the existence of social law.

'In the realm of law, will is the soul of personality,'[51] Gierke argues. And, as the above exposition indicates, the concept of person, or rather the specific German understanding of that term, is one of the bases of Gierke's conception of law. Whether he is correct in arguing for a divisibility of the concept of the person depends upon the question to what extent law does or should reflect political and social conditions. If law is a separate and unrelated discipline, then the abstract Roman concept of the person can be accepted. This acceptance is based on the premise that natural and legal personalities can be separated. It is not impossible, as the Roman example indicates, to establish legal categories and use this *a priori* categorization to deal with private law, its law of persons, and its law of things.

But if the concept of person is understood to mean not only a legal status but a real living human being which is part natural and part moral and which possesses a free will unhindered by all considerations except ethical and social ones, then

48 *Ibid*., p. 39.
49 *Genossenschaftstheorie*, p. 642.
50 *Genossenschaftsrecht*, II, p. 42.
51 *Ibid*., p. 475.

the German conception of the person, as expounded by Gierke, seems a great deal more realistic. It does not confine the concept of person to the legal realm alone but brings it into correlation with political, social, and psychological factors. No man can be a legal island, and no person can exist, in reality, without others. The existence of other persons, particularly the existence of their rights in contradistinction to the rights of others, is really a mutual limitation of these rights. No man, in other words, can have the 'plenitude of rights.' There are contending claims inherent in his own personality as well as in those of others. In order to attain some form of harmonious existence not only on the legal but also on the political and social levels, a certain compromise on the part of the person is called for. The individual has to allocate part of his personal rights to the exigencies of communal existence. He is obliged, to divide his personality into those segments that pertain to his social obligations and those that relate to his private being.

It is a temptation at this point to accept the rigid Roman distinction between private and public law. After all, it may be convenient to relegate the person to a realm of its own and bar its possible capricious behaviour from the sphere of public law. But, as Gierke sees it, this distinction cannot be maintained without resorting to the spurious theory of the fictitious person. And whether one accepts Gierke's theory of the real unity of life of the group-person or not, it is hard to subscribe to the Roman premise that associations can manifest themselves only through guardians and legally appointed spokesmen. In practice, such groups as fellowships, associations, and corporations may produce a common will that is more than just a mere expression of the sum total of individual wills. A group's life can continue regardless of changes in its membership and for legal purposes it is perfectly possible to ascribe a distinct will and personality to such a group.

On a philosophic plane it is possible to argue that 'human personality is something ultimate' and that 'No philosophic systematization of the contents of human experience can abolish the unique individuality of each self-conscious, willing human being who has that experience.'[52] But law, confronted with the mundane exigencies of social life may well be obliged to accept Gierke's assumption that the person, in its legal manifestations, is divisible, indeed that it has to be divisible for certain given ends. This process of dividing in no way interferes with the uniqueness of the individuality, nor does it detract from its self-consciousness and will. As a matter of fact, the opportunity to branch out into the spheres of both private and public law enhances the value of the person.

In reality, man's 'asocial sociability' draws him in two directions: towards his own private self and, simultaneously, towards an association with other men. So-

52 Hallis, *Corporate Personality*, p. xxiv.

cial and political imperatives oblige him to divide his energies between himself and the plurality that surrounds him. A division in interests, desires, ambitions, and goals is inescapable yet this does not necessarily lead to a schizophrenic personality. It is perfectly feasible to envisage, with Gierke, a division of powers within one legal person. Some of these powers are devoted to individual endeavours and some to communal undertakings, and these two aspects of a single person do not necessarily lead to disharmony.

Personality, legal or otherwise, is innate to man. Basically, law merely confirms, assists, and, to a degree, regulates the play of personal forces in society. There is no need to endow the person with a fictitious quality for it is a social as well as legal reality that needs no excuses. If it wants to or is obliged to direct its attentions into two or more directions, individual and communal, then it ought to be free to do so without any intervention by the law. Gierke, as he surveys the development of the German concept of person, is indubitably biased in favour of his native development and he may be correct in his stance. Yet the accomplishments he detects are, at times, more imaginary than real. When he speaks of freedom as one aspect of the German concept of person, he is on theoretical rather than on sound historical ground. It was only after the absolutistic state receded that he could, in the nineteenth century, speak of the freedom of the person both in theory and, partially, in practice.

Thus Gierke's references to Germanic and German freedom are prescriptive rather than descriptive, and that is understandable only in so far as one remembers that he is advocating the acceptance of a new general code of civil law. This civil law was to be based upon the principles of German historical as well as modern social law and not upon the precepts of the Roman code. But is is not irrelevant to his argument that his concept of the person is accorded an unlimited right to divide its powers because that in itself is a step towards the realization of civic freedom. With the rigid distinction between private and public law removed, the individual person is seen as being active in both realms. Nor is it insignificant that Gierke sees these two realms as the two sides of a single coin. The political consequences of this view are clear. The time is past, Gierke and his predecessors and followers indicate, when public law could be viewed as the exclusive reserve of the state. The person was, in the Roman context, confined to the realm of private law. It is now invited to participate in the foundation and functioning of public law.

This new role is a very measurable political improvement upon the legal conditions of the period extending from the sixteenth to the early part of the nineteenth century. In practice it means that political freedom, or lack of restraint upon the person, is extended through a legal device. But this extension of rights ought not to be considered an act of concession. Rather it is a recognition of an existing condition, or at least what Gierke perceives to be an existing condition. To concede to a person an attribute that he already possesses is a meaningless act. The free right to associate, to form groups, and to direct their internal affairs is indigenous to German law. And it is this act of self-administration that Gierke sees as one of the major manifestations of the person's free will. It is a concrete and practical expression of the otherwise somewhat nebulous concept of freedom that stands in need of legal and political verification. This verification is contained in Gierke's understanding of the concept of person. It is a condition wherein the ancient legal mask may be discarded in favour of a real personality that is both natural as well as legal.

3

State and Law

The political and legal community thus consists, for Gierke, of a chain of persons, some of them individuals and some of them associations. The state represents the highest entity in this aggregation of persons and is distinguished by the fact that there can be no higher personality present. It is, by its very nature, the only person that can represent the universality of the whole community, a role no other association is able to fulfil.[1] The Romans envisaged the state as an incorporation of an absolute will. Gierke, on the other hand, sees it as the embodiment of an ethically free will. Being the embodiment of the common will, the state must be and indeed is the sovereign communal person[2] that encompasses all other associations by providing them with a legal matrix and assuring them of a secure sphere for their endeavours. The state commands the sovereign 'plenitude of powers' (*souveräne Machtvollkommenheit*)[3] but, most important, is not above but under the law.[4] This relationship does not diminish the status of the state. Like any individual person it has to act according to the law for it is a 'state of laws,' a *Rechtsstaat*. Not being an absolute, moreover, it does not exist for and in itself, but stands in reciprocal relationship with its individual members. The relationship between the state and its members is identical with the relationship that exists between any association and its constituent organs. The same transference of individual and group-personality takes place, a similar communal group consisting of the will of its members comes into existence and the resulting new, though pre-eminent, association gains an inner unity of life of its own. Thus, it can be said, that Gierke's 'theory of the state is simply an extension of his *Genossenschaftstheorie*.'[5]

1 *Genossenschaftsrecht*, II, pp. 41, 831.
2 *Genossenschaftstheorie*, p. 642.
3 *Wesen*, p. 33.
4 *Genossenschaftsrecht*, II, p. 41.
5 Hallis, *Corporate Personality*, p. 148.

As Gierke surveys the history of the relationship between individual person and the state he finds three basic configurations. In classical antiquity man existed for the sake of the state. The individual lived not for himself or his group but for the sake of the universal whole. The state, viewed in this light, appeared as a complete and independent entity composed of subordinated parts. It attained its character and unity by and for itself without reference to its constituent members.[6] Consequently, it was irrelevant whether the state was a natural manifestation, a result of a divine act, the expression of a sovereign will, or the incorporation of an idea.[7] Roman jurisprudence viewed the state as a universal and absolute person that granted a status to certain individuals. Being isolated in the realm of private law, however, the latter contributed but little to the course of public law and policy. Thus an interaction between the wills active in the private and public realms was negligible. Plainly, the individual's and the group's influence were subordinated to the will of the absolute Roman state.

The second configuration discerned by Gierke is what he calls the individualistic theory of the state. Originally derived from the mediaeval theory of natural law, it maintained that the state existed for the sake of individual human beings. According to this theory, 'Only the individual was real, had its own purpose, and was endowed, by nature, with a unity.'[8] The state was viewed as a means for the attainment of individual ends, with little thought given to the interests of the whole. Even when linked into corporations, wills, according to the individualistic theory, remained isolated in their origin and essence. It was assumed, in contradiction to Aristotle, that the individual preceded the state, that indeed the part was more ancient than the whole.

Thus, in the post-mediaeval epoch, the state was perceived as the result of a creation of isolated human wills of hitherto unassociated individuals who banded together in a contract to obtain the advantages accruing from the existence of a legal commonwealth. This state did not possess any inherent organic unity of its own and, 'Therefore the state could not be considered a person but was a sum of individual persons, some of whom ruled and some of whom were being ruled.'[9] If any personality was ascribed to the state at all, it was done by resorting to the fiction theory that made the state into a necessary but synthetic tool or even into an abstract theoretical notion devoid of any real life. Under such conditions, natural individuals were confronted by an artificial state-individual, and the essential organic tie between these two entities was totally disregarded. Theoretically, moreover, public law was subordinated to private law, and while the idea of

6 *Grundbegriffe*, p. 88.
7 *Ibid.*
8 *Ibid.*, p. 90.
9 *Ibid.*

law gained status through this approach, the idea of the state lost in stature.[10] The result, according to Gierke, was an increasing tendency towards a materialistic, mechanistic, and atomistic view of political society.

The third model pertaining to the relationship of the individual and the state is represented, according to Gierke, by the modern German theory of the state.[11] Its basic premise is the duality inherent in man's nature. He is an individual *per se* but, at the same time, he is a member of a generic association. These attributes are innate and irrevocable and inseparably rooted in human nature. As Gierke puts it, 'Man can have no consciousness without being simultaneously aware of his particularity as well as of the fact that he is part of a universality.'[12] The result is that there are two spheres of existence, individual and communal. The individual spirit is balanced by such manifestations as the communal mind, communal will, and communal consciousness. But these phenomena do not, indeed cannot, lead to an absolute uniformity among men. Innumerable social organisms put in an appearance reflecting the individualistic urges within the whole. The urges manifest themselves in the multi-faceted, articulated, and colourful profusion of associations that undergo a constant change, birth, and death.

The state itself belongs to this panorama of communal human existence.[13] Its major task is to carry out the provisions of the common will. Thus the state has to have at its disposal sufficient, indeed sovereign, powers to tend to the goals of the community. It is given the 'plenitude of powers' in order that it may carry out the designs of a territorially demarcated body politic. But, as argued, the state is not a self-contained absolute nor is it the arbitrary creation of individuals. Nor is it the union of individual wills as propounded by the advocates of the social contract theory. The state is a creation of a non-contractual common will that is the expression of the sum total of the elements of the common will that reside in all individuals. The state is the epitome and the union of the portion of sociability that resides in every individual. This sociability formulates itself into a common will that, as the culmination of social instincts, establishes the foundations of the state. The creative act of forming the state is therefore not based on individual volition but on what may be called the natural associative instinct that is part of every individual's personality. Most important, individual volitions formulate themselves into groups and associations in general before the state is created. Hence the groups act as intermediaries between the individual and the whole body politic, and their permanent importance is assured by this fundamental role.

10 *Ibid.*, p. 91.
11 *Ibid.*, p. 92.
12 *Ibid.*, p. 93.
13 *Ibid.*, p. 96.

Because of its derivation, the state appears as a complex of communal life that is composed of social organisms.[14] Its unity is derived, first, from the associative instinct of man. Second, it emanates from its organic rather than mechanistic nature. Third, its unity is assured by the voluntary subordination of its members that endowed the state with its life. This subordination is not to be understood as the total annihilation of individual life. Despite its claims to universality and power, the state does not and cannot absorb all facets of human life.[15] It does not, for instance, interfere with the cultural developments taking place within its boundaries nor can the state fully represent the natural and political notions of the *Volk*.[16] Even though sovereign, the state is but one of the organisms serving the community. It is the nodal point for legal and political activities, but the fundamentally important inner unity of the people is also derived from generic ties, independent or semi-dependent lesser communities and the family. There are further manifestations of spontaneous life. Foremost among them are the great religious associations, the churches. But there are also such intangible yet powerful factors as social and ethical ideas and artistic and literary movements that exert power through their associations. Thus there is a wealth of group-activity that flourishes on its own volition. In view of the fact, however, that all this activity is taking place within a legally formulated whole, all groups, regardless of their independent origins, are subordinated to the legal powers of the state.[17]

It is the precondition of orderly communal existence that the state act as the legal source of regulatory measures that pertain to the groups.[18] But, as we have seen, the state does not create associative life but only declares it, guards it, and supervises it.[19] It cannot legislate into existence the associative life that preceded its appearance but must incorporate it into its legal matrix. It is therefore inevitable that consideration be given to the relationship between state and law.

It is the nature of the law that it acknowledges and limits the rule of the state as it pertains to human associations. As soon as such a group is founded, it requires a legal order that will assist it in its endeavours. Without the presence of law, social life becomes unimaginable. Thus law, in its objective manifestations, consists of a complex of norms. In its subjective form it is a complex of rights and duties.[20] As a positive norm, it embodies the external rule over existing wills.

14 *Ibid.*, p. 98.
15 *Ibid.*, p. 99.
16 *Ibid.*
17 *Ibid.*, p. 100.
18 *Genossenschaftstheorie*, p. 648.
19 *Ibid.*, p. 652.
20 *Grundbegriffe*, p. 102.

As a subjective law, it is the expression of the freedom of the multitude of wills that are assigned a sphere of activity. This sphere incorporates right, as an element of freedom, and duty, as an element of limitation upon freedom.

The link between the state and the law is irrevocable, but neither precedes the other. The state is no more the creation of law than law is the creation of the state.[21] Each has independent roots although the two institutions develop side by side and become interdependent upon reaching maturity. Indeed, ultimately, in the modern state, law becomes dependent upon the state's recognition.[22] The source of law is not the state but the spirit of the people (*Volksgeist*). It is the development of this spirit over history that produces the appropriate legal norms for a community. It is not the state but the communal consciousness of a people that leads to the evolution of positive law. Law expresses that which is deemed right by the community, and the state formulates and promulgates, in legal terms, the desires of the consciousness of the people. Under these conditions the state attains a near-monopoly over law but it is nevertheless dependent, because of its derivation, upon the common will. Viewed in this light, the state is the depository of that concept, and law is the result of a general social consciousness.[23] The state's task culminates in political acts while law concerns itself with setting limitations upon individual wills. Its culminating accomplishment is the legal recognition, if not the creation, of the constituent groups.

The state's major characteristic is power, while law, without power, still remains law. But the healthy state seeks to establish itself upon the basis of law in order that rule be viewed as a legal enactment in accordance with the common will and consciousness. It follows, that the state will be limited by law, aware of its own rights and duties like any other juristic person or subject. For its part, law requires the assistance of the state's coercive power because, as conditions in the realm of international law indicate, law without coercive power is ineffectual.[24]

While inextricably linked, state and law have, to a certain degree, different purposes. The contemporary state, as Gierke sees it, is a 'state of culture' (*Kulturstaat*) that does not limit itself to legal pronouncements but also concerns itself with the fulfilment of the cultural goals of the community. At the same time, the most pre-eminent association is a 'state of laws' (*Rechtsstaat*) in so far as it apportions rights and at the same time voluntarily acknowledges the limitations imposed upon it by the legal order.[25] *Rechtsstaat* and constitutional state are two closely related concepts. Both distinguish between private and public law, both

21 *Ibid*., p. 103; Gierke, *Johannes Althusius*, Aalen, 6th ed., 1968, p. 318.
22 *Genossenschaftstheorie*, p. 18.
23 *Grundbegriffe*, p. 105.
24 *Ibid*., p. 106.
25 *Ibid*., p. 107.

place the state under the law, and both emphasize the constitutional character of public law.

Constitutional law, according to Gierke, is part of public law but is most definitely separated from private law.[26] It views the state as a universality and encompasses individuals and groups as articulated members of the state. It acts as a mediating and arbitrating force between the organic groups that constitute it. In view of its special position, constitutional law alters some concepts that were originally derived from private law. Thus the concept of person, in constitutional law, refers primarily to the personality of the associations and other groups. Not only does it recognize these entities as persons but it also regulates their conduct. It emphasizes and encourages those tendencies that lead to the creation of the unified group-persons who contribute to the life of the state. Constitutional law also determines the degree of absorption the groups are subjected to and guards their independence as far as possible. The reserve clause, operative in private law, is also active in constitutional law. The process of absorption that the groups undergo is not to be confused with their obliteration within or by constitutional law. Groups retain part of their personality and their inner living unity even in the face of constitutional law. They keep a segment of their independent essence despite the exalted position of the law they are confronted with. There are spheres within the realm of group-life that cannot be tampered with by private, public, or constitutional law,[27] and the reason for this is clear.

The groups, whether they be called fellowships, associations, or corporations are organs that act as mediators between the individual and the state and its laws. As the complexity of the state increases, so does the multitude of its organisms. Their tasks and goals differ but they are linked by a common denominator. They contribute part of their personality to the constitutional life of the whole. Their mediating function is regulated by the state in so far as it touches upon constitutional issues. The state, for instance, through its constitutional law, decides upon the degree and manner of co-operation it requires from each group. It is logical, that not all organs are of equal value to the state. Fundamental institutions such as the crown, the legislature, and the judiciary rank above the group of administrative officials and their sphere of activities.[28] Some organs are directly tied to issues concerning the state and therefore are of primary importance to constitutional law. Other, lesser, groups are only indirectly involved. The major tasks of constitutional law consist of the classification of all elements into a legal order, the recognition of their legal implications, and the regulation of both their mut-

26 *Ibid.*, p. 113.
27 *Ibid.*, p. 118.
28 *Ibid.*, p. 126.

ual relationships and their contacts with the state. It is of paramount importance that in such a *Rechtsstaat* the limits of group-activity as well as the limits of state activity be clearly defined and demarcated. For though the modern state may be the primary association among the multitude of other groups, though it may be endowed with sovereign powers for certain specific purposes, ultimately it is dependent upon the activities, the purposes, and the creative associative instinct of the constituent groups.

Describing the fundamental political principle of the Middle Ages Gierke says, 'Omnis multitudo derivatur ab uno – ad unum reducitur';[29] the multitude is derived from the one and to that one it returns. The modern state cannot subscribe to that principle. The number of individuals and group-persons has increased so substantially and the tasks of the modern state are so numerous that it cannot exist on an individualistic basis any more. But Gierke, in his admittedly ambiguous assessment of the state, also rejects the models supplied by ancient Greece and Rome, as these systems failed to give sufficient scope to the individual. As he sees it, this entity was totally obliterated by the Greek and Roman state. The individual's life was not lived for itself but for the state, a position that Gierke finds unacceptable. This, however, is an exaggerated view. Individualism, as for instance represented by Socrates, was indeed known and practised in classical antiquity. It was also reflected in Protagoras' contention that man was the measure of all things. Even though classical philosophy held that the fullest development of human nature could only come about within the framework of the appropriate state, Greek thought and Roman law did attribute a measure of intellectual and legal freedom to the individual. The concept of the group-person was alien to Greek thought and only incompletely exploited by Roman jurisprudence. But this shortcoming did not prevent the existence and proliferation of individualistic associations and corporations in Rome. Admittedly, these groups suffered from a legal constraint expressed in the concession theory, but at least they existed and at times even flourished.

As for the conditions relating to the individual and the state in the Middle Ages, Gierke's position may again be somewhat exaggerated. Despite the imposing amount of material Gierke compiles, it is not shown conclusively that the individual reigned supreme in that age. In fact, the individual served two, at times warring, masters: first the gradually emerging state that functioned under the names *regnum* or *imperium* and second the *sacerdotium*, the spiritual realm. The complicated relationship of these two entities, moreover, prevented the clear emergence of the state as the sole sovereign legal and political power. While rudi-

29 *Genossenschaftsrecht*, III, p. 515.

mentary forms of the nation-state manifested themselves in England and France by the twelfth century, Germany lagged far behind in that development. Not until the sixteenth century did some of the principalities assume a constitution that resembled that of a nation-state. In the absence of a national home, that supremacy of the individual to which Gierke refers is very difficult to discern. Indeed, the opposite may be closer to the truth. Exactly because the nation-state was present in an incomplete form, the individual was subject to the direct rule of monarchs and princes. Gierke bases his contention upon the fact that many of the rulers and indeed the prevalent legal and philosophic tone of the Age of Enlightenment was couched in the language of the theory of natural law, a mediaeval legacy that had been elaborated upon. But the individualistic implications of the *jus naturale* did, in practice if not in theory, apply primarily to the exalted position of the individual ruler. Its libertarian and egalitarian implications were not translated into reality until the latter half of the eighteenth century. But to say, as Gierke does, that the model of the Middle Ages and the heritage it passed on to successive generations was individualism nearly unhampered by public law is an exaggeration.

Similar objections can be raised to Gierke's treatment of what he calls the individualistic theory of society that ruled supreme in the seventeenth and eighteenth centuries. Again, the facts indicate that the individualistic potential was confined to the ruling circles and that it had little effect upon the common man. Gierke is on firmer ground when he ascribes to that age a mechanistic and atomistic view of society which denied the organic links that are the true foundations of Gierke's community. One of the weaknesses of the individualistic theory of society was its insistence upon the contractual origin of the state or society, a view most thoroughly rejected by Gierke. Modern legal thought, as he sees it, must divest itself of the idea of contract as the basis of a community for, ultimately, such a contract's nature is as nebulous as the theory of the fictitious person. Therefore he rejects the notion that the state can be based upon the sum of voluntary wills banded together for the sake of the protection of life and liberty. Yet his own theory of the state, which is an extension of this fellowship-theory, does not escape the taint of contractualism.

Hobbes' contract is based upon man's desire for self-preservation,[30] and in this respect Gierke's notion of the founding of the fellowship differs from Hobbes' contract. Locke's contract is motivated by man's desire to secure his 'life, liberty and estate,'[31] and these motives are not far removed from the goals of the potential members of the associations, large or small. Gierke can, together with all op-

30 T. Hobbes, *Leviathan*, chap. 17.

31 J. Locke, *The Second Treatise of Government*, para. 87.

ponents of the contract theory, reject the basic notion of the contract as being historically unsound. But as to the motivating forces that induce men to join a contract, his 'fellow' is not far removed from Locke's man who joins civil society.

The distance between Rousseau and Gierke is, however, greater. There is the temptation to see Gierke's common will as a derivative of Rousseau's general will. And, in so far as both concepts are derived from the consciousness of a people, they are indeed related. But Gierke's common will does not require that man give himself totally to the community founded upon contract. He retains part of his personality for the pursuit of his private ends. Rousseau, on the other hand, speaks of 'the total alienation of each associate, together with all his rights, to the whole community.'[32] In view of Gierke's basic contention that man's personality is divided into private and associative sectors, such a total alienation cannot come about. Nevertheless, the social urges that persuade man to form associations can, at one point, express themselves in the form of a contract. Guild-members, trade-union associates, and members of a religious group, for instance, do band together for the sake of some common aims. They do form groups, and there is both an agreement and consent in this act as well as a corollary element of obligation. Even if Gierke's association is a natural rather than a premeditated *a priori* contractual creation, the element of consent required for the functioning of the association has a contractual aspect. Thus his scheme is not free of all the ambiguities that accompany that theory.

Gierke's argument about the state's sovereignty is equally ambiguous. He argues that his state is an association among other associations and herein he resembles Aristotle.[33] It is, moreover, the most eminent of all associations and in this Gierke again agrees with Aristotle to whom the *polis* is the highest association. Nor is there a disagreement on the point that the state is a territorially limited association that knows no higher legal and political authority. But there the similarity with Aristotle ends, for to Gierke the state is also a juristic person as well as an entity endowed with a will and the capability to act on its own.

These assertions can be accepted so long as one agrees with Gierke's understanding of the reality of the legal person. His position becomes more ambiguous when the sovereignty of the state is examined. His state possesses the 'plenitude of powers,' but is also under the law. The state does not create the law, moreover, for that process is left to historical and social forces. Not being its source but merely its declarer and being divested of the power of concession, the state's absolute sovereignty, or what appears as the state's absolute sovereignty, becomes a vague proposition. For legal if not necessarily for political reasons, Gierke may

32 J.-J. Rousseau, *The Social Contract*, Bk. I, chap. 8.
33 Aristotle, *Politics*, 1252a.

be justified in ascribing sovereignty to one party or another. Law does need a focal point, a source, and a matrix, and the modern state, regardless of its political form, meets these requirements. The political theorist may choose to reject the idea of sovereignty entirely[34] but he does so at the peril of denying the existence of an ultimate and legitimate law-giving power within a community.

As argued, Gierke does not see the state as the source of law. But the state most certainly is the sovereign guardian of the law. Yet, owing to the derivation of the law, Gierke's concept of sovereignty is divided in a manner that resembles his concept of the legal person. The state commands the highest power in the land. Yet there are competing though somewhat unequal groups that are near-sovereign in their respective spheres of activities. This semi-sovereignty is not due to a concession or legitimization by the state. Rather, the status of the groups that compete with the state is derived from the ultimate force in Gierke's societal construct, the will of individuals and group-persons. The ambiguity inherent in Gierke's treatment of the state is not explained by merely quoting him as saying that the state is the 'highest right on earth.'[35] If that were the case, the state would indeed be sovereign. If, however, the state is dependent for its existence upon the will of its individual and group-members, then its sovereignty is limited.

Gierke holds that the state is the necessary product of the social forces that are active in individuals. We can carry this further and argue that these social forces, that is the will of individual and group-persons, express themselves directly through their respective associations. They contribute to the life of the state; indeed, in Gierke's thought, there can be no appropriate state without constituent group-persons. Being then dependent upon forces that provide it with life and the necessary social dynamism, the state is hardly as sovereign as the expression the 'plenitude of powers' indicates.

Indubitably the state has a monopoly on legitimate organized power within its territorial limits. Unquestionably the state does supervise the relationships of the associations within its realm. This is only to be expected in any modern system in which groups of political, social, economic, and even religious nature abound. But precisely because the state depends upon these groups it is hard to accept the verdict that Gierke's theory supports state-absolutism.[36] At the same time, Gierke cannot be ranked with the pluralists either. He does not subscribe to the pluralist rejection of the concept of sovereignty even though some of his ideas resemble pluralist notions. The emphasis on an articulated political society in which groups

34 For a recent discussion of the subject see W.J. Stankiewicz, ed., *In Defense of Sovereignty*, New York, 1969.

35 *Wesen*, p. 31. Cp.R. Emerson, *State and Sovereignty in Modern Germany*, New Haven, 1928, p. 139.

36 Hallis, *Corporate Personality*, p. 159.

are given free reign to pursue their ends in an unhindered fashion is a pluralist conception that is not far removed from Gierke's ideas. But it can be argued that even the most pluralistic state must find an ultimate source of legitimate power regardless of its intention of dissembling or denying the notion of sovereignty entirely. This does not make the pluralist model of the state conform to the monist idea and the same can be said of Gierke's conception of the state. In the final analysis his state is supreme in such fields as constitutional law, external affairs, and the acknowledgement and fostering of the life of its constituent groups. It may, in some aspects, represent the highest power in the land, but that power is not absolute but dependent upon the contributions of its organs. It may be even argued that ultimately Gierke's state is subject to a concession emanating from the common will of its organized populace.

To resolve the ambiguity inherent in Gierke's idea of a state that is a *Kulturstaat* and a *Rechtsstaat* at the same time, it would be simple to classify him as a monist or pluralist. It may even be questioned whether a *Rechsstaat* can or should act for or in the name of the culture of a people, and Gierke is certainly not clear on that point. But as for the monist or pluralist views, it must be seen that he takes a position between these two models. He adheres to a juridical conception of the state that is fairly familiar because it rests on the assumption that sovereignty can be divided.

The question arises, immediately, whether such a hybrid state can exist in political reality. Is it necessary instead to agree with the pluralist denial of the concept of sovereignty or is it mandatory to envisage the state as the absolute possessor of the sovereign plenitude of powers? Gierke's attempted solution is not to deny the concept of sovereignty but to diffuse it in a manner reminiscent of his treatment of the individual person. This individual contributes to the common will but in the process does not lose his individuality. There are two sides to his being, and this duality, we saw, does not necessarily lead to a schizophrenic condition. He is both a public and a private person, sovereign in some matters, subject in others. The state, in Gierke's conception, is not free to act in an arbitrary fashion either. In some of its aspects it acts and wills on its own. In other aspects, however, it is bound by the law as it emanates from its constituent members and their common will. Not even the common will is supreme for it too is divided among the individuals and group-persons that serve to make up the social fabric. Without the social instincts that persuade man to form into groups that eventually culminate in the appearance of the state, the latter is but a fiction and its personality a synthetic fabrication.

As for the question of divided sovereignty, that has, in practice, been resolved by the existence of federal systems whose continued presence is a proof that sovereignty does not have to be an absolutely monolithic concept. In practice it can be diffused and divided without denying that there is an ultimate source of legitimate power in any land. In Gierke's case, the power is not distributed between the central and the regional governments but between the person of the state and the person of the individuals and groups that express their social instincts in the form of a common will. If these social instincts disappear, the state ceases to exist, for it is not Hegel's 'divine idea as it exists on earth,'[37] but a dependent social organism void of metaphysical atrributes.

The reference to Hegel and his idea of the state is not coincidental. Few German jurists of the nineteenth century could afford to disregard Hegel's work, primarily his *Philosophy of Right*. Certain affinities and differences exist between Gierke's and Hegel's conception of the state and the role of its constituent groups. The differences emanate from Hegel's philosophic derivation of the state, a view Gierke does not share. Hegel places the state into the category of the objective mind that is but a stage towards the attainment of the realm of the absolute. Gierke does not follow these specific metaphysical assumptions. Also absent from Gierke's exposition is Hegel's category of civil society, for to Gierke society and state are but two sides of a single coin. But if there are differences, then there are also strong affinities between the two thinkers. Both show admiration for the historical forces that produce the law of the land; both men admire the intrinsic value inherent in the concept of the *Volk* and both men speak of the spirit of the *Volk* (*Volksgeist*) that is the motivating force of the state. There is a further agreement between them in so far as both wish to see the institution of a general civil code of law in Germany.

One of the major points on which Gierke differs from Hegel is in his treatment of the concept of person. Initially, there is an agreement between them, for both men look upon the person as a moral, willing, and acting individual. Gierke, as a jurist, then goes on to accept the Roman notion of *persona* but enlarges upon it by endowing it with a supra-individual unity of life. Moreover, as seen, he transposes the characteristics of the single person to the group and sees both entities as legal subjects. Hegel, on the other hand, bitterly attacks the Roman concept of person[38] when used in a strictly juristic sense. He charges that by relegating the person to the realm of private law, by making individuals right-bearing entities only as private persons,[39] the Roman system excludes the individual from politi-

37 G.W.F. Hegel, *Vorlesungen über die Philosophie der Geschichte*, Stuttgart, 1928, p. 71 (*The Philosophy of History*, J. Sibree transl., New York, 1956, p. 39).

38 For a further discussion of this subject see my 'The Sources and Significance of Hegel's Corporate Doctrine,' Z.A. Pelczynski, *Hegel's Political Philosophy*, Cambridge, 1971, pp. 111-35.

39 *Philosophie der Geschichte*, p. 154 (*Philosophy of History*, p. 107).

cal participation. This process makes the individual, as far as Hegel is concerned, an abstraction, an entity divorced from the philosophic, political, and social reality of his time. It is Hegel's ambition to end the isolation of the individual who is considered a mere legal category. It is his goal to bring the individual, hiding behind the enforced mask of the *persona*, into the light of social relationships. On this issue there is no disagreement between Gierke and Hegel. Even though the former does not object as violently as Hegel to the usage of the concept of person, he too wants to see the person being active in both private and public law. Moreover, both men agree on the undesirability of the theory of the *persona ficta*. According to them, a man is not a person because that status has been conceded to him by the state but because he is a free moral agent and a willing and acting being.

But the issue upon which both men agree most thoroughly is their conception of the state as an articulated organism wherein associations, fellowships, corporations, and foundations (*Stiftungen*) act as intermediaries between the individual and the totality. Both men abhor the idea of the atomistic individual being lost in the multitude of the modern state. Hegel makes his view perfectly clear in arguing that the 'atomistic and abstract point of view vanishes at the stage of the family, as well as that of civil society where the individual is in evidence only as a member of a general group. The state, however, is essentially an organization each of whose members is in itself a group of this kind, and hence no one of its moments should appear as an unorganized aggregate.'[40] Only by joining a group, Hegel argues, does the individual become 'somebody'[41] who thus attains rank and dignity.

The benefits derived from the corporate model, moreover, are not confined to the individual alone. The state, on its part, gains strength and permanence from its subsidiary, constituent organs. If a state eliminates these organs, then it suffers dire consequences and Hegel points to Napoleonic France as the example. Rather than legislating them out of existence, as had been done in that country, the state must encourage the existence of the subsidiary groups for 'the proper strength of the state lies in these associations.'[42] Gierke, writing some five decades after Hegel made that pronouncement, does not disagree. He notes, 'By according an organic nature to the associations, jurisprudence was obliged to accept the idea of a real communal personality.'[43] This, according to Gierke, was one of Hegel's ideas that influenced successive thinkers. It should be noted that, although Hegel did not speak in terms of 'real communal personality,' his conception of

40 G.W.F. Hegel, *Philosophy of Right*, T.M. Knox transl., Oxford 1942, para. 303.
41 *Ibid.*, para. 253.
42 *Ibid.*, addition to para. 290, p. 290.
43 *Genossenschaftstheorie*, p. 6, n. 1.

the state as the universal totality in the realm of the objective mind is but a philosophic formulation of the idea of the reality of the group-person. For, ultimately, Gierke's state with its divided sovereignty is essentially a group-person among other associations that, despite its ambiguity in logic, is a very real model of the modern state.

4

Natural and Historical Law

Gierke was 'from first to last a soldier in the Germanist section of the School of Historical Law.'[1] This means that Gierke rejected the philosophic approach of law as propounded by the adherents of the *jus naturale*. It also means that he was intent upon obtaining and establishing a truly indigenous German body of law that had been at least partially purged of the tenets of the *Corpus Juris Civilis.*

One of the most lasting ideas of that *corpus* had been the introduction, dissemination, and eventual victory of the idea of natural law. The roots of that school of thought reach back to Aristotle's distinction between 'particular,' (that is, positive) law and 'universal law,' (that is, 'the law of nature').[2] The notion gained pre-eminence with the Stoics and Cicero and was enshrined in Justinian's pronouncement, 'The law which natural reason appoints for all mankind obtains equally among all nations. ... '[3] This fragment contains the essential elements of the concept of natural law for it refers to its derivation from nature and from reason and to the universal applicability of these notions. There is the reference to natural reason common to mankind or, as Cicero had put it, 'True law is right reason in agreement with nature; it is of universal application, unchanging and everlasting. ... '[4] Reason was considered the common and uniform possession of mankind, the attribute that set it apart from the animals.[5] It was the supreme arbiter open to all rational appeals and so prevalent and transcendental that it

1 Barker, 'Introduction,' *Natural Law*, p. lvi.

2 Aristotle, *Rhetoric*, 1373b. See also Barker 'Introduction,' pp. xxxiv ff.

3 *Institutes*, 1.2.1.

4 Cicero, *De Re Publica*, C.W. Keyes transl., London, 1928, 3.22.

5 Ulpian's definition of natural law differs at this point, stating that 'this law is not peculiar to the human race, but belongs to all animals ... ' (*Digest*, 1.1.1.). This denies the pre-eminence of human reason and, on the whole, was disregarded by the *jusnaturalist* school.

had a meaning to all those who cared to exercise their natural rational faculties. Nature contained this reason and, in the mediaeval interpretation, came to be looked upon as an extension of the divine will. Being a universal postulate, natural law, whether ancient or mediaeval, was cosmopolitan in its appeal, and, on the political level, could apply to both the ruler and the ruled. In the post-mediaeval era it could lead to Hobbes's absolutism[6] as well as to Locke's economic liberalism.[7] It was its libertarian and egalitarian strain that served as the basis for the effective radical theories of the American and French Revolutions.

Regardless of the interpretations attached to natural law, however, one of its features remained pre-eminent. It never lost its cosmopolitan connotations. By its very nature it had this universal appeal for it was born at the time when the small, intimate *polis* was being replaced by such larger territorial and political units as the Hellenistic and the Roman Empires. Because of this metamorphosis, the individual found himself as a very small part of large and atomized societies. With the intimacy of the *polis* lost, the individual could find solace by subscribing to one universal ethical law that stood beyond and above the law of the land. He could, figuratively speaking, consider himself a citizen of the world, of the cosmopolis. His primary point of reference was neither his own community nor his generic association but the brotherhood of man under one supreme law, an idea bolstered by the victorious emergence of Christianity. Despite the fragmentation of the European community in the Middle Ages and the successive centuries, natural law, in theory, surmounted feudal and then national boundaries for, by its definition, it was of universal applicability.

In the latter half of the eighteenth century the Romantic reaction set in, questioning the tenets of natural law. Encouraged by such philosophers as Johann Gottfried Herder, men turned their attention to the study of their native environment, their own language, their indigenous literature, and eventually to their own native customary law. As Gierke puts it, 'Confidence was lost in the dream of a universal law just as confidence disappeared in the attempt to find a universal language.'[8] Similarly, faith in the existence of universal reason disappeared, and instead emphasis was placed on the concept of the *Volk*, its consciousness, and its spirit in all of its native ramifications. Natural law, Gierke admits, led to some great achievements,[9] but it disregarded the indigenous law of the people. In the course of history, Roman, canonical, and Italo-Roman law and their *jus naturale* had been grafted upon the body of German law. This process did not always produce fortunate results. Indeed, 'Untold damage was inflicted upon the German

6 *Natural Law*, I, p. 106 (*Genossenschaftsrecht*, IV, p. 394).

7 *Ibid.*, I, p. 113 (IV, p. 409).

8 *Naturrecht*, p. 13.

9 *Ibid.*, p. 14.

people by the lengthy rule of foreign Roman law,'[10] Gierke maintains in one of his more personal pronouncements.

A very special relationship existed between Roman and German law, reaching back into the age of the great migrations and the contracts between the late Roman Empire and its remnants and the emerging Germanic kingdoms. Once the former nomadic tribes had settled in their respective domains, which were often carved out of former Roman provinces, they attained a degree of political and social sophistication. They required laws suitable for their changed conditions and it was natural that they turned to the precepts of Roman law and grafted them onto the tribal laws that had been valid in their migratory stages. The *Lex Romana Burgundionum* and the *Lex Visigothorum* (*Breviarium Alaricianum*)[11] of the sixth century represented Roman codes pertaining to Germanic peoples. The Carolingian rule and the establishment of the Holy Roman Empire led to further intermingling of advanced Roman legal concepts with the somewhat vague and ill-defined Germanic folk-laws. The process was not received everywhere and at all times with great enthusiasm. Repeatedly, attempts were made to return to Germanic folk-law, notably in the thirteenth century that witnessed the publication of the indigenous *Sachsenspiegel* and the *Schwabenspiegel*.[12] But these attempts at reinstating the folk-law were relatively ineffectual owing to the Roman cast of the canon law and the elasticity of the *Corpus Juris Civilis* that lent itself to wide adaptations. Thus, in mediaeval Germany, Roman law still served as the model for a legally advanced community, although the folk-law retained some hold upon the community. The two systems of law coexisted in a haphazard fashion until the sixteenth century. Then came the Reception of the entire body of Roman Law into the German realm,[13] that is the general adoption by the various German principalities of the entire *Corpus Juris Civilis*. In fact, as Gierke points out,[14] the *corpus* of law that was 'received' was not classical Roman law or the Justinian compilations alone but also the body of Italo-Roman law that had been developed by the canonists and jurists in the school at Bologna.

The reception and the adoption of the Italo-Roman law led to a dichotomous position. The 'new' law was fostered, promulgated, and disseminated by the rulers whose absolutistic tendencies were well served by Justinian's statement, 'That which seems good to the emperor has also the force of law.'[15] Their court officials,

10 Gierke, *Recht und Sittlichkeit*, Darmstadt, 1916, p. 49.

11 P. Vinogradoff, *Roman Law in Medieval Europe*, Oxford, 1929, pp. 16-30.

12 H. Mitteis, *Deutsche Rechtsgeschichte*, Munich, 1956, pp. 150-1; Vinogradoff, *Roman Law*, pp. 124-5.

13 *Genossenschaftsrecht*, III, p. 672.

14 *Ibid.*, p. 646.

15 *Institutes*, 1.2.6.

their judiciary, and their administrators could thus act upon the assumption that law and the word of the ruler were one and the same. Moreover, Roman law, or what was assumed to be Roman law, became the province of the learned jurists and their courts who paid no heed to the older common law of the land. 'Learned' law and folk-law competed for a while but eventually the latter was overcome by the subtle clauses of the former.

One of the consequences of this development was the resulting pressure put upon the ancient fellowships, associations, and corporations that had constituted the mediaeval body politic. The absolutistic state viewed such intermediary groups with a jaundiced eye, seeing them as possible competitors for absolute sovereignty. On a juristic level, the notion of the fictitious person and the concession theory became prominent again with all the accompanying implications. The association, viewed as a lifeless *universitas*, was accepted only as a legal subject in the form of a *persona ficta, repraesentata, imaginaria*, as a mere juristic concept without any real organic essence.[16] While nominally subscribing to natural law, the Reception thus robbed the German concept of person of its real living unity and its own *raison d'être.* On a political level this meant the denial of the ancient free right to associate, a concept that had been central to German folk-law. Despite its libertarian connotations, therefore, natural law, as introduced by the Reception, came to exert a repressive and illiberal force. Moreover, it undermined the ancient concepts of folk-community and fellowship and substituted for them a form of arid individualism that served as a model for an atomized and mechanistic view of state and society. Thus the rule of Roman jurisprudence with its concept of natural law was, in the German experience, a legacy of somewhat dubious value. To replace the plethora of Roman principles and to revitalize the indigenous cultural and legal life of the community became the major goal of the school of historical law.

One of the earliest and most prominent exponents of the new trend was Gustav Hugo who first 'realized that the law of the people could only be understood through the national life itself, since it was itself a part and expression of that life.'[17] This theme was espoused with great enthusiasm by such men as Karl Friedrich Eichhorn and, above all, Friedrich Carl von Savigny. It was the latter who argued that 'Law grows with the *Volk*, it formulates itself according to the *Volk*, and finally dies, if the *Volk* loses its character.'[18] Gierke argued that neither arid jurisprudence nor the arbitrary decrees of rulers are the source of the law. Rather, law is an essential ingredient of communal life and is inextricably linked

16 *Genossenschaftsrecht*, III, p. 726.
17 G.P. Gooch, *History and Historians in the Nineteenth Century*, Boston, 1959, p. 39.
18 *Vom Beruf*, p. 11.

to such other manifestations of group-existence as language, religion, morality, custom, economics, and native art and science.[19] Law is thus the product of an organic communal life that culminates in the 'spirit of the people' (*Volksgeist*).[20]

The *Volksgeist*, moreover, is not a haphazard and arbitrary manifestation of a group of isolated individuals but stands for the consciousness of a community as it developed over history. The historical view is, according to Gierke, unalterably and irrefutably correct,[21] for law is not and cannot be an *a priori* creation. Determinedly, the school of historical law rejected the idea of a Lycurgus or a Solon, or the figure of any other great law-giver who instituted a code that emanated from the mind of a single individual. Reality, as Gierke saw it, simply did not bear out the theory of the great legislator and innovator when it came to the birth, growth, and flourishing of a native code of law. It was this code and its origins, as well as its history and development that had to be studied and then applied by modern legal science.

Gierke saw practical advantages accruing from this approach. Precise studies in the record of Germanic and German law would lead to a more accurate and penetrating understanding of the present.[22] And what his time required was the establishment of a general code of civil law based upon the tenets and findings of historical research. The new civil code was to be drawn up in harmony with the ancient principles that had been brought up to date and applied to both private and public law. Nor was the new jurisprudence to make its way in isolation. Its findings were to be supplemented by men active in such fields as literature, history, and linguistics, men such as Grimm, Ranke, and Arndt.[23] With their assistance the influence of the *receptio in complexu* was to be banished and a German law established that was on the same level as Roman law. The new national law was to be independent of the Roman past and its verification based solely on a series of German precedents.[24]

The formative years of the school of historical law in the first half of the nineteenth century witnessed the appearance of a schism within the school itself. The source of the schism was the disagreement over the desirability of eliminating Roman law completely. The so-called Germanist wing of the school was intent upon following just such a radical course. But the Romanist wing, under the leadership of Savigny, was not so certain. The question was not one of academic re-

19 *Naturrecht*, pp. 7-8.
20 *Ibid.*, p. 9.
21 *Ibid.*, p. 14.
22 *Die historische Rechtsschule und die Germanisten*, Berlin, 1903, p. 22 (hereafter *Historische Rechtsschule*).
23 *Ibid.*, p. 20.
24 *Ibid.*, p. 22.

moteness but had real, practical implications. Admittedly, *Volksrecht* and *Juristenrecht*, or common law and 'learned' law, had become separated, as maintained by Gierke's mentor, Georg Beseler.[25] But it was also a fact that Roman law and its derivatives had become an integral part of the fabric of German law. With some modifications, many of its provisions had been incorporated in the common law of the land, as Savigny pointed out.[26] To remove these elements from the body of German private law appeared as an imprudent step. Therefore Savigny argued that Roman law not be disregarded but rather that it be incorporated into the new system.

However, he thereby placed himself in an ambiguous position. On the one hand, he was the acknowledged leader of the school of historical law before the advent of Gierke, arguing that law was the result of social action[27] and the derivative of the *Volksgeist*.[28] On the other hand, he maintained that German legal science was not yet sufficiently advanced to discard the lessons taught by Rome. He stated, 'We can dispense with examples when we have learned to handle juristic matters with the freedom and the mastery that we admire the Romans for.'[29] It is a false sense of pride that makes a nation reject the lessons of history even if these lessons come from a foreign source. Therefore Savigny cautioned against the improper use of the surgeon's scalpel in excising all principles of Roman law from the *corpus* of German law.[30] It was for this reason that he set out to examine, in the greatest detail, the entire system of Roman law as it existed in his time and to derive from it those facets that were of permanent utility to the new science of German law. He found no contradiction between his endeavour to perfect the knowledge of Roman law and his own dictum that the law was derived from an indigenous *Volksgeist*. As Savigny saw it, the orderly development of German law would have been impossible without references to the Roman system.[31] Savigny also doubted that the time was appropriate for the codification of a general civil code.

This argument, together with his insistence upon the retention of a substantial portion of Roman civil law, produced the schism in the school of historical law. It developed a Germanist wing under the leadership of Eichhorn. This wing was intent upon producing a purely German version of a planned general civil code. The original co-operation that had existed between the Romanist and Germanist

25 *Volksrecht und Juristenrecht*, Leipzig, 1843.
26 *System*, I, pp. 4-5.
27 *Ibid.*, p. 21.
28 *Ibid.*, p. 20.
29 *Ibid.*, p. xxxl.
30 *Vom Beruf*, p. 115.
31 *Vom Beruf*, p. 38.

factions disappeared in the tumultuous days of 1848, when the question of the civil code was very much a centre of discussion. Then, 'it was renewed, with less ardour but in more practical form, when a definite scheme for a new civil code for the German Empire was published in 1888.'[32]

Gierke belonged to the second generation of the school of historical law. As professor of jurisprudence in Breslau (1872), Heidelberg (1884), and then Berlin (1887), he placed himself at the head of the Germanist branch. Deeply involved in the argument concerning the cast and the nature of the new civil code, he maintained, as he had done in all of his works, that the historic interpretation of law was not a new speculative system but the irrevocable truth.[33] All true philosophies of law had to be based upon history[34] for only in that way could a truly national law emerge. Despite his attacks upon the influence of Roman law, he retained a respect for the accomplishment derived from the *Corpus Juris Civilis.* But this respect was tempered by an awareness or the conviction that time had made the Roman law a thing of the past. History never ceases to introduce changes and new forms and explications. So far as Gierke was concerned, these explications could not be derived from Roman law anymore for the national consciousness of his people had surmounted the past and had arrived at the modern age. The changes were not only of legal but also of political character, a further aspect that separated the Romanist from the Germanist branch of the school of historical law.

The Romanist branch, with Savigny at its head was, Gierke argues, essentially conservative, while the Germanist branch represented liberal ideas.[35] Savigny, in his insistence upon the fictitious person and the correlative concession theory, was prepared to accept the absolute sovereignty of the state. The Germanists, on the other hand, with their emphasis upon the importance of the group-person, the constituent associations, and the free right to associate, opted for a more balanced state where the weight of the central authority was mitigated by the existence and the real life of the groups. Their constitutionalism centred upon the attainment of a unified, national state, a notion not in contradiction to liberal ideas in the nineteenth century. When that unification was achieved and the national civil code eventually enacted in 1896, the schism between the Romanist and Germanist branch of the school of historical law was not healed. But certainly the violent altercations between the two factions ceased. In retrospect, Gierke admits, both factions had served their cause well and had contributed to the level

32 Barker, 'Introduction,' *Natural Law*, p. lv.

33 *Naturrecht*, p. 7.

34 *Historische Rechtsschule*, pp. 34-5.

35 *Ibid.*, p. 26.

of jurisprudence in their country and ought, therefore, to be studied with care.[36]

The school of historical law had some valid points. It also exhibited some potentially dangerous tendencies. One of its major accomplishments was to replace the theory of natural law with a body of thought that was more aware of the historical and social realities of its time. Its division into Romanist and Germanist branches was very significant for it illustrated the tenacity and strength of Roman law. When Savigny argued for the validity of the clauses of the *Corpus Juris Civilis*, he spoke for a tradition that had withstood the test of time for about two thousand years. The reason for the extraordinary tenacity of the influence of the *corpus* can be explained by its considerable elasticity and adaptability. Whether in the guise of canon law or under the influence of Bologna, it proved itself capable of serving as a model for innumerable legal systems and institutions. It was not as thoroughly organized as Savigny envisaged it and that may be one of the explanations for its survival. Its clauses, or at least some of its clauses of private law, served as a useful model for the continental nations even as they discarded, over time, those elements of Roman law that had become irrelevant. Thus for instance, the absolute power embodied in the *patria potestas* could be changed to more humane interpretations of family law without rejecting the entire *corpus*. Above all, Roman law had contributed to the civilization of Germany and could not be discarded lightly. In this respect, the Romanist position was justified. But the Germanists had some valid arguments also.

One of the most powerful influences exerted by Roman law had been in the advocacy and dissemination of natural law. Gierke correctly surmised some of the fallacies inherent in that school of thought. There were historical contradictions in a *corpus* that made references to a universal law with egalitarian and libertarian connotations and yet condoned the institution of slavery. Roman jurisprudence was more successful in applying the tenets of natural law to the *jus gentium* that provided the matrix for an orderly legal intercourse between the Roman state and its non-Roman population. But Gierke is correct in maintaining that the theory of natural law produced an atomistic view of state and society. The Roman *jus singuli* and natural law exhibited marked similarities, and certainly individualism could be interpreted in an absolutistic as well as in a liberal fashion as shown by the examples of Hobbes and Locke. Gierke is correct in tracing the various consequences of the *jus naturale* and maintaining that the theory lent itself to a wide variety of interpretations, some of them liberal, some illiberal.

36 *Ibid.*, p. 36.

Natural law implies the existence of natural rights. These rights played an important role in the Middle Ages when they were utilized to place the monarch under the rule of law. While this tenet frequently remained in the realm of theory, it implanted the notion that there were rights of individuals that limited those of others regardless of their status. The identical theoretical position appeared in the Age of Enlightenment and in the thought of the *monarchomachi* who spoke for the right of lawful rebellion against the ruler. It was this idea that culminated in the American and French Revolutions. Natural law and natural right became tangible political forces of tremendous importance. Yet, as Gierke points out, the individualistic and atomistic models of the seventeenth and eighteenth centuries had marked shortcomings. As it has been said, 'The discovery of nature or of the fundamental distinction between nature and convention is the necessary condition for the emergence of the idea of natural right.'[37] Convention, on the other hand, is one of the elements that can only be produced over time. While adapting itself to changing historical circumstances, natural law, with its *a priori* postulates, did not give up those of its tenets that tended to disregard the dynamism inherent in history.

Conventions are subject to alterations and natural law disregarded one such development, the awakening of the national consciousness in Germany in the eighteenth century. So far as Gierke is concerned, that was not the only fault of the theory of natural law. As he sees it, the Germanic peoples had a natural right, the free right to associate, long before they were exposed to the clauses of Roman law. This was not an individualistic but a communal right that could not or ought not to have been buried under the learned tomes explicating the *jus naturale*. It was a convention as indigenous and basic as the natural rights of individual men. In Gierke's historical perception, moreover, the communal right to associate preceded the right of the individual and it was the task of his school of thought to press home this point.

Conditions were favourable to this approach. Romanticism, as indicated, spoke of community and the *Volk*, its spirit, its consciousness, and its communal accomplishments. In comparison, natural law appeared as an arid and lifeless legal formalism. It was overcome by the tide of romantic communal feeling and thought. Whether this was really an advance in social and legal thought is a contentious issue. Romanticism, despite its pathos and emotionalism, did represent a real historical development, the search for a new and possibly better community that was responsive to the awakening national consciousness not only of Germany but of many other central and eastern European countries. In this respect, the school of historical law, and particularly its Germanist branch, mirrored the

37 L. Strauss, *Natural Right and History*, Chicago, 1953, p. 93.

legitimate aspiration of a people. At the same time, romanticism was highly susceptible to zealousness, bigotry, and even xenophobia, the latter being quite absent from the cosmopolitan character of natural law. These facets led to the excesses of nationalism that deteriorated into chauvinism, a phenomenon all too familiar to the twentieth-century observer.

There are thus dangers in making convention the basis of law. Gierke mitigates this danger by speaking of a constantly changing and responsive social law that mirrors not only the past but also the conditions present in a modern state. Yet his insistence that a people's consciousness, as expressed in the *Volksgeist*, is one of the sources of law places the onus on an exceedingly vague notion. Who or what represents the *Volksgeist*? The whole people or only those who express the wishes of the majority? What of the dissenting minorities? Are they to be expelled from the body of the *Volk*? Gierke's reply is reassuring only in so far as he advocates and indeed insists upon a proliferation of groups within the body politic. It is logical to expect that not all these groups will have identical ideas and ambitions and that there will be a fruitful interchange between the contending factions before some sort of harmony is attained. The condition of this interchange is provided for by the existence of a *Rechsstaat* that guards the existence of all legitimate subsidiary groups. But if the *Rechtsstaat* is replaced by a mere *Volksstaat* as propounded by the national socialists in Germany in the twentieth century, then immeasurable harm is done. At such times, a return to the immutable individualistic tenets of natural law would have been justified.

Yet, as the example of English common law indicates, convention as a source of law can be most acceptable. Gierke was confronted with a different and a more difficult problem, for, as indicated, German common law had been subordinated to Roman law. The quest for an indigenous code of law, based upon historical precedent, custom, convention, and, as far as that is determinable, the common will, is a legitimate approach to the law. That some of its features, such as the idea of the *Volksgeist*, were perverted by some men of the twentieth century cannot be held against Gierke. But it cannot be denied that the Germanist branch of the school of historical law endowed successive ages with an ambiguous legacy.

In considering Gierke's work in general, it must be taken into account that he represents a tradition that is not always familiar to the English-speaking world. Continental Europe in general and Germany in particular had a legal development different from that of England and those countries that inherited its legal principles. Nowhere is that more evident than in Gierke's concept of the fellowship, association, and generally the group-person. While other legal systems also recognize such entities, Gierke sees the entire development of the historical and juridical structure as a result of man's associative instinct. There would be nothing novel to this view were it not for his contention that the groups have a life and an inner unity of their own that makes them autonomous persons in their own right. This is a unique and peculiar transposition of man's 'asocial sociability' for, as argued, the ultimate test of the existence of this life is an act of faith. Whether it is possible to build a valid juristic system on such an assumption is a matter of conjecture.

First, there is the question of this faith in the real life of the group-person, as Gierke understands it. It is difficult to separate the life of the members of the group from the life of the group itself. It is their will that creates the group and without that will the group may well become a *persona ficta*. In terms of commercial law, what is the joint stock company without the contributions and wills of its shareholders? Or, to put it on a wider plane, what is the state without the voluntary or reluctant co-operation of its citizens? There is a danger in ascribing a distinct personality to such entities as corporations and the state. The danger is not so much of a political nature, for, it can be argued there is little risk in assuming that the state has a personality of its own. If it does have one, then it is, in Gierke's scheme, under the law. It is a legal subject no less than the individual citizen. It may represent the highest right and therein Gierke is correct, for it is difficult to argue that the state is not the pre-eminent legal and political association in today's world. It is also quite acceptable to see this state as the ultimate source of legitimate power, for power must have a source and a nodal point before it is diffused and distributed. The danger lies in the possibility of being carried away by a faith in the group-person at the cost of the individual. Yet Gierke makes it clear that the bases of the groups are individual wills which come together for a specific purpose. As long as they retain control over their groups and the groups in turn retain their influence upon the state, there is the possibility of attaining a balanced system, a *Rechtsstaat* in the best sense of that word. This process does not necessarily require a blind faith in the supra-individual unity of life but can be seen as a practical and valid formula.

Second, there is the question of social law. This is, for all intents and purposes, the saving grace that makes Gierke's whole system of law comprehensible. There may be repeated references to *Volksgeist, Volksseele* (the soul of a people), and a common will, but these romantic notions do yield to a sense of juristic sobriety in Gierke's own definition of the fellowship. It gains even more realism when law is seen as a derivation of social interactions and relationships within a geographically delimited community. In its legal practices, this community does not have to fall back upon history and convention alone but can derive a fresh legal impetus from legislation derived from and directed by the tenets of social law. These tenets are nothing else but the legal conclusions drawn from the daily practices of the community itself. It is free of *a priori* postulates and therefore flexible and presumably sensitive to the wishes of the constituent individuals and groups. Gierke's romanticism wanes and his juristic realism gains by the processes of social law. His historicism yields to the sober requirements of the modern state. It is noticeable that there is no clear distinction between the supervisory role performed by social and constitutional law respectively. The omission, however, does not measurably influence the final result of his thesis.

Third, his model of the state, that consists of the idea of an articulated society diffused into constituent groups, is in harmony with the realities of the day. Even though Gierke lived in and was part of the great nationalist movement in Germany, his juristic sense kept him from demanding a monolithic state that would be intolerant of intermediary groups. There is an interesting ambiguity in his conception of the *Volk* and the groups. The *Volk* is the totality of the cultural, political, social, and economic ambitions and accomplishments of a people. Theoretically it would be easy to turn this concept into a monolith to be worshipped by all of its members. Yet Gierke, with his strong sense for and faith in the group-personality, fortunately refrains from accepting the monolithic model. No state that is obliged to give as much freedom of action to its constituent groups can be considered monolithic, despite Gierke's ambiguous treatment of the concept of sovereignty.

Admittedly, the state is in a privileged position in so far as it can and does recognize the groups and their life. But it cannot turn upon them and obliterate them, for in doing so it would vanquish itself. The law is still the best guardian against abuses, and it seems that Gierke is more concerned with possible abuses emanating from the state than with the centrifugal power exerted by the groups. The reason for this is his firm conviction that articulation is more important than centralization. The spontaneous creation and real or imaginary life of the groups supercedes the claims of the whole for the simple reason that there can be no whole without constituent organs. It is not necessary to subscribe to the organic theory of state and society to perceive the advantages of his model of the articulated political community. There is no act of faith involved in such a process. It is indisputable that modern man would be lost in the multitude of the contemporary state if he were denied the opportunity to form and join subsidiary political and economic groups. The precondition of such a process is the recognition of and respect for the legal subjectivity of the person. The person, behind his juristic mask, is the thinking and willing individual who expresses himself according to his ethical volition and the ethical postulates of his community.

Finally, a few words about Gierke's own treatment of the idea of association in classical antiquity and early Christianity. It is best to let Gierke speak for himself, but his basic premises as enumerated above must be kept in mind. When he writes about Greek, Roman, and early Christian associative law, he has really two purposes in mind. One is the historical compilation of the record of the groups under their respective systems of law. The other purpose is to test the accumulated material against his own convictions and findings as derived from Germanic and German law. His reservations about the deep Roman schism between public and private law are evident in his presentation. He determinedly rejects the concepts of the fictitious person and the concession theory, not because he thinks that the Romans ought to have known better but because history, in the German realm, had proved these theories to be fallacious. Above all, he cannot forgive the Roman system for its insistence on deriving private law from the single isolated individual when historical and social circumstances failed to support that view. His conclusions, like all historical judgments, are based upon *ex post facto* observations. Therefore they must be understood with these reservations in mind.

THE ASSOCIATION IN CLASSICAL ANTIQUITY AND EARLY CHRISTIANITY

Otto Gierke

Translator's Note

Unlike Savigny, Gierke has a style that is exceedingly complicated and at times convoluted. Therefore the translator was faced with the dual task of rendering the text in a comprehensible manner while still retaining Gierke's original thought. While breaking up Gierke's long sentences, paragraphs, and frequently his composite words, the translation attempts, with a few abridgments, to be as faithful a transposition as possible.

There are some terms that require elucidation. *Genossenschaft* has, following the examples of Maitland and Barker, been translated as 'fellowship.' Only that term can convey the special meaning which Gierke and the German language attach to the word. *Recht* has been translated both as 'right' and 'law,' as the meaning of the argument warranted. This dual rendering is in keeping with the Roman tradition that uses the term *jus* both as 'law' and 'right.' Thus the *Institutes* speak of the *jus naturale* while its translator refers to it as the 'law of nature.'[1] Gierke uses the term *Gesetz* (law or *lex*) relatively infrequently. Generally he prefers the word *Recht* even when speaking of positive law. Hence the necessity for translating *Recht* as both right and law as the meaning of the argument dictated it.

The term *publizistisch* has, in keeping with Maitland's practice, been translated as 'political.' The modern connotations of 'publicity' are too much with us to permit the use of the word 'publicistic.' After Barker's example,[2] the terms 'collective' and 'collectivity' have been avoided as much as possible. They are used when speaking of the Roman *universitas* in so far as it is the prototype of an inorganic, purely formal collection of individuals and their rights. In Gierke's thought, it is the antithesis of the organic fellowship. The term 'group-person' has been used when the occasion warranted it. *Verband* has been translated as 'association,' '*Körperschaft*' as 'corporation,' and *Gesammtheit* as 'totality.'

1 Justinian, *Institutes*, T.C. Sandars transl., London, seventh ed., 1956, 1.2.

2 'Introduction,' *Natural Law*, p. xci.

Gierke's voluminous footnotes have been edited and, whenever possible, abbreviated. In some instances he fails to supply the date and place of publication. and these have been provided wherever possible. However, there are some works whose publication data are not available, and these have been rendered according to Gierke's text. References to some minor secondary sources have been omitted for they have lost whatever little importance they may have had.

References to the *Digest*, the *Codex*, the *Novellae*, and the *Institutes* have been changed to accord with the English mode of citation. Lengthy quotations from classical texts have been omitted for Gierke gives their references and the interested reader can check the relevant passages.

Scriptural references are from the New English Bible.

I

The Concept of Association in Ancient Philosophy

Greek views on the state and law served as the basis for the speculations of ancient philosophy about the nature of human associations. In Greek thought, the concept of human associations coincided originally with the concept of the *polis*. The state appeared simply as *the* human association. All social ties were entirely derived from it; they were considered as parts of the whole organization. Thus a science of social life came to the fore, a philosophic theory of the state that, in reality, was a universal theory of society. What the Greeks did for the legal concept of association and what they passed on to the Romans must be discussed with regard to its theoretical background.

In Greek philosophy as well as in popular conception, the state in general was, from its inception, a given independent whole of unique and original substantiality. As parts of it, human beings were fully contained in the state. Individual existence was, of course, recognized as something particular, but it was brought to fulfilment only within communal life which was the natural and higher order of existence. This existence was incorporated in the state and the individual therefore derived from the state his particular measure and goal. At no point did he transcend its limitations. The individual had ultimately no autonomous purpose but he functioned as a means whose purpose was derived from the whole. This view is intimately related to the peculiar limitations of Greek legal thought. Law was understood exclusively as the harmonic ordering of communal life within the state. Therefore, the concept of law resolved itself basically into objective law. Rights had no independent meaning but were only the reflections of an order that existed for and through the whole.

The Greek spirit accomplished something immortal for the idea of objective law. The Greeks were the first to develop the conception of the 'state in which laws rule' and this they passed on to posterity. They attributed to law a majesty and raised it above the ruler as well as above the ruled.[1] Simultaneously they removed the substance of law from the sphere of human caprice and viewed it as an expression of righteousness contained in an objective principle. The Greeks considered it as a principle that encompassed the state and the individual in an ethical world order. According to popular conviction, the divinely inspired 'unwritten higher laws' were the source of all human law. Nothing was further removed from this conviction than the idea that will can be the creator of law.[2] In conjunction with the deterioration of public life, various philosophical views developed that disputed this view and sought to maintain that laws were of human origin.[3] Nevertheless, the true national philosophy of law devoted its greatest powers to proving that there was an eternal, unshakable principle (be it God or

1 K. Hildebrand, *Geschichte und System der Rechts – und Staatsphilosophie, das klassische Alterthum*, Leipzig, 1860, I, pp. 28 ff. At the same time there existed the conception that the perfect ruler as the personification of the rationality of the laws made them superfluous and that the immediate realization of the legal idea was to be preferred to rigid, rule. In this sense Xenophon in his *Cyropaedia* calls the true ruler the embodiment of law. Plato establishes the rule of laws in the constitutional state, while in the ideal state the ruling class is not bound by external law but is guided by the immediate idea of the good. In exceptional cases, Aristotle permits absolute monarchy without laws. But for normal conditions Aristotle expresses the thought that law is the real sovereign, *Politics* 4.c.4; 3.c.15. Similarly the Stoics; cp. Chrysippus' statement which reached the *Corpus Juris Civilis* through Marcianus, *D.* 1.3.2.

2 Cp. Hildebrand, pp. 29 ff., who correctly emphasizes that it was alien to pure Greek thought to regard law as the product of the will of the people. 'The agreement of the people could not be absent but the content of the law was not legitimized by the will of the people. Rather it was assumed that the people had willed it because it appeared as legitimate to them.' In this sense Aristotle, above all others, notes that democracies in which laws rule have been formulated by popular decision. He refuses to recognize a democracy of that nature as having a true constitution. (*Polit.* 4.c.4). Demosthenes' definition of law reached the *Digest* through Marcianus (*D.* 1.3.2). In it it is argued that the force of law is applicable to all human beings primarily owing to the divine origin of the laws. Only on a secondary level was law derived from the insight of wise men and through popular decisions (the common agreement of the city). To an even lesser degree law was considered the product of the will of excellent men who served as legislators. On the other hand, customary law was given a legislative standing because of its derivation from mythical personifications; it was only the voice for the revelation of the legal idea, and it was wisdom and not power which was ascribed to it.

3 The controversy centred on the argument whether the just was derived from nature or from human promulgation. The latter view was maintained by Archelaos (Diogenes Laertius, 2.16). The argument appeared again, in different forms, in the Sophists, the Cyrenaics, and the Sceptics (cp. esp. Diog. Laert., 9.61). Cp. Hildebrand, pp. 47 ff., 70 ff., 502 ff., 518 ff. The Epicureans derived the concept of the just and the unjust from a contract entered upon in order to obtain security. They maintained that this contract was a result of a natural demand and an indirect derivation of the just from nature (Diog. Laer., 10.150 ff.); cp. Hildebrand, pp. 514 ff.

Nature or the Idea) that served as the original source of justice.[4] Greek philosophy thus produced the concept of natural law which became increasingly separated from positive law.[5]

But Greek natural as well as Greek positive law was essentially an objective and not a subjective law. As a result of an ethical world order it contained but it did not extend rights. To the Greek consciousness the notion of natural rights remained alien as did the idea of acquired rights. Therefore the attempt to separate positive law from natural law on the one hand, and from customary law on the other, could not be undertaken. This feature was so basic to Greek legal thought that the Romans, who in their positive law took subjective law as a starting point, failed in their legal philosophy to overcome this difficulty.[6] Only when Roman jurisprudence mastered the concept of *jus naturale* could it then introduce into this sphere the notion of the subject and thereby elevate itself to the acceptance of natural rights,[7] without fully overcoming the Greek derivation of that concept.[8]

4 On this point Socrates, Plato, Aristotle, and the Stoics agree. See the discussion of their philosophy of justice in Hildebrand, pp. 89 ff., 122 ff., 196 ff., 303 ff., 509 ff.

5 M. Voigt, *Das jus naturale, aequum et bonum und jus gentium der Römer*, Leipzig, 1856-75, I, pp. 81-176 (*Lehre vom jus naturale in der griechischen Philosophie*). The distinction between natural and positive law is already hinted at by Socrates, developed by Aristotle (*Eth. Nicom.* 5.c.10), and fully expounded by the Stoics.

6 This applies especially to Cicero's philosophy of justice; see its discussion by Voigt, I, pp. 176-226, and by Hildebrand, pp. 560-81. Also J. Stahl, *Die Philosophie des Rechts*, 3rd ed., Heidelberg, 1856, I, p. 48 calls attention to the fact that Cicero raises neither the idea of subjective right nor the separation of law from morality to a scientific level. All his categories are ultimately of Greek origin. This applies without qualification to his concept of *lex naturae* as the eternal divine universal law and the *jus naturae* which is derived from it. This *jus naturae* is equally valid; it is above human arbitrariness and remains unalterable. But even the *jus civile* is considered as belonging to the concept of an objective order. This order establishes norms with a formal authority which is derived from natural law, which in turn is adjusted according to the place and the standards of the time. In Cicero, the *jus gentium* appears as a median between natural and positive law; he sees in it a copy of natural law which has been accepted by humans but he does not think of developing its specific Roman elements.

7 This occurs in the well-known passage of the Code where the *jus naturale* is defined as a universal human law and where the freedom and the equality of all humans is proclaimed (*Inst.* 1.2; *D.* 1.1.4; 1.5.4.1; 50.17.32). An enormous step from Aristotle's conception of 'slaves by nature.' Therefore it can be claimed that in fact Roman jurisprudence envisaged man as a subject under the law. The *jus civile* pertaining to the citizen, the *jus gentium* to the free man, and the *jus naturale* to all of humanity. Cp. Voigt, II, p. 856, Hildebrand, p. 633.

8 If the concept of *jus naturale* had been completely penetrated by Roman jurisprudence, then Ulpian could not have defined it as the natural order of humans and animals (*D.* 1.1.1); its separation from the entire ethical realm would not have taken place

The Greeks did not know the independent concept of subjective law. Therefore the autonomous concept of a legal subject was equally absent. This difficulty was evident in the treatment of the individual as well as of the state.

The individual, according to Greek thought, was endowed with his own essence but never with a true legal personality. Whatever his rights and duties, the individual was not himself considered an original centre of autonomy. Rather, his rights and duties derived from his being a part of the whole. An independent private law did not exist. Private legal relationships appeared as direct concomitants of the political association. Entirely absent was the idea that the individual will had, in its own right, a sphere of action which was recognized and guarded by the state or indeed that such an expression of a will could prove to be a creative principle of law. The entire concept of individual freedom, which was untouchable in so far as the community was concerned, remained alien to the Greeks. All freedom was political freedom. It was participation in the freedom of the state.[9]

Plato, in his ideal state, carries this fundamental bias to its ultimate consequence by advocating the total absorption of the individual into his community. It is also noteworthy that Aristotle, in his thorough polemic against the collective ownership of wives, children, and property, bases his argument throughout on the clearly conceived interest of the whole and not upon the right of the individual. He is unaware of the right of personality. He too is in accord with the view that the citizen does not belong to himself but to the state.[10] Wherever individualism appeared in Greek philosophy it did so in contradiction to the existing order of the state and the law. Even in the process of the dissolution of the traditional Hellenic idea of state and law, the principle of personality understood in a positive sense remained undiscovered.[11]

(Voigt, I, p. 342); Roman thought would not have ascribed to it a universality and immutability (*D.* 1.1.11; *Inst.* 1.2.11) and at the same time maintained the postulate with regard to the legal subjectivity of all human beings which was to be transcended by the *jus gentium*. This supports Voigt's thesis (I, pp. 243, 258 ff., 269 ff.) about the assumed derivation of the *jus naturale* from the Greek concept of the 'naturally just.' If Hildebrand (p. 600) believes in the independent derivation of the *jus gentium*, this concept of the jurists is a generalization of the historical *jus gentium*. In fact, the *jus gentium* is a philosophic and legal idea of the Romans just as the *jus naturale* is that of the Greeks. Therefore, for Gaius the *jus naturale* and the *jus gentium* coincide (Gaius, *Inst.* 1.1). But in the *jus gentium* the subjective Roman legal concept is fully developed.

9 Cp. especially Stahl, pp. 45 ff., and Hildebrand, pp. 26 ff.

10 Aristotle, *Polit.* 2 c.1 sq. and also 8.c.1.

11 This by the Stoics, Cynics, Cyrenaics and Epicureans; cp. Hildebrand, pp. 70 ff., 499 ff., 517. The beginnings of the idea of the mediation between state and individual is found only in the Stoics; *ibid.* pp. 506 ff.

This conception of the individual was decisive for the Greek idea of the state. It resulted in the Greek mind's classical exposition of the idea of the nature of the state. But it did not ascribe any personality to the state.

The unique essence of the state was the central principle in Greek political thought as long as it remained consistent with itself. Any derivation of the state from individuals was alien to it. Aristotle's famous dictum that the whole is prior to the part and that therefore the state precedes man,[12] was merely the concise formulation of an ancient Greek view. Thereby philosophy did not presuppose the existence of a pre-historical state. Rather it envisaged the state as originating in the family and then organically expanding from it. In part also, philosophy considered the state as the product of conscious human activity that contributed to its foundation. The state was also considered a natural phenomenon. It was assumed that its origin was due to a mixture of older forms but the development of the state was seen as the unfolding of a completed organism which had contained its full potential from its inception. In so far as the state was considered the result of human labour, Greek philosophy did not envisage it as a process of wills directed towards the elimination or combinations of heretofore individual essences of life. Rather it saw it as the conscious realization of an idea that had been posited *a priori*. It viewed it as a higher purpose of existence that had been recognized by reason.[13] Accordingly, the state was not considered as a means for the development of individual goals but rather as an end in itself. It saw the purpose of the state-community as an evolution towards a self-sufficient harmonious life

12 Aristotle, *Polit*. 1.c.2.

13 Plato derives the *polis* from the need of a division of labour and from the conscious formation of institutions (*Republic* 2.369 sq.). He does not conceive the formation of the state as an act of will but rather he sees it as the realization of the idea of organized reason. Aristotle's contention that the state precedes the citizen is also relevant here. Aristotle views man as a naturally political being and sees the state as a product of nature since it is only the completion of the natural ties of kinship and neighbourhood; however, he does not exclude the creative act in which the natural drive is realized. (*Polit*. 1.c.1-2; 3.c.6.). The Stoics find the origin of the state in the natural unity of the world in general and of the human race in particular. Here too Cicero depends on the Greeks. The basis of the state for him is the rational social nature of man and the natural society derived from it (*De Fin*. 3.20.65, 4.2.4; *De Leg*. 1.10.28 and 12.33; *De Off*. 1.4.11-12 and 44.157; *De Republ*. 1.25.39). He thinks of the historical development of the state as the organic development of a germ contained in the family (*De Fin*. 5.23.65). He connects thereby the idea of a conscious foundation of the state with need and particularly with the requirement for legal protection that persuades the originally isolated beings to unite (*De Off*. 2.21.73, 3.5; *De Republ*. 2.1; *Pro Sestio* 42).

attained through virtue. The state was considered the realization of the ethical idea for its very own sake.[14]

This conception of the state as a self-contained communal life led the Greeks, at an early stage, to an organic view of the whole of the state. The notion of the state as a living organism was expressed philosophically in diverse conceptions. Each of the diverse theses was significant for the development of the concept of the unique essence of the association. But the concept of the unique personality of the state was absent.

Plato propounds the idea that the state is man's enlarged image.[15] Between the macrocosm of the world and the microcosm of the individual, Plato places the mesocosm, the state, which consists of both mind and matter linked by a third element, the sensuous principle related to the animal. Thus his doctrine of the state revolves around an anthropomorphic transposition of his psychology and ethics into the communal sphere.[16] The three classes of the ideal state are the specific orders of life and correspond to the three incorporated parts of the powers of the human soul.[17] The perfection of communal life consists of the growth of the four cardinal virtues towards a condition wherein they become the subjective character of the state.[18]

14 This is particularly emphasized by Plato, cp. *Laws* 3.702 and 8.828. Also the statements in *Rep.* 4.420 sq. and 7.519 sq., according to which the happiness and the virtuous beauty of the city is attained through the single citizen's sacrifice of his individual happiness. Perfection is attained when the citizen devotes himself to the fulfilment of his determined functions. Aristotle, on the other hand, argues that it is impossible to separate the happiness of the whole from the happiness of all or from that of the majority. He envisages the end of the state to consist of a virtuous, happy communal life through which the citizen as an individual attains virtue and happiness. But he identifies the common good with the good of the state in a social and not in an individualistic sense. He does not consider the state-community as an end but as a means for the individuals and the close associations. But he emphatically elevates the state to the point of having its own purpose, by ascribing to it the most noble characteristic, i.e. self-sufficiency as the best of final ends. Cp. *Polit.* 1.c.2, 2.c.5, 3.c.6 and 9, 7.c.1, 2, 4, 5, 8, and 15. Cicero essentially repeats the Greek concept of the state designed for public welfare and virtue. Cp. *Ad Att.* 8.17; *De Republ.* 4.3.3.

15 Hildebrand (p. 88) assumes that in view of the fact that Socrates demanded self-recognition on part of the state, he saw it as an enlarged image of man.

16 Plato in his *Republic* takes the inverse course in so far as he first seeks to establish justice in the state and then transfers it to the singular (2.368 sq.). In all other similar questions he proceeds in a similar manner.

17 The ruling class of philosophers is the rational, the working class is the desirous, and the warrior class the mediating life-principle of the soul of the state; cp. *Rep.* 2.369 sq., and then the analogy of the individual soul 4.435 ff.

18 The virtues of the single soul belong partially to its different elements and are, partially, common to all. The city is wise, courageous, and temperate 'through a

All constitutional deterioration is the result of the perversion of the soul of the state.[19] The state is analogous to man and differs from him only in size.[20] Its perfection increases the more it approximates man by its organization.[21] Hence the demand for unity in the state which, as that of the individual, is as simple as possible. It is a unity in which the parts are fully contained and are valuable to the whole. It is this unity that ultimately leads to communism.[22] Despite this, there is no indication of the notion of the personality of the state in Plato. His state is the concrete totality of everything it contains. It is understood as a uniform whole but never as a unity *in* the whole. The state is the multiplicity transformed into a unity but it is not understood as the independent unity, the person, that resides in the multiplicity. Towards its members the state has no rights and duties – just as man has no rights or duties towards the parts of his body. It is therefore impossible to attribute to either party a personality in this relationship of state and individual. Neither the state as a whole nor the individual considered as a whole is endowed with a personality. The Platonic view of life lacks the idea of a difference between the central unity of the subject and the multiplicity of its manifestation. Ultimately, the state, just as the individual remains an artificial aggregation of contending parts whose assumed unity is reduced to a conception of relations between classes.[23] Where the question of the relationship between the parts of the state arises, it is made clear that the parts appear as quasi-subjects of certain specific functions assigned to them by an ob-

part of itself,' in so far as wisdom is produced exclusively by the ruling class, courage is produced by the warrior class, and moderation is produced preferably by the class of the ruled. Justice is attained when each part fulfils its assigned function. Cp. *Rep.* 4.427 sq. and then the completion of the analogy of the individual *ibid.* 434 sq.

19 The parallel of the gradual deterioration of the constitution and the ethical degeneration of the human soul is discussed, in detail, in the eight and ninth books of the *Republic*.

20 Cp. e.g. *Rep.* 2.368, 4.435.441, 5.449, 7.543; also *Laws* 3.689.702, 8.828.

21 *Rep.* 5.462.

22 Plato argues in various passages of the *Republic* that unity is the highest good of the state and everything divisive is the greatest evil. The state must be large enough to be self-sufficient, small enough to be united. It is necessary that each citizen perform that task for which he is best suited, so that each one does what is proper for him and thus becomes one instead of many, and so that the entire city grows to be one instead of something divided. The completed unity is derived from the common ownership of wives and property (among the guardians) in so far as no one can utter the words 'mine' and 'not mine.' The community of the state experiences directly and exclusively that pleasure and pain that its parts experience. cp. 4.422.423 and esp. 5.462.

23 Aristotle (*Polit.* 2.c.5) criticizes the contradiction in which the analogous unity of the individual finds itself in the real constitution of Plato's ideal state and distinctions between (component) elements.

jective order of law. Nowhere do the parts appear as organs of a uniform, communal will that permeates the whole. Nowhere do the parts appear as representatives of an ideal subject of law. Therefore Plato, in his formulation of the ideal constitution as well as in his classification of the empirical, imperfect forms of the state, remains a captive of the distinction between ruler and ruled. He identifies the power of the state with either its collective or its single physical representative.[24]

Aristotle, too, considers the state as a living organism.[25] He refuses, however, to consider the state as a magnification of man and argues against the premise that the nature of the state is, as nearly as possible, analogous to the unity of the individual. He thus reaches the conclusion that the state is a composite organism which is transformed into a higher and more self-sufficient whole by an arrangement of the heterogeneous parts that complement one another so as to form a basis for reciprocal equality. The whole, in its manifestation as the state, precedes the individual whose concept is based upon the multiplicity of the unity.[26] Aristotle does not succeed in deriving the concept of personality from his view of the relationship between the individual and the multiplicity. For him the state is a multiplicity gathered into a unity whose existence, owing to its unique organic bonds, succeeds in producing a collective being with an independent communal life.[27]

Aristotle, in a manner that was of historical importance, speaks of the distinction between the whole and the sum of its parts. He further distinguishes between totality and multiplicity and he posits an essential difference between a collective and a distributive view of the united multiplicity. Aristotle emphasizes that

24 In the *Republic*, with regard to the ideal constitution (5.473 sq.), and the four empirical forms, i.e. timocracy, oligarchy, democracy, and tyranny (8.544 sq.). Also in the *Laws*, where the idea of the mixed constitution appears (3.690 sq. and 756 sq.).

25 This view is derived from his theory about the origin of the state (see note 13 above) especially as he sees the individuals as parts of the state. He uses the comparison of the hand and the foot which, if the whole man is dissolved, do not exist anymore except in name (*Polit*. 1.c.2.).

26 Cp. *Polit*. 2.c.2. and 5. In the argument against the common ownership of wives and property it is postulated that the state, by nature, is a multiplicity which can be considered a unity only in certain aspects. Thus the most thorough unification would remove the concept and the advantages of the state when viewed as an entity specifically distinct from individuals and families. It is further argued that the true unity of the state is unthinkable without a dissimilarity of its constituent parts and that the composite is more self-sufficient than the individual. This view of the necessary differentiation between the parts of the state's organism is reflected in the argument against an equality in property (*ibid*. c.7.) and is utilized later for the whole positive construction of the constitution (cp. e.g. 3.c.4 and 4.c.4).

27 Cp. e.g. *Polit*. 2.c.2 and 5.

what pertains to the whole does not necessarily pertain to each part. Conversely, something can be posited of the part which is irrelevant to the whole. But to him the contradiction is exhausted in the dual meaning of the word 'all,' so that it can denote all individuals living in the state and also the collectivity of them as being the state.[28] Thus the state remains in the conceptual realm of society or community. The state is a social construct that encompasses all human relationships. But even though Aristotle cedes a certain freedom of mobility to the related elements of the state; basically his *polis* is not what we call a 'state' but a 'civil society.'[29]

In the light of this basic view, the idea of group-personality cannot develop. Moreover, with Aristotle, communal existence and the individual do not confront one another as subjects of law. For him too the relationship is one of order and not a true legal connection. Aristotle, in opposition to Plato, attempts to draw the boundaries between the communal and the individual spheres of life and he attempts to formulate a certain equilibrium. The result, however, is essentially an objective order which is necessary for the harmonious development of the whole. There is no recognition of two independent subjective centres of law.[30] The state as a whole is not personified. There is, in Aristotle, the determined effort to illustrate the material structure of the state, its basis, its articulation, and the organic tie that links its various parts. Despite this he is unable, in his completed scheme, to arrive at a substantial subjective unity. Instead he formulates only a collective, formal, and purely logical unity.[31] Thus the material unity of the state is conceived as consisting in the relationship of various categories of orders within the multiplicity. An essential element of this relationship of orders is the distinction between ruler and ruled,[32] an analogy Aristotle derives from his reference to the composite whole and especially to every organic structure. Thereby

28 *Polit.* 2.c.3, also 7.c.15.

29 *Polit.* 1.c.1, 3.c.6, 7.c.8.

30 Compare the discussion about the property relationships (2.c.5) and ultimate identification of human with civic virtue (3.c.4 and 18). Also the fragment of the ideal constitution (7-8). The idea of private rights does not appear anywhere. Equally absent is the concept of private personality and its opposite. The reference is always to the community and to individual rights, as distributed and apportioned by the community. The notion that individuals can confront the state in which they are more than mere parts of the whole is entirely absent.

31 Cp. notes 26-8 above. The state as a unity can have attributes other than those of the sum of its parts. But the good of the state and the general good of the individuals, the virtue of the state and that of the citizen, the best of the state and that of private man, the goals of man as an individual and his goals in the community – all these simply coincide. Cp. esp. *Polit.* 2.c.5, 3.c.6-7, 7.c.2 and 13-15.

32 *Polit.* 1.c.5.

he arrives at a number of important conceptual conclusions. He posits the notion of the constitution as the rule of the sovereign body,[33] and he develops the concept of sovereignty as the highest rule.[34] He establishes the classification of forms of the state both with respect to the locus of sovereignty on the one hand and its use on the other.[35]

Aristotle distinguishes between the activity of legislation and executive and juridical decisions and sees them as diverse components of the art of governing. He exposes, in detail, the articulation of the participating administrative segments of the state according to their authority and offices.[36] But none of these concepts is designated as the ideal subjective centre. Aristotle does not think of the constitution as an expression of a uniform collective will but sees it as the expression of the state's total sovereignty. He does not consider the ruler as an organ of the state or the manifestations of the rule as the function of the state. Throughout his theory, he retains the conception of ruling and the ruled as parts of an objectively ordered whole. Whenever the question of rights and duties that we would ascribe to the state as such arises, the concept of the subject is not derived from the real and visible activity of the relevant part of the state according to Aristotle. As soon as he conceives of the state as an active essence, he substitutes the active part for the whole.

Accordingly he arrives at a new definition that perceives the state as nothing but the substance of citizens, and citizens as only those inhabitants who actively participate in the rule of the state's territory.[37] This citizenry, which is identified with the state, is seen by Aristotle as being legally and actively capable only as it

33 Cp. *Polit.* 3.c.6.

34 *Polit.* 3.c.6, 7, 10. According to Aristotle, the sovereign power does not exclude the independent participation of other factors in the administration of the affairs of the state.

35 *Polit.* 3.c.7 sq.

36 *Polit.* 3.c.14-16.

37 *Polit.* 3.c.1: 'A *polis* or state belongs to the order of "compounds," in the same way as all other things which form a single "whole," but as a "whole" composed, nonetheless, of a number of different parts. This being the case, it clearly follows that we must inquire into the nature of the citizen (i.e. the part) before inquiring into the nature of the state (i.e. the whole composed of such parts). In other words, a state is a compound made up of citizens. ...' Hence the definition of the citizen as that man who participates in governing and then the observation that ' ... a state, in its simplest terms, is a body of such persons adequate in number for achieving a self-sufficient existence.' Cp. *ibid.* c.5. (the exclusion of the artisans) and 7.c.4. Most relevant are the discussions in 7.c.8-9, where a distinction is made between the entire indispensable substratum and the living members or parts of all composite natural beings. Consequently, in the ideal state, the classes of the farmers, artisans, and wage-earners are seen as the passive substratum, and the effective part is limited to the rulers and warriors.

becomes or as it can become the real assembly of the collective whole.[38] If other assemblies or individulas are constitutionally enabled to carry out the laws of the state, they relate to the assembly of the citizens and to one another as ruler and ruled and appear in a similar manner as subjects or quasi-subjects of those powers of the state that had been legally transferred to them.[39] And if, instead of the totality of citizens, only a minority or a single entity is designated as the sole possessor of sovereignty, the active essence of the state coincides completely or primarily with either of these.[40] The result is that the legal subjectivity of the state remains with its ruling part. Aristotle posits the following thesis which was to be of great importance for the future. The ruling collectivity of the state is not a heterogeneous multiplicity but in essence an organizationally collectivized unity. Any possible single ruler wields communal rights not as a private person but as the head of the whole. However he has been created, he never executes political power on the basis of his own right but does so only as a part of an organic whole which is based upon an objective order.

Finally, there is the imperative postulate contained in the idea of law which obliges the ruler to utilize the power not for himself but for the community.[41] But Aristotle fails to detect the true subject hidden behind this quasi-subject. Consequently, the identity of the communal being is destroyed not through a change in the rule of the communally constituted single individuals nor, apparently, through a change in the person of the monarch; rather, the communal being is destroyed when a change in the ruling part of the state takes place. Therefore, there is no continuity of legal subjectivity that connects the state before and after a constitutional change.[42]

38 Cp. e.g. *Polit*. 3.c.11 (where the frequently used parallel between the united multitude and a man with feet, hands, and many senses is made); 4.c.4: 'The people then becomes an autocrat – a single composite autocrat made up of many members, with many playing the sovereign, not as individuals, but collectively.' Also 3.c.13 and 15, 4.c.6. Therefore Aristotle can envisage a free communal existence only in a city of moderate size and here too he attempts to delimit the citizens' rights. The notion of representation, moreover, is entirely absent (7.c.4 sq.).

39 Cp. *Polit*. 4.c.1 sq; Aristotle, as all other Greeks, was fully conversant with the concept of the mixed constitution (*ibid*. 2.c.6).

40 *Polit*. 3.c.13-17; 4.c.5 sq.

41 In so far as Aristotle applies these views to all good constitutions, he manages to avoid the pitfalls inherent in the theories of contract and popular sovereignty. Yet he does not transcend these theories but rather lags behind them. He attains the idea of the constitutional state through the absolute power of an impersonal order in which subjective liberties, all personal wills, and all independent rights vanish.

42 *Polit*. 3.c.3. Aristotle indicates that he is dissatisfied with the consequences of the solution to the question which he raised at the outset of this discussion. He considered whether previously contracted loans should be repaid after a change in the

This philosophic formulation of the concept of the state corresponded to the Greek popular view which consistently envisaged the state as a living, organic communal being. The unity of this organism was derived from the connection between the related parts and the state, as an acting subject, and was identified with the assembled citizenry.[43] In its era of decline, the Greek mind produced views according to which the state was merely a means for attaining individual goals, a useful invention, an arbitrary creation of power or a contract. But the resulting theories of the state, which are familiar to us, had no measurable influence upon antiquity.[44]

However, of lasting significance was the fact that Stoicism, the mediating factor between the Greek and Roman realms of thought, developed the concept of the state further and thereby approached the native Roman concept of the state. Although the Stoics, like their predecessors, looked upon the state as an organic community, they attributed to the individual an autonomous value. On the other hand, so far as the essence of the association was concerned, they introduced the idea of unity and its articulation as the highest principle of the whole world.[45] In so far as the subordinated communal being belonged to the general category of bodies composed of diverse parts (*corpora ex distantibus*),[46] they simultaneously ascribed to the individual and his association an independent corporeal unity with its own essence of life. They created the concept of the *corpus reipublicae* that they extensively utilized themselves. But the idea of an immanent personality residing in this unity remained entirely alien to them. They considered the inherent unity of the body of the state as an ethical and legal bond which held together the relevant parts but failed to discern the subject of this unity; rather,

constitution. His closing words are: 'It is a different question, and another matter, whether it is right or wrong for a state to repudiate public obligations when it changes its constitution into another form.'

43 The thesis of Bolze, *Der Begriff der juristischen Person*, Stuttgart, 1879, pp. 112 ff., is correct.

44 This is especially true of the beginnings of the contract theory as expounded by the Sophists, so far as it can be surmised from Plato, *Republic* 2.358-9 and from the developed contract theory of the Epicureans. Their legal and political theory saw the power of the state as a means of contractual security arrangements among humans; Diog. Laert., 10.140 and 150 sq; cp. Hildebrand, p. 517.

45 For the theory of state of the Stoics cp. Hildebrand, pp. 505 ff.

46 Cp. Göppert, *Über einheitliche, zusammengesetzte und Gesammtsachen nach römischem Recht*, Halle, 1871, pp. 10 ff. Marcus Aurelius (*Meditations* 9.9) views the constitution as being composed of diverse elements. Similarly, Seneca (*Epist*. 102.6) and Pomponius (*D*. 41.3.30) rank the *populus* among bodies consisting of diverse parts (*corpora ex distantibus*).

to the Stoics, the subject remained the collectively united group formed by such a bond.[47]

Roman philosophy accepted the Greek concept of the state and reformulated it. Even though the result was an unintentional adaptation of alien thought, the basic Greek matrix remained unchanged. Thus, especially Cicero sees the state as an organism with a specific identity in which the unity of the whole *corpus* is distinguishable from the multiplicity of the parts.[48] For Cicero too the unity of the state is derived from the union of the parts. Frequently he declares the state to be a partnership (*societas*), 'an assemblage of men having come together' (*coetus hominum congregatus*), a united multitude (*multitudo*). In civil society (*societas civium*) that grows out of the natural community of men, Cicero sees the formation of a happy and virtuous communal life. He discerns the real substance of the state as the multitude associated in a bond (*vinculum*) which he characterizes as the agreement of law and the communality of interests.[49] But Cicero does not develop the idea of the personality of the state. However, he cannot entirely prevent the concisely developed idea of the subjectivity of law from influencing his speculations about the philosophic doctrine of the state. But Cicero's philosophic exploitation of this concept is prevented by his close adherence to Greek examples. He ascribes to the individual a sphere of independent and protective law *vis à vis* the community. Consequently, the singular and the totality of the state are posited, against one another, as subjects of law.[50]

However, in doing so, Cicero is unaware of the basic divergence from the Greek example which this theory represents. As far as the state as a whole is concerned, Cicero introduces into its organism the concept of the subject of law when he declares that the law of the state is, ultimately, the subjective law of the *populus*. Basic to all of his deliberations about the forms of constitutions is his definition of his state (*respublica*) as the people's possession (*res populi*).[51] He is inclined to treat the magistrate as the representative and the administrator of the law of the

47 The Stoics derived the state from the natural community of men and the community from the unity of the world with the human race. But unlike a simple body, the state, according to the Stoics, was not endowed with a soul that was a uniform part of the world-soul. The single concept, the *spiritus unus*, was specifically denied to the bodies composed of diverse parts, even though the Middle Ages maintained the opposite.

48 Cp. Cicero, *De Off.* 1.25.85; *De Republ.* 3.25.

49 Cp. *De Off.* 1.17; *De Republ.* 1.25.39, 1.26.41, 1.32.49, 3.31, 3.33, 4.3, 6.13. Cicero also repeats the Greek simile that compares the state's unity with the harmony in music, *De Republ.* 2.42.

50 Cp. e.g. *De Off.* 2.21.72, 2.21.73, 2.22.78, 2.24.84-5.

51 Cicero, *De Republ.* 1.25.39, 1.26.41, 3.31-5; cp. 1.26.41: 'the state is the constitution of the people.'

populus[52] and indeed, in speaking about him, uses the term 'representative of the state' (*persona civitatis*).[53] On the one hand, the *populus*, which he identifies with the active *civitas* or *respublica* and which is endowed with all the characteristics and abilities of an individual,[54] coincides with the real or imaginary popular assembly, with the collectively united multiplicity, of citizens.[55] On the other hand, however, in his discussion of the state's organization, he disregards the concept of a central subject of law.

Cicero repeats, in unaltered form, the Greek theory about the three possible seats of sovereignty (*summa rerum* or *summa potestas*) and the three different constitutional forms and their corollary degenerations. He discusses all this without raising the question of the real subject of the state's power.[56] He declares the mixed constitution to be the best and describes it in detail, but contents himself with distributing the state's powers among its various parts. However, he does not examine the relationship of this division of the state's powers to the subjective unity contained in the totality of the state.[57] Finally, Cicero presents the notion that the true *respublica* must be a *res populi*, a turn of phrase which changes the

52 These views emerge repeatedly in the planned magistracy in the third book of the work *De Legibus*; cp. esp. *De Leg.* 3.12.27-8.

53 Cp. the passage in the above note; *civitas* here, as elsewhere, is equated with *populus*; e.g. *De Republ.* 3.17 and 18.

54 Cp. e.g. *De Republ.* 1.44.68, 3.15, 3.17, 3.18, 3.23, 3.33; *De Leg.* 3.12.

55 Always the rights of the people's assembly (*potestas populi*) opposed those of the senate and the administration. Never did the people's assembly appear as an organ of the *populus*. Throughout, the *populus* conceived as a legal subject, was the substance of the enfranchised citizens. But it was not seen as an organically articulated people and was therefore referred to as 'multitude' and 'all.' Cp. e.g. *De Republ.* 1.26.42, 1.27.43, 1.32.48-9, 1.35.55, 1.40.62, 1.42.65, 1.44.68, 2.32.56, 3.13.22-3, 3.25.37, 3.33.45; *De Leg.* 3.12.

56 Cp. *De Republ.* 1.26.44. Even in an aristocracy and a monarchy Cicero appears to derive the rights of the rulers from the people. But he does not think of a continuous people's sovereignty. Only in the *respublica popularis* does he ascribe to the *populus* a *summa potestas*. Among the simple forms of constitutions, he prefers, however, a monarchy because it is a copy of the universe ruled by one God and because it possesses all the powers of the soul through reason. Otherwise he does not conceive of the sovereignty of the ruler as a special right but sees it as a delegated power just as he accepts the classification of constitutions according to their just or unjust applications. Throughout, there is an ultimate absence of a [legal] subject which would fill the void created by the absence of the state's personality.

57 Cp. *De Republ.* 1.29.45, 1.45.69, 3.13.23; *De Leg.* 3.12. Cicero assumes a real partition of the *summa potestas* without finding anything objectionable in it. This is borne out by the statement that 'a sort of bargain is made between the common people and the powerful' (*De Republ.* 3.13.23). Other writers of antiquity who praise the mixed constitution are in agreement, e.g. Polybius, *Histories* 6.

people from being the state's legal subject in their own right to mere means to the state's own end. But the substantial unity of the state, following the Greek example, he again describes exclusively as a realized objective order derived from the idea of law.[58]

Along entirely different lines and quite independently from Greek thought, there developed the juridical conceptions of positive Roman constitutional law. From the point of view of later theoretical formulations it was of at least negative significance that the Romans had no philosophic conception of the state to depend upon but that of the Greeks.

If we enquire about the ideas with regard to the positive and legal nature of other associations formulated by ancient philosophy, we encounter everywhere the basic premise that identifies the concept of the state with the concept of civil society. Consequently, it was, under no circumstances, possible to attribute to the state as a whole a partially co-ordinate associative nature. Rather, associations could exist only in so far as they either contained the state or were themselves contained by it.

Originally, only the world-totality conceived as an organic unity was recognized as existing above the state. The idea of the *cosmos* as a universal living organism, of which the state was a part, became of great importance to the history of political theories. The construct of the state was influenced by this theory because a model relationship to the universe was derived from it. Moreover, natural law was derived from this view in so far as it was considered to be the result of the universal union of the state and *cosmos*. It was thought of as a notion of such impor-

58 Cicero devotes the entire third book on the state to the proof that if the *respublica*, according to its concept, is a *res populi*, every justly governed state is endowed with the character of a *respublica*. Unjust rule leads to a condition where the *respublica* becomes *vitiosa* (faulty) or even a *nulla respublica*. For this reason he argues that, on the one hand, not only the sovereignty of the *populus universus* but, to an even higher degree, the sovereignty of the *optimates* [the ruling 'establishment' of the late Republic], and most of all that of the king, is compatible with the essence of the *respublica*, so long as the ruler acts according to the idea of justice internally and externally. On the other hand, Cicero undertakes to show that it is not only the rule of a tyrant or of a *factio* (faction or party) but also unlimited popular rule that excludes the concept of the *res populi*. Even if the condition of the *omnia in populi potestate* is present, the *populus*, in the absence of a guiding legal principle (*juris consensus*), does not qualify as a true *populus* (*De Republ.* 3.33.45). Thus the concept of the *res populi* is understood in a sense which can mean the 'concern of the entire people.' But *populus* can also be understood as meaning subordination to an objective legal principle according to a constitutional order. With regard to the latter, it is noteworthy that in Cicero the impersonal *lex* occupies the place of a living personality of the state; cp. e.g. *De Leg.* 3.1.2.

tance that all human legislators had to yield to it. The cosmic universal bond was, understandably, placed beyond the realm of the legal sphere. In antiquity, as a corollary to the above view and particularly owing to Stoic philosophy, the common unity of gods and men and the rational substance of the universal order was seen in the light of the earthly state.[59] Between the universal world order and the individual *polis* there existed, according to traditional Greek thought, no organic unity. Gradually, however, there developed from this originally negative view the idea of a universal citizenship. This was expounded by the Stoics and accepted by the Romans so that the idea of a positive union of mankind came to be known as a *societas generis humani*.[60] This conception led to the postulate of a universal state encompassing all humanity and also to the assumption of a common binding law applicable even to peoples separated by state boundaries. These assumptions, however, did not bring forth a new and unique conception of legal association. The ideal realm of man was envisaged as a *polis* encompassing the whole world, whose houses consisted of individual cities.[61] In fact, the idea of a universal state was partially realized by the Romans as the territory of the Roman city-state gradually changed into a unitary construct which applied to the whole Empire. However, the city-state remained its model.

From the legal community of peoples separated according to states, Roman jurisprudence derived its philosophic concept of the *jus gentium*. But the legal community under the *jus gentium* was not considered as an externally organized association but rather as a symbol of an inner unity of humanity expressing itself through some common juristic pronouncements.[62] Similarly, the observation that

59 Cicero, *De Deor. Nat.* 2.62; *De Fin.* 3.19-20; *De Republ.* 1.13 and 36, 3.22 *De Leg.* 1.7.23. Seneca, *De Otio Sap.* 31; *De Vit. Beat.* c.20; Marcus Aurelius, *Meditations* 4.4, 6.44. The conception of the ancient city-state reappears everywhere. The divine rule of the world is seen as the realization of an eternal law standing above gods and men. The substantial associational unity is found in the objective unity of the rational order of the world. Cp. Chrysippus, *D.* 1.3.2, a statement based upon the famous verse of Pindar, *fr.* 11.48.

60 The idea of world-citizenship as referred to by Socrates (Hildebrand, p. 88) and as further developed by the Cynics and the Cyrenaics (*ibid.* pp. 500 ff.) had an individualistic meaning. With the Stoics the idea was transformed into civil rights in a human commonwealth (*ibid.* p. 511). Similarly in Cicero (*De Leg.* 1.23.61), where the partnership of the human race or the partnership of all men appears as the final stage of the temporal associations; *De Off.* 1.17.53, 3.5.21-2 and 17.69; *De Fin.* 5.23.65; *De Leg.* 3.1.3.

61 Thus Zeno according to Plutarch, *Moralia, De Alexandri Magni fortuna aut virtute*, 1.6; Marcus Aurelius, *Meditations* 3.11.

62 Cp. Gaius, *Inst.* 1.1 and *D.* 41.1.1; Ulpian, *D.* 1.1.1.4. Just. *Inst.* 1.2. Essentially the *jus gentium* was a 'law common to all mankind' and it was 'preserved uniformly among all.' The inner basis of this agreement was derived from the

there existed between humanity and the city-state some national entities did not produce a special concept of legal association.[63] Thus the conception of the state as derived from the *polis* remained, in theory, unaltered, while in fact larger state-organizations based upon the federal principle did emerge. The city-state as a complete and essentially self-sufficient communal being, as defined by Aristotle, was capable of entering into lasting contractual relationships with similar communal organizations. As a member of a permanent league, the city-state could limit or expand its powers and, according to the nature of its arrangements, gain or lose its sovereignty. But the idea that out of such an organization of member-states a higher communal organism or an autonomous associational being could be derived remained entirely alien to ancient theory.[64]

Ancient political science knew of associations that did or could contain the idea of the state and throughout adhered to its basic notion that the state coincided conceptually with human society. The force of this fundamental premise manifested itself in the energy with which ancient philosophy subsumed all other associations as parts of the state. In fact, the Greek view according to which the individual was totally contained in the state had to lead, of necessity, to considering all associations pertaining to the individual as being essentially specific parts of the state. Plato tolerated only those societal relationships among the citizens that were formed by and for the state. Aristotle ascribed to the family, the village community, and the arbitrary fellowship an original and specific identity. Therefore it is significant that Aristotle emphasized that each special association was a part and a tool at the disposal of the self-contained and self-sufficient political association. He stressed thereby not only the distinction in size but also in the nature of the societies and referred to the necessary subordination of all close communal life to the life of the state.[65]

unity of the human race in so far as everywhere the same common natural reason and the same needs prevailed. It was formally realized by the recognition extended to it by the individual peoples. The idea of deriving the *jus gentium* from legal persuasion or from manifestations of the will of the peoples' community was alien to the Romans.

63 The 'community of peoples, nations, and speech' appears in Cicero as a step in the human order; *De Off.* 1.17.53, 3.17.69; *De Leg.* 3.1.3.

64 Cp. Brie, *Der Bundesstaat*, Leipzig, 1874, pp. 8 ff. It was important for posterity that Aristotle (*Polit.* 3.c.9.) made the distinction between a *polis* and an alliance and declared the latter to be a mere contractual relationship. For the beginnings of the federal state see Polybius, *Histories* 2.37; cp. Brie, p. 10.

65 Cp. *Polit.* 1.c.1 (the state is a certain type of association but it is the most sovereign and encompasses all other associations. Family and village community are distinguished from it not merely by size but also generically); 1.c.2 (family and community are the preconditions, but the state is the completion and therefore prior to them for the whole consist of parts); 1.c.3-13 (the household as

Among the original associations, Aristotle concerned himself only with the household community and its three elements, the matrimonial, the parental, and the societal relationships of the master. The domestic association was, to Aristotle, an essential member of the social organism and therefore appeared not only as the pre-condition but as the permanent basis of the state. On the other hand, Aristotle saw the community as a basic stepping stone and a passing phase of the development of civil society. In relation to the origin of the state, he spoke of the village which disappeared in the *polis*. But in his theory of the state he never returned to the concept of the community. He did not exclude the arbitrary fellowship[66] but referred to it as accidental and created only for specific purposes. In his ideal constitution he clearly envisaged a state-ordered articulation of the citizenry according to vocational groupings and table-fellowships.[67] In this respect Aristotle expressed the common Hellenic view, and Roman philosophy was guided by this model.[68]

In so far as it is possible at all to ascribe to the association a specific identity, it was a diluted copy, a partial analogy, of the specific identity of the state. In fact Aristotle and the other Greeks subsumed the state and all associations under the general concept of society and the Romans used the word *societas* in the same general sense. On the other hand there was the inclination to perceive in every community an organic element through which the united multitude appeared as a whole. But the concept of the personality of the association was not developed. Rather a distinction was made between universal law and the law pertaining specifically to everyone. This was, generally, a model of a collectively united multitude whose legal sphere fell partially within the common and partially within the private sphere. Thus it is noteworthy that ancient philosophy united, under one heading, family relationships of all types, unions of friends and com-

a part of the state); 3.c.9 (the distinction of the state from defensive alliances and contractual companies formed for commercial purposes; all associations within the state serve its purpose); *Eth. Nicom.* 8.c.9. and 11 (tribal, district, and sacrificial associates, army communities, and associations for the sake of various undertakings are derived from the social nature of man. All are parts of the state. The state exists not only for the sake of its parts but for the sake of the collectivity; it exists not only for a single human purpose but for the sake of the totality of purposes. It concerns itself not only with the aim of the moment but with that of the entire life).

66 The suppression of all associations and assemblies of citizens he sees as a means used by tyrants to maintain their rule; *Polit.* 5.c.11.

67 *Polit.* 7.c.10-12.

68 As an organic intermediary between individual and state, Cicero sees only the domestic community as the 'principle of the city and, in some sense, the seedbed of the state.' He mentions its growth through family relationships and neighbourhood but without developing the concept of community or the public corporation; *De Off.* 1.17; *De Fin.* 5.23.

munities, commercial societies and sacrificial (religious) associations, social assemblies, permanent political associations, and the state. All of this was done without distinguishing between a real group and a mere communal or commercial relationship.[69]

Obviously Greek positive law was unfamiliar with the clearly formulated distinction between *universitas* and *societas* which was known to the Romans. Undoubtedly, the specific legal subjectivity of the state, of communities, and of corporations was utilized in practice and in court.[70] But the concept of the juristic person was not thereby developed. Rather, conversely, in social and communal relationships the absence of the legal subjectivity of the whole was expressed in terms of individualism.[71] Typical of this view is the familiar Solonic law which was partially transferred into the Twelve Tables and then transmitted by Gaius into the *Corpus Juris Civilis* (*D.* 47.22.4). Thus in Gaius the recognized conception of the corporation is placed on the same level as communal commercial

69 Cp. the reference to Aristotle in note 65 above; even more vague in the category of *societas* in Cicero (cp. references in note 68 above).

70 Like the state, the tribes, the *fratries*, and the *demes* and other communities of the Athenians had real and other property. There were also sacral properties that, in a manner of banks, lent money and rents and accepted deposits. They also instituted manumission of slaves through their sale to the deities. Obviously, some arbitrary fellowships and corporate organizations had also the same rights, especially the permanent religious associations that were organized fellowships formed for the purpose of regular communal feasts which were financed through common funds. There were also associations formed for mutual support against poverty and there were associations organized for helping to release prisoners etc. Similarly, there existed unions under the guardianship of a deity, associations that collected regular contributions and held meetings. Like the state, these corporations could, through officials or through individual members, sue or be sued. Cp. Meyer and Schömann, *Der attische Prozess*, Halle, 1824, pp. 540-4; Büchsenschütz, *Besitz und Erwerb im griechischen Alterthum*, Halle, 1869, pp. 63 ff., 64 ff., 73, 114, 174 ff., 312, 331, 443, 506-9, 533.

71 Lacking any other form of authorization, the associations were permitted to appoint liquidators of estates and partnerships. The fellowships were also permitted to collect for sacrifices, meals, and feasts, and their surplus funds were disposed of accordingly. It also appears that all sorts of vocational societies and unions were liable to suits as a result of their societal obligations; cp. Böckh, *Staatshaushalt der Athener*, I, pp. 264 ff. and 360; Meyer and Schömann, pp. 378 ff. and 536. Subsequently the Roman notion of *societas* was equated with the Greek understanding of that idea, while the *collegium* and *corpus* were compared to a Greek, less formal type of association. There is no great technical difference between the Greek and Roman understanding of these terms.

undertakings and commercial speculations and reference is made to the contractual legal determinants among the participants.[72]

In the light of these facts it becomes understandable that the numerous general philosophic views about unity in multiplicity and multiplicity in unity did not immediately relate to the question of legal subjectivity. This applied particularly to Stoic philosophy that set the tone for Roman jurisprudence. The Stoic view about the possible unions of individulas within the multiplicity was expressed in the common three-fold division of bodies into simple bodies (*corpora unita, continua*), compound bodies (*corpora connexa, composita*), and communal bodies composed of diverse parts (*corpora ex distantibus*).[73] This three-fold division was accepted by the Roman jurists. The human individual, as well as the totality of the world, was placed into the category of simple bodies whose common characteristic was the uniform manifestation of the world soul (*spiritus unus*) that penetrated the entire universe. To the category of compound bodies, whose bond of unity was found in the spatial connection of simple bodies, the Romans relegated lifeless things. In the category of communal bodies, whose bond of union the Roman jurists attributed to the inner, physical connection of spatially separated bodies,[74] they placed, among others, human associations.[75] Thereby a meaningful expression of the Greek conception of the peculiar essence of associations was made available to the Roman jurists. Because in so far as an association was considered a *corpus ex distantibus* it was thought of as a whole, distinguished from its parts. A corporate unity was ascribed to this whole, to which individuals, otherwise regarded as independent bodies, related as members.[76] Thus, despite a complete change in membership it became possible to subsume, under a uniform point of view, the identity of a college of judges, a legion, or a people. Regardless

72 'If either the people or clan brothers or members of the sacred rites or sailors or sharers of common burial plots or members of a religious guild should go for plunder or for trade, if there be a property arrangement among them with each other, this arrangement shall have the force of law unless contradicted by the public law' (*D.* 47.22.4).

73 Cp. the thorough examination by Göppert in the above (note 46) work.

74 Cp. Göppert, pp. 49 ff. According to this convincing argument, the *corpus ex distantibus* was derived from the natural social instinct. Therefore it is not accidental that only animate things are mentioned as examples.

75 Cp. the sections in Göppert, pp. 10 ff. Plutarch, *Conjugatia Praecepta*, 34; Sextus Empiricus, *Adversus Mathematicos*, 7.102 and 9.78; Seneca, *Epist.* 102.6; Marcus Aurelius, *Meditations* 9.9; Pomponius, *D.* 41.3.30; Paulus, *D.* 6.1.23.5; *Inst.* 2.20.18.

76 Cp. Seneca, *De Ira* 2.31; Marcus Aurelius, *Meditations* 7.13. The Stoics conceived of the association as a real body. This is shown by Göppert, p. 51. Among the Roman jurists it was Paulus who perceived most clearly the correlation of the double corporeal unity of the whole and of the members, *D.* 6.1.23.5.

of changes in its planks, a ship retains its identity and, similarly, the human identity is preserved despite changes in its atoms.[77]

But the communal whole did not provide an answer to the question whether and to what degree the association had a subjective unity, a legally relevant will and an independent personality. Rather the concept of the *corpus ex distantibus* remained relevant to a herd of animals as well as to a human association. It pertained to a group acting with a uniform goal as well as to an organic association.[78] Within the general category, special groups were distinguished but none was given a distinct attribute that contained the concept of group-personality.[79] Roman jurisprudence received from philosophy that peculiar expression of the Greek conception of association that was void of personality. In certain instances the jurists were able to utilize the concept of the *corpus ex distantibus* in their doctrine of the legal object by considering directly the objective unity of the whole.[80] This notion they could have utilized in the doctrine of the legal subject. This, however, did not come about. But it was not unimportant in the history of the theory of corporations that the term and the conception of a united *corpus* with an essentially interchangeable membership became a legally recognized subject for Roman law. But the idea of an inner organic unity of such a corporative body was not fully developed and further elaborated upon by the Roman jurists. Rather they contented themselves with a purely superficial and formalistic view. This is illustrated by that definition of the *corpus ex distantibus* in which Pomponius places all emphasis upon the unity denoted by the term.[81] The conception of a uniform communal body remained limited to the substratum of the or-

77 This is the content of the influential exposition of Alfenus in *D.* 5.1.76, where a complete parallel is drawn between the change in membership inside the whole body and the change in the parts of a ship. (A distinction between an organic unity as opposed to a composite unity). Pomponius asserts the same and compares the unity of the whole to a herd. He greatly emphasizes corporeal unity. *D.* 41.3.30; *Inst.* 2.20.18. Cp. also *D.* 6.1.3.

78 See notes 75 and 77 above.

79 It was of importance for mediaeval theory that Marcus Aurelius (9.9) divided collective bodies into rational human associations and contrasted them to the lower unions among non-rational beings and to the higher system of the constellations. But all possible kinds of human associations were seen as being similar. Seneca also ascribed to the associations the characteristic of being joined together by right and duty, but the question remains unanswered whether it is possible to ascribe subjective unity to such legal and ethical unions.

80 Göppert, pp. 94 ff.

81 *D.* 41.3.30. Cp. Kuntze, *Exkurse über römisches Recht*, Leipzig, 1880, 2nd ed., p. 454. While the association was undergoing a change of membership, its identity remained unchanged. This peculiarity is indicative of the superficial and formal concept of a union held by the Romans.

ganized union as a legal subject. Legal personality, meanwhile, was not derived from the inner essence of such a social organism by the Roman jurists. Rather it was derived from the special Roman concept of the legal subject, a concept averse from the organic view.

This will become clear as we turn to the concept of association in Roman law.

II

The Concept of Association in Roman Jurisprudence

The Romans were the first people on earth to found a great independent science of law. Of decisive importance for this was the distinction that the Roman mind made at an early stage between the two categories of legal thought and, further, the fact that they brought these two categories to a level of relative independence. The Romans as well as the Greeks perceived the idea of objective law as corollary to the early conception of the state. They viewed this law as a binding order relevant to all communal existence beyond and above all human caprice. But they only arrived at the independence of law from state and ethics by simultaneously grasping the idea of subjective law. They clung to this notion most determinedly, basing their system of authority on the ancient realm of original human freedom.

From the outset, the Romans considered the will as the centre of law. Active will, as recognized and delimited but not as produced by objective law, appeared to the Romans not to be a contradiction but a creative principle and the living embodiment of legal thought. The idea of subjective law and its central significance was part of the Roman consciousness from the earliest times.

Roman legal subjectivity concentrated, from the beginning, on two sharply isolated carriers of the will. The force of will in law, understood as *jus*, was derived from either the *populus Romanus* or from the single *paterfamilias*. In this sense the roots of law were divided into two independent spheres. In the one the sovereignty of the people prevailed, while in the other the sovereignty of the single will of an individual ruler predominated. This distinction, never thought of by the Greeks and attained by the Germanic peoples only at the end of a complicated evolution, stood at the beginning of Roman jurisprudence. It was the fundamental division between the *jus publicum* and the *jus privatum*. The successes as well as the failures of Roman law were due to this sharp and unmediated distinction.

The distinction was grasped originally by the Romans entirely in accordance with the subjective principle. It is therefore not analogous to the modern differentiation between public and private law. Rather, the *jus publicum* was the *jus populi* even though it may have entailed the ability to hold property. The *jus privatum* was the *jus singulorum* referring to the power relationships or the punishments arising out of the concept of *inter privatos* (among private individuals).[1] Essentially, the subject of the specific right determined to which sphere of law it belonged. The norms of the two spheres of the *jus publicum* and the *jus privatum* were endowed with their own concepts, institutions, and procedures. The unity inherent in the distinction was not resolved, and the inner components, that resembled one another, were never mediated. There was therefore no urge juristically to grasp nor legally to formulate the common basic principles derived from the division. Every Roman legal principle was therefore originally conceptualized and developed from either the *jus publicum* or the *jus privatum.*

The central concept of legal subjectivity was not seen as something relevant to both spheres and it was not formulated in an uniform fashion. Rather it was developed one-sidedly and separately for each sphere. Precisely this approach proved itself decisive for the peculiar development of the concept of association in Roman law.

The Roman *paterfamilias* was the focus of private law.[2] Here individuals who were citizens appeared as the only human beings fully recognized by the Roman state. They were the sole, self-determined, and in their sphere sovereign representatives of the concept of right. The objective order determined the limits of freedom abstractly and equally for all. Within the assigned sphere, the free individual will created its own specific realm.

There existed a multiplicity of equal wills each of which ruled not only over a household but also confronted each other as centres of power. Consequently, there soon manifested itself a juridical determination and formulation of an equal and common legal subjectivity. There developed within and for private law the Roman concept of person, derived from the old artificial expression *caput*[3] (head)

1 The subjective point of view is also retained when the norm derived from the people is denoted as *jus publicum* and when it is opposed to the autonomous formation of the legal relationships through the exercise of the private will.

2 At one time, even in Rome, the individual possessed a legal subjectivity not only as an individual *per se* but as a 'member of the self-contained and externally united fellowship of the *gens*'; cp. R. Ihering, *Geist des römischen Rechts*, Leipzig, 1873, 3rd ed., I, pp. 183 ff; A. Pernice, *Marcus Antistius Labeo*, Halle, 1873, I. pp. 93 ff. Cp. Kuntze, *Exkurse*, pp. 413 ff.

3 Cp. Savigny, *System des heutigen römischen Rechts*, Berlin, 1840, II, Appendix VI; Walter, *Geschichte des römischen Rechts*, Bonn, 1860, 3rd ed., II, paragraph 457; Pernice, I, pp. 97 ff.; Kuntze, pp. 61 ff. and 427 ff.

which, in jurisprudence, received an abstract conception through the use of the word *persona*.

The Roman concept of person was thus originally used in a strictly individualistic manner. Its content was the abstract attribute of the single Roman citizen. It meant the capacity to exert the power of the individual will within that private sphere that was recognized and protected by the Roman state. It was formulated, plainly, for the single human being. And the individual human being was thought of as an isolated, self-contained unity of will which was subject only to external limitations. All organic ties were thereby disregarded. As an unassociated and as an essentially co-ordinated single being, the individual received his legal *caput* and, in the legal realm, was viewed as a *persona*. Naturally, the position of the individual as a person was not without its significance when his relations to such organic associations as the family, the body politic, or the people were considered. But the connections that were at the basis of these ties were not incorporated in the concept of personality and they were exploited unequally.

The full development of legal subjectivity was confined to the *paterfamilias*. His entire freedom under private law was not derived from his position as head of a household but from his position as a legal adult (*homo sui juris*).[4] The household association was not the basis but rather the result of his full personality so that the concept of the *paterfamilias* could be applied fully to a family that had formulated itself into an individual.[5] As far as the law was concerned, the household was not an association consisting of a head and of members but rather a sphere of rule (*Herrschaftssphäre*) that consisted of the expression of the absolute authority of a totally free individual.[6] Conversely, the subjugation of the legal minors (*homines alieni juris*) according to family law, represented a limitation upon the personality and this was a diminution of the notion of *caput*.[7] But this diminution was essentially the result of the external interference of the domestic power. It was not an expression of an organic position of a member of the household association. Thus the abstract *persona*, attributed to the child of the house, represented a limitation upon its activity.[8]

4 This would apply to the concept of person as expounded by jurisprudence, provided the assumption of Lange (*Römische Alterthümer*, I, p. 157) is correct that the expression *caput* referred originally to the head of the family and that it related only to that entity. It is more likely, however, that the word *caput* was also derived from the idea of the individual and that, from its inception, it stood for the head of a human [association] recognized by the state. Cp. Kuntze, p. 42.

5 *D*. 50.16.195.2.

6 Ihering, pp. 156-217; Pernice, I, pp. 108 ff.

7 It is evident that according to the concept of the *capitis diminutio*, the *caput* of the *homo alieni juris* was diminished; cp. Savigny, II, paragraph *D* 68 ff.

8 Savigny, II, paragraph 67; Pernice, I, pp. 103 ff. and 158 ff.

In a similarly one-sided manner all relationships involving dominance within private law were construed as the expressions of individual rights and were not permitted to enter the law as articulated associations. The slave lacked personality, hence he could not be considered as having a subjective value within the whole of the association.[9] Personality as derived from private law was owed to the free man only as an isolated individual, and certain limitations were imposed upon him as a result of the rights reserved for the head of the family.[10] Originally, all legal subjectivity was determined by citizenship. Eventually the Latins and the non-Romans were recognized as subjects to private law without being granted all the advantages accruing from that law. This meant, however, the gradual grant by the Roman state of a subjective legal standing to alien individuals without its making the decision to accept the personality of the organic communities in which these individuals lived.[11] Wherever Roman law distinguished between legal ability, it either failed to recognize or only partially recognized legal personality. It had no conception of personality as an immanent union of wills. Rather it imposed limitations upon that individual who had been elevated to the status of a person. In a fully abstract manner, Roman law ordered human beings into social bodies as subjects of a law which treated them only as simple, indivisible individuals confined to themselves.[12]

In contradistinction, a glance at the role of the Germanic development of law shows the importance that was ascribed to the unity of the family and the relationships of rule and the orders of the community. It is therefore a fact that the frequently cited tendency of Roman law towards arid individualism is true. According to its dominant idea and in its fully articulated structure, Roman law was predominantly a law that pertained to the advantage of the individual and it did not recognize 'organic unities.' Accordingly, individuals were fully isolated autonomous subjects of specific spheres of law. All institutions and forms of the *jus privatum* were designed for such isolated individuals. The interlocking ties and bonds of the individual will in its legal existence produced a jurisprudence that, with admirable art, dissected and construed all relationships of private law. These relationships led back to the abstract content of power as a right, free of

9 The slave had neither *caput* nor *persona*. The gradual recognition of his actual personality by the law (cp. esp. Pernice, I, pp. 113-58) left the principle unaltered. However, we do find a start towards legal subjectivity.

10 Cp. Savigny, II, paragraph 65. It is irrelevant whether the association of *clientes* had any legal significance.

11 Cp. Savigny, II, paragraph 66. The perceptible *caput* was envisaged either fully or to a lesser degree, while the more abstract *persona* could only be acknowledged or negated.

12 Cp. above, p. 96.

obligations and in harmony with the strictly individualistic understanding of the concept of person.[13]

Because of this fundamental view of the legal subject, Roman private law could not develop a legal concept of association. Rather it reduced all communal ties within private law to the right and duty of the multiplicity of subjects. It always conceived of the multiplicity as the sum of isolated individuals who were bound essentially and externally by the identity of their rights or their circumstances but who did not represent, in any way, a subjective whole.[14] Thus the Roman community never surmounted the concept of the *communio* in which unequal parts agreed upon this one point: each participant was, within a specific sphere, individually endowed with rights and duties. Every formation of a society was subsumed under the form of *societas* which was viewed as a purely obligatory and externally unbreakable contractual relationship but not as a voluntary contract based upon the content of the legal essence of the personality. Roman private law refrained from accepting those conceptions that viewed a multiplicity of persons as an associated group and a community as having a 'common hand.' It failed to view a 'society' as a group with its own unity that could be endowed with rights and duties.[15]

Roman law knew nothing of the communal extension of rights and obligations familiar to Germanic law. Owing to its basic conception of person, it was plainly obliged to place all associations of subjects under the objective compe-

13 Cp. Pernice, I, p. 108; esp. Ihering, II, pp. 139-217; III, pp. 182 ff., 194 ff. Ihering argues for the 'one-sided recognition and completion of the point of view that might and rule' without the balancing force of morals is the only 'juricial' and 'absolutely correct 'interpretation (II, pp. 139-41, 293 ff.). Nevertheless he emphasizes the lack of moderation in the Roman concept of power that did not acknowledge any duties ameliorated by rights. This feature negated the notion of the 'idea of reciprocity' as the only 'transitory' feature of Roman law (*ibid*, p. 297).

14 Windscheid, *Pandekten*, paragraph 51; Pernice, I, p. 19.

15 In the case of communal relationships the Romans spoke of a unity of the legal personality (*unitas personae*). Joint owners appeared in the place of a single man (*unius loco*) (*D.* 10.1.4.7). Those joined (*conjuncti*) in the law of inheritance enjoyed the power of a single legal personality (*unius personae potestate funguntur*) (*D.* 30.34) and acted as though rendered into a single body (*quasi in unum corpus redacti sunt*) (*Cod.* 6.26.1). The correlated creditors were viewed as acting in place of one (*unius loco*) (*D.* 2.14.9) or as though in place of one (*quasi unius*) (*D.* 9.4.19). Cp. esp. *D.* 2.14.9 where those believed to be co-defendants (*correi credendi*) were considered to take the place of an individual (*unius loco haberi*) because one thing was owed (*quia unum debitum est*). In the same manner there were references to several guardians of a minor who was a creditor (*plures tutores pupilli creditoris*) and to a single guardian of several wards (*unus tutor plurium pupillorum*). These were held to take the place of one legal subject.

tence of the sovereign individual. It would have been necessary to negate the Roman concept of liberty in order to be able to look upon a private community as a substantial limitation upon the individual will in favour of a communal sphere of will. Furthermore, it was unthinkable that a Roman community based upon private law could formulate itself, of its own volition, into a corporate association whose unity was a subject of law distinct from that of the sum of its members. The concepts of *communio* and *societas* were unable to deprive the individual of the smallest measure of sovereign independent existence. Lacking even a trace of such thought, the Roman system could generate no development leading to a formulation of a new personality distinct from the individual.[16] This would have been an incomprehensible step. The single Roman individuality was posited purely in itself and essentially for its own purpose. Its freedom was recognized by the state as an objective concept endowed with an unchangeable content and protected from all incursions. However, a Roman individual did not receive that kind of autonomy which was required for the genesis of the communal will, for he was not granted the autonomy to form a union of individual wills.[17] Roman law therefore did not cede a specific legal essence to any association derived from private law. It knew no associations that were based upon private law nor did it have the potential to do so.

An exception to the prevailing doctrine in Roman law did however exist in the case of the associations of the *publicani*.* But that these societies gained recognition as having an existence independent of its members was due to the fact that they came under the aegis of the Roman state's financial administration. As such they were under the jurisdiction of the *jus publicum*.[18] They may be considered as vocational corporations[19] but not as bodies derived from private

* The *publicani* were a group of men who financed buildings, road construction, mining, and other similar enterprises. In exchange, they were permitted to collect taxes. Their enterprises were of such magnitude that they had to form associations, partnerships, and syndicates in order to meet their obligations.

16 One merely has to consider the exemption of the *communio* from suits for division of property (*D.* 10.3.14) and the extension of the condition to the inheritors in the *societas* (*D.* 17.2.59). Naturally this applied only to the communities and societies under mature Roman law. Originally the Romans confounded the germ of the corporation with sociability, placing both concepts into the matrix of communal living.

17 Ihering, *Geist*, II, pp. 218 ff. Here he develops the consequences of the Roman concept of freedom as a legal institution of objective content untouchable by its own subjects. He disregards the concommitant result, i.e. the unyielding nature of Roman freedom which would be unacceptable to modern legal consciousness.

18 Cp. Pernice, I, pp. 295-8.

19 The *societates publicanorum* were viewed as acquisitive corporations and were distinguished from other corporations by their lack of a *causa perpetua*. They differed

law. Rather they appeared as political bodies that included the social relationships of private law.[20] Despite the greater permanence of the *publicani* and a certain type of organization permitted to their societies, they belonged to the category of a purely obligatory *societas*.[21] At the same time, the *corpus* permitted to the associates was a college of vocationally linked members, as legal agents entirely divorced from their societal contracts.[22]

The Roman concept of association was therefore exclusively relegated to the *jus publicum* and has to be located in that realm.

Strictly speaking, the Roman *jus publicum* recognized only one legal subject – the Roman state. The Roman state, for its part, appeared as an association of the whole that encompassed and delimited all personalities. It was, however, never referred to or thought of as a personality.

According to the original Roman conception, the state as subject coincided with the *populus Romanus*.[23] The *populus Romanus* was the assembled or theoretically assembled totality of the Roman citizens. As was the case with other developing peoples, the Romans in the early stages of their history, did not distinguish between a group-unity and a collective multiplicity. Everywhere in Roman law traces were encountered of the view that a state was the sum of the citizens. The law of the community was the common law of all. The obligation of the totality was the obligation of the individuals. The public legal order was the mutual legal relationship of the citizens, and the sovereignty of the people was

from a *societas privata* in so far as they had a juristic personality. Savigny, *System*, II, p. 255; Puchta in Weiske, *Rechtslexikon*, 'Corporationen', Arndts, *Pandekten*, paragraph 42; Böcking, *Pandekten*, I, p. 238; von Hahn, *Die materielle Uebereinstimmung der römischen und germanischen Rechtsprincipien*, Jena, 1856, pp. 346-50; Bruns in Holtzendorff, *Enzyklopaedie*, 3rd ed., p. 359; T. Mommsen, *de collegiis et sodalitiis Romanorum*, Kiel, 1843, pp. 84-6, also *Römisches Staatsrecht,* 2nd ed., II, p. 102, pp. 978-9.

20 At any rate, it is not acceptable to move the Roman concept of corporation into the realm of the concept of society as known to private law.

21 Thus Weiske, *Praktische Untersuchungen*, 1847, III, p. 137; Pfeifer, *Juristische Personen*, 1847, p. 40, note 2; M. Cohn, *De natura societatum juris Rom. quae vocantur publicae*, Berlin, 1870, and *Zur Geschichte des römischen Vereinsrechts*, Berlin, 1873, pp. 155-85. A decisive argument against the corporate nature was that the censor entered into contractual relationships not with the society but with the purchaser or contractor (*manceps*) or the leading man among the *publicani* (*princeps publicanorum*) and the originator of the partnership (*auctor societatis*) who alone received duties and rights from the state. Cp. J. Marquardt, *Römische Staatsverwaltung*, 1875, II, p. 290.

22 In the *Corpus Juris Civilis*, certain associations recognized as *corpora* are referred to as *societas*. (*D*. 3.4.1, 46.1.22, 47.2.31.1). This practice was of importance to the history of the modern theory of corporations.

23 Whenever the state was referred to as a subject, the expression *civitas* meant the citizenry. *Respublica* did not stand for the state in the subjective sense but meant communal property; Mommsen, *Staatsr.*, II, p. 1035, note 7.

rooted in the contractual union of wills of the fellowship of the people.[24] In a naïve manner the Roman jurists confused the people as a unity with the people as a multiplicity. They derived customary law from the tacit consent or the tacit agreement of all citizens. In order to reinforce this view, they assumed that legislation arrived at by popular resolution was identical with the manifestations of the sovereign will of the people.[25]

At an early stage, Roman consciousness decisively and energetically separated the totality of citizens from its individual parts. It viewed the totality of citizens as the carrier of a uniform and indivisible common will. In a most determined manner the law of the Roman state expressed the idea that all legal will and action of the sovereign people were tied to constitutional assumptions and forms. In their assemblies the people were constitutionally enabled to express their will and to act accordingly. Every resolution was arrived at by the taking of votes. The institution of multiple systems of assemblies assured the possibility of expressing the popular will through different legislative bodies. As a result of the class struggle, the ancient fully enfranchised citizenry blended with the separately organized *plebs* into a united people within one state. Thus a fully efficacious system of representation was attained by the assembled *plebs*.[26] However, no assembly of the community could meet or vote without the supervision of the duly appointed magistrate.[27] It became obvious, therefore, that the subject of the state's power was not the sum of the citizens but rather the citizenry in its legally ordered unity.[28]

The concept of *publicum* denoting the competence of the people could, at an early stage, discard all traces of the old identity of the public with the total community. Originally the law of the people and the law of the individual had been placed in opposition to one another in a communally established and distributed general law. This position was arrived at by formulating the important difference between *publicum* and *privatum*, signifying the plainly contradictory categories

24 Cp. Ihering, *Geist*, I, pp. 207-25, 103 ff., 176 ff.; II, p. 236; R. Ihering, *Der Zweck im Recht*, Leipzig, 1877, I, pp. 549-50.

25 *D.* 1.3.32.1; Hermogenianus, *D.* 1.3.35; Papinianus, *D.* 1.3.1; Modestinus, *D.* 1.3.40.

26 Cp. Mommsen, *Staatsr.*, I, pp. 17 ff.; II, pp. 261 ff., 462 ff., 269-71.

27 Cp. Mommsen, I, pp. 1 ff., 187 ff., 193 ff., 270 ff., 452; II, pp. 282 ff.

28 A different point of view was put forth by Augustus who maintained that it had been the unanimous will of the citizens that conferred upon him the right to govern. It was this interpretation that formally legalized the election or removal of the emperors by the alleged will of the people. Cp. Mommsen, I, p. 671; II, pp. 814, 1077. This atomistic theory indicated the dissolution of the ancient Roman concept of the people. It led to a constitutional condition wherein the state became separated from the concept of the people despite the fictitious sovereignty of the populace.

of communal and individual legal rights.[29] Only in this way was it possible to perceive the totality and the individual as sharply isolated subjects and to provide each, in its own sphere of competence, with full sovereign powers. As a *privatus* the individual had his inalienable and specific rights that, in principle, could not be interfered with by the *populus*. He could enter into true legal relationships with the *populus* because he was not part of it but rather an independently constituted whole confronting the larger totality.[30] On the other hand, as *civis Romanus*, the same man was essentially a part of the whole. So far as the laws of the *populus* were concerned, he was their living embodiment but he could not play an independent legal role as a citizen. The rights of the full citizen to vote and to hold office enabled him to participate in the exercise of the power of the state. However, this enfranchisement was never understood as a subjective sphere of autonomy but as a legal enablement derived from an objective order.

In the same manner, individuals utilized the *res publicae* only as members of the people and in that capacity were carrying out the laws of the people.[31] They protected not their own rights but the people's rights when they intervened against the violation of customary rights.[32] According to the older view, popular interdicts and actual popular complaints were treated as private complaints in the interest and to the advantage of the plaintiff.[33] In accordance with the principle of giving 'anyone of the people' the status to sue, any member of the public was assumed to partake of the communal property or communal rights that furnished the basis for a complaint.[34] In fully developed Roman law every complaint

29 Thus the *ager publicus* and *privatus*, *res publicae* and *privatae*, penalties of the *populus* and the injured *privatus*. Therefore it was not important that the law was called a *sponsio* (promise) and the private disposal and contract was referred to as *lex*. The attributes *publica* and *privata* explained the generic differences adequately.

30 Frontinus, *De Aquaeductu Urbis Romae*, c. 128, 'that within his own sphere each man shall have his own right as a state or private corporation would ... ' Cp. Ihering, *Geist*, II, pp. 67 ff.

31 *D.* 43.8.2.2.

32 *D.* 43.8.2.2 and 43.9.1.1. The exercise of customary law was obviously an 'individual' right but only if it was recognized and protected as such. It could have asserted itself against the *populus* but there were no traces of such a development. The exercise of customary law appeared, essentially, as the exercise of the rights of the *populus*, utilizing the *res publica* in and through its members. The individual citizen, when defending customary law against a fellow citizen, appeared as a member of the people acting in his own interest. The exercise of the rights of the *populus* did not appear as a concession on part of the abstract state, nor was it a concession to the sum of the subjects.

33 Bruns, 'Die römischen Popularklagen,' *Zeitschrift für römisches Gesetz*, III, 1864, pp. 341, 370 ff., 388 ff., 401, 405.

34 This is the correct assumption of Bruns' argument (p. 408). But one cannot agree with the idea of a 'form of communal property of the collective citizenry' in which the indi-

of this kind represented a means extended to the individual citizen to protect the rights of the *populus*. The point is made explicit in the *Digest*: 'A suit is denoted as popular or belonging to the people which upholds the people's right' (*D*. 47. 23.1.1). This formulation differed only in its procedural structure and not in its legal-material basis from the numerous cases in which the 'anyone of the people'-principle was utilized by the proconsuls to allow suit in the name of the people (*pro populo*).[35]

Similarly, the [older] juristic treatment of the public lands which had originated as communal fields involved the conception of partial ownership. [In later law] this concept of public lands disappeared without a trace. Each change from communal land to private property was considered a manifestation linked to a complete change in subject and was never viewed as a partition or a distribution of portions.[36] Under no circumstances was the political sphere of the individual identified with the private sphere, as understood as a specific and independent realm of autonomy. Finally, under no circumstances was the political sphere of the individual identical with the specific and independent concept of authority assigned to him by private law. Rather, his status was the result of his constituted position as a member of a legitimized totality.[37]

Roman consciousness never progressed beyond this point. The people's totality posited as a unity remained identical with the state as a legal subject. The idea that the state in its totality could be a living organism, whose subjective unity was represented by the assembled citizenry as its highest embodied expression, did not appear in Roman law.[38] Therefore the concept of the organ as a relationship of a particular political expression with respect to the activity of the state's associational whole was not developed. Rather, one can speak only of a legal mandate to exercise those laws pertaining to the totality of the citizens. The senate was legally only the adviser of the community. But from Tiberius onward, its

vidual 'as *civis* and *jure civitatis* exercised his rights.' Mere 'popular utilization' did not represent 'communal property' because it failed to limit substantially corporate property by references to the pluralistic individual rights.

35 Cp. Bruns, *ibid*, pp. 363 ff. and 400 ff.; Mommsen, *Staatsr.*, I, p. 160 ff., 179 ff., 180 note 1; also Gaius, 4.82; *Inst*. 4.10.

36 Mommsen, *Staatsr.*, II, pp. 607 ff., 955 ff.

37 Roman administrative justice occupied a place between the *populus* and the *privatus*. But there was no analogous legal relationship between the *populus* and the *civis*. In the Roman community, civic duty was essentially unlimited, while civic rights were without influence. That is why Mommsen can speak of arbitrary taxation and the withdrawal of citizenship on moral charges. *Staatsr.*, II, pp. 320, 363 ff.; see also Mommsen's exposition of the nature of Roman criminal jurisdiction I, pp. 153 ff.

38 Cp. also Bruns, *Enzykl.*, 3rd ed., p. 96.

opinion was the definitive expression of the popular will. It could therefore be considered as representing the people's decayed assemblies.[39]

The collective Roman magistracy appeared, from the outset, as the legally constituted representative of the community for executing those tasks that were unsuitable for direct resolutions in the assembly.[40] In so far as the community as such was considered capable of exercising its will and acting in this field, the position of the magistrate approximated that of a guardian.[41] The magistrate, however, always remained the mere representative of the totality. He supervised its laws and in the name of the whole exercised the full measure of its legal powers. The totality's action was, legally, equivalent to the magistrate's action.[42] Thus the *principate* could initially establish *de facto* the rule of an individual within the framework of the magistracy, in theory without interfering with the sovereignty of the people.[43] As before, the state as a legal subject was equated with the *populus Romanus* whose right was exercised by the *princeps* in conjunction with the senate.[44] With the decay of the assemblies the real subject of the state's power became entirely unable to will and to act,[45] so that the sovereign people appeared as a minor under a guardian. Thereby the view of the totality considered as a subject had to divorce itself from the conception embodied in the assemblies. It had to seek refuge in the abstract concept of a collective totality that disregarded the multiplicity of its components.

Eventually the idea of the monarchy was accepted and it became easier to modify and continue with the old view as to the legal subjectivity of the state.[46]

39 Of importance to later political theories is Pomponius' statement, *D.* 1.2.2.9. Similarly, *Inst.* 1.2.5.

40 Mommsen, *Staatsr.*, I. pp. 73 ff., 227; II. p. 22.

41 Mommsen (I, p. 227) exaggerates when he assumes that by republican times the community was generally incapable of action. Cp. also II, p. 22.

42 Cp. Mommsen, I, p. 227; Seneca, *Controversiae* 9.25.

43 Mommsen, *Staatsr.*, II, pp. 726 ff.

44 For this reason, a crime against the emperor was considered a crime against the *populus Romanus* (*D.* 48.4.4).

45 The appointment and the removal of the *princeps* by the army or the senate could be considered an expression of the popular will. (Mommsen, II, pp. 764 ff., 1076 ff.). But this was, in reality, not a substitute for the constitutional manifestation of the collective popular will. Besides the magisterial competence of the *princeps*, there existed the independent competence of the senate that encompassed a series of the sovereign rights of the *comitia* (*ibid.*, pp. 826, 840, 847, 857, 876, 877 ff., 984). Yet it cannot be maintained that these represented the organized will of the people. Rather, the representation of the legally incapacitated totality was divided between the emperor and the senate in a unique manner that Mommsen characterizes as a 'dyarchy.' (*ibid.*, p. 725).

46 For the sources and the evolution of the monarchical idea, see Mommsen, II, pp. 732 ff.

The notion came to prevail that there was a lasting transferral to the emperor of all the rights which had once belonged to the people's assembly.[47] The emperor represented now what the people's assembly had once been. He was the entire and exclusive carrier of the abstract totality, the visible incorporation of the common will, the sole manifestation of the state's legal subjectivity. The reformulation of the corporate unity of the people into an institutionalized unity was thereby completed. But the idea that the state could be the legal formulation of the organic unity of the whole people remained as remote as ever.

This view of the state's legal subjectivity prevented the Romans from arriving at the concept of the personality of the state. They remained with the subjectivity of the *populus* and later with that of the emperor. Unique of its kind, this subjectivity was not subordinated to any higher generic concept.

From its inception, Roman constitutional law knew no other specific law but that of the *populus Romanus*. The *populus Romanus* as the sovereign, uniform, and indivisible embodiment of the common will did not recognize any other independent representative of the public will. Certainly the traditional Roman conception of the sovereignty of the citizenry was not identical with the total absence of legal restraint. Rather, constitutional law appeared as a conception of legally binding norms in and through which the people themselves or their representatives exercised the state's powers.[48] But only those rules of objective law existed which were related to changes in the common will. Separately recognized subjective law was not developed in this sphere. The Romans refrained from thinking that the relationship between an organized associated whole and its

47 The *lex regia* that granted comprehensive powers to the individual *princeps* may have originated with the *lex tribunica* of the early Empire. (Mommsen, II, pp. 838-41, 871-7). In the *Corpus Juris Civilis* the following exceedingly important juristic announcements are made. 'By means of an ancient law that is called the royal law, all the rights and power of the Roman people have passed over to the power of the emperor' (*Cod*. 1.17. 1.7). Or, 'By the royal law that was passed concerning the emperor's power, the people have conferred upon the emperor all of their power and dominion' (*D*. 1.4.1, 1.2.2.11; *Inst*. 1.2.6).

48 If they contradicted the existing legal order, popular decisions were declared invalid; cp. Mommsen, *Staatsr.*, I, pp. 97, 187, 270 ff., 452, 615 ff., also note 27 above. Ultimately the formal powers of the legislator enabled him to surmount all legal barriers. But the Romans hardly seemed to have been aware of this condition as Ihering asserts in his polemic against Cicero (*Geist*, III, pp. 229 ff.). In any case, the conviction prevailed that, in reality, the will of the people was limited by constitutional and legal barriers and that it was illegal to go beyond these boundaries. Cp. Ihering, I, pp. 59 ff., 67-77. Roman laws that prohibited their own abrogation (*ibid*, III, p. 231 and Mommsen, I, pp. 690 ff.) were already criticized by Cicero (*Ad Att*. 3.23.2). But they show the intensity of the Roman conviction that the constitution bound the sovereign will of the people.

members as such could be seen not only as an objective relational order but as a true and mutual subjective legal connection. Hence the *persona* of man remained relegated to the category of the *privatus*, and there is no trace of an expression of that aspect of the individual that confronts the whole. There is no indication of a public person (*persona publica*) or a reference to a 'civic personality.'[49]

The power of the magistrate was envisaged as being lofty and unfettered,[50] but there was no notion of a subjective executive and legal power distinct from that of the people.[51] Absent from Roman law was the conception of the sphere of competence of the executive. In vain one seeks for a complex of authoritative rights and its institutional expression.[52] Roman constitutional law concerned itself totally with the relationship of orders and remained unfamiliar with the theory of mutually contradictory subjects of law. It knew of only a single collective legal subject represented by an associational whole. Precisely for this reason the *populus Romanus* was, without further hesitation, considered a living being endowed with the highest subjective majesty and power.[53] This legal subjectivity was not derived from a general concept and could not be compared with the personality assigned to the individual. The Roman understanding of 'person' was plainly a matter of contradiction but not a higher developmental form.

As the *princeps* gradually changed from the representative to the unique possessor of the state's legal subjectivity, he adopted this subjectivity in an exclusive and concentrated way. Now there could be no reference to a political authority opposed to the emperor. The sovereign common will found its simple and constant expression in the manifestations of one man's will. The principle of objective legal ties seen as the manifestation of the will of the state disappeared. The emperor now united in his person the legislative and executive functions. As the

49 Cp. note 37 above.

50 Cp. Ihering, *Geist*, II, pp. 260-92; Mommsen, I, pp. 73 ff., 672 ff.

51 By attacking the magistrate, the individual harmed not only the laws but also the right and the majesty of the people; the people themselves could act unconstitutionally by intruding upon the sphere of the magistrate, but this act did not violate a subjective law. While acting as a magistrate, not even the *princeps* could fall back upon the right of investigation (*jus quaesitum*) (Mommsen, II, pp. 1077 ff.). Most significantly, the Romans appointed an extraordinary magistracy to deal with the reserved and constitutional rights of the community; cp. Mommsen, II, pp. 569 ff., 626 ff. This illustrated the community's ties with the legal norms. It demanded the execution of all popular decisions through magistrates but it also indicated the absence of a governing institution independent of the people.

52 Cp. Mommsen, I, p. 679.

53 This is particularly evident in the concept of the *majestas populi Romani*. Cp. Cicero, *De Invent. Rhet.* 2.17.52; *De Partit. Orator.* 30.105; *Philipp.* 3.5.13; *De Leg.* 3.12 and Livius, 8.33.17.

successor of the assemblies, he could dispense with the formal norms and expressions of the sovereign popular will. The statement 'That which seems good to the emperor has also the force of law' (*Inst.* 1.2.6) expressed the transfer of communal rights to the emperor and signalled the end of all formal limitations upon imperial legislation.[54] As a corollary, the relevant statement 'The emperor is not bound by law' (*D.* 1.3.31) acquired an ominous meaning in so far as it became the formula for future absolutism.[55] Simultaneously, the traditional separation of the sovereign and the executive functions disappeared, as they were now united in the emperor. Also, the constitutional independence of the magistrate was no longer recognized in practice. There remained only the imperial officialdom with its delegated powers.[56] Roman constitutional law culminated in a purely administrative order. But this was not the only consequence of its basic bias. The state's legal subjectivity required a juridical formulation even less than it did in republican times. The conception sufficed that the emperor was the incorporated universality, that he was, as Justinian claimed, the 'living law' (*Novellae* 105.2.4). In his private affairs the emperor was considered as a person but publicly he was the symbol of the abstract unity of the state and as such he was above and outside the concept of person.[57]

In Roman constitutional thought, the law of nations appeared in a different light. Here the legal subjectivity of the *populus Romanus* was confronted by the legal subjectivity of external wholes and rulers on an equal basis. In this realm, however, classical antiquity never distinguished basically between a collective unity and a collective multiplicity. Rather it treated nations as mutually exclusive bodies whose respective beings emanated from their specific totality.[58] Thus the *jus gentium* recognized independent human associations under the generic concept of *gens*[59] but refrained from the idea of ascribing to other states a per-

54 *D.* 1.4.1; *Inst.* 1.2.6; *D.* 1.2.2.11, 1.2.2.12. For the development of the legislative powers of the *princeps*, cp. Mommsen, II, pp. 845 ff., 867-77.

55 *D.* 1.3.31; *Nov.* 105.2.4. For the original, limited meaning of the sentence and its gradual generalization cp. Mommsen, II, pp. 727-30.

56 G. Kretschmer, *Über das Beamtenthum der röm. Kaiserzeit,* Giessen, 1879, esp. p. 36 ff.

57 The concept of a personality of the state that was distinct from the sovereign remained alien to the Romans. This was illustrated by the treatment of the problem arising out of the question whether the successor was bound by the acts of the government of his predecessor. Mommsen, II, pp. 1067-76. It was precisely from this premise that the Middle Ages developed the idea of the personality of the state.

58 Ihering, *Geist,* I, p. 215; Mommsen, *Staatsr.*, I, p. 243.

59 Hermogenianus, *D.* 1.1.5.

sonality under the aegis of the law of nations.[60] In all peaceful and hostile contacts, and in treaties and alliances, the concerned and obligated nations were equated with human complexes that had constituted themselves into states. It was therefore relevant to the law of nations whether the legal subjectivity of a particular state was represented by the *populus* or, in its place, by a *rex*. It was equally relevant in what manner this *populus* or *rex* could be represented in legal actions.[61] But the internal relationship between the national totalities and the individuals they contained was a matter of indifference to the law of nations. Externally viewed, the individuals were simply contained by their respective collectivities. Therefore the *populus Romanus*, even though viewed by the *jus gentium* as one of the *populi*, remained the only entity that had received Roman law in its entirety.[62]

As far as the legal subjectivity of the Roman state in the realm of private law was concerned,[63] the state possessed, besides its specific powers, those rights that allowed it to be represented as an individual. In the field of property matters it entered into mutual and real legal relationships with individuals. Originally, the state was not considered as belonging to the category of a person under private law.[64] As long as the *populus* was represented fully and exclusively by the state, its ability to hold property was part of its political nature. The *populus'* property rights were those that had been transferred from the *jus privatum* to the *jus publicum*. It was public not only in the sense of a subjective enablement of the *populus* but also in the sense of an objective political qualification. This qualification applied to all property of the Roman people marked as *res publicae*.[65] It ap-

60 The lack of any distinction between the maxims of the *jus gentium* and the laws treating individuals on an equal footing, a feature prominent in the *jus gentium*, is evident (cp. chapt. 1, note 62).

61 For Roman constitutional rules with regard to the sovereignty of the community in contractual matters, cp. Mommsen, I, pp. 237-44; with regard to the Empire, cp. II, pp. 913 ff.

62 The legal character of the *jus gentium* need not be examined here. Its sanctions were based on religious grounds.

63 Cp. Pernice, I, pp. 263-77; Mommsen, I, pp. 162 ff., II, pp. 952 ff.

64 Savigny (II, p. 247) correctly surmises that the concept of the juristic person was not formulated by the state but rather was transmitted to it.

65 Therefore Gaius states, 'Those things that are public do not belong to anyone's personal property but are the goods of the association itself. Private property is that which belongs to individuals' (*D.* 1.8.1). This frequently cited quotation obviously did not distinguish between the *res patrimonio populi* and the *res in publico usu*. Therefore it cannot be quoted as signifying the lack of property of the latter without denying the property of the former. It does support a view that excludes the *universitas populi* from the concept of the person and it does generically distinguish between the property of the *populus* and private property.

plied to the public land (*ager publicus*),[66] to the public treasury (*aerarium publicum*),[67] and to the slaves of the state (*servi publici*).[68] Therefore the distinction of the *res publicae* into the people's patrimony (*res publicae in patrimonio, sive pecunia*) and public property set aside for the people's use (*res publicae usui destinatae*)[69] was essentially of a political nature. It did not apply in any way to the property of the totality that was derived, in both instances, independently from individual rights.[70] Rather its purpose was the maintenance of the property of the people, a purpose based upon a public legal order which was continuously and universally operative and uniformly applicable.[71]

Similarly, requirements and relationships in the sphere of property whose subject was the *populus* came under public law.[72] The whole relationship of the state with private persons did not follow the forms of procedure that held among private individuals. Rather, from the beginning, the relationship developed out of a series of specific public legal transactions. Owing to the practice of using con-

66 The fact that it was public property distinguished the *ager publicus* from private property. It indicated that all private property was, through *adsignatio*, derived from common property and that, to a certain extent, it remained as such (Cicero, *De Off.* 1.7.21; Seneca, *De Benef.* 7.4). This view was evident in the practice of treating provincial holdings as the property of the Roman people and also in the absence of a special concept relevant to the sovereignty inherent in the property of the *ager publicus.* Cp. Pernice, I, pp. 263, 268; Mommsen, II, p. 957.

67 Mommsen, II, pp. 531 ff., 970 ff.; Pernice, I, pp. 265-6; Marquardt, II, pp. 147 ff.

68 Cp. Mommsen, I, pp. 306-17.

69 *D.* 18.1.6, 41.1.14, 50.16.17, 43.8.2.3-5.

70 It follows that the *res publicae in publico usu* was the property of the *populus. D.* 1.8.6.1, 43.8.2.21, 43.12.1.7, 43.1.1.

71 The formal *publicatio* of an edict issued by an official and aimed at bringing something into common usage (*D.* 43.8.2.21) was not a disposal and it did not produce a subjective right. Rather it was an obligatory proclamation issued in the name of the people and valid until withdrawn. Such a proclamation designated some things for public usage, and they were thus permanently removed from the *commercium.* As a *res extra commercium* the things were endowed with a special quality removing them from the sphere of business transactions (*D.* 18. 1.6, 45.1.83.5, and 137.6). It also removed the things from the private sphere despite possible previous ownership (*D.* 41.3.9) and made them immune from creditors (*D.* 50.16.17). The principle of possession, however, was not destroyed by this approach. Pernice (I, p. 273 ff.) shows that even the *flumina publica* (public rivers) were treated no differently than other *res publicae.*

72 It was a matter of indifference whether the claim of the state for money originated with a contract or was derived from a public duty or was incurred as a penalty. Similarly, all liabilities of the community, whether arising from public demands or from contractual obligations, were made in the form of payments coming from the *aerarium*. All debtors and creditors of the *populus* were listed in the *tabulae publicae*. Pernice, I, pp. 265-6; Mommsen, *Staatsr.*, I, pp. 170-80; II, pp. 419-43, 535 ff., 539 ff.

tractual forms derived from precedents dealing with cases relating to individuals, a formal and materially less rigid structure was imparted to these relationships.[73] In obtaining its rights, the *populus* was not bound by the limitations of civil law. Thus, for instance, despite the legal inability of a person of uncertain status (*personae incertae*) to inherit, the ability of the Roman people to 'take under a will' (*testamenti factio passiva*) was never theoretically questioned.[74] The entire administration of state property was carried out through the *jus publicum*, in keeping with the principle of legal competence established in accordance with the exercise of the laws of the *populus*.[75] The *jus publicum* and not private law, with its rules about mandates or unauthorized transactions, determined the extent and activities of the representation of the people by the magistrates. Thus free self-representation, a principle alien to civil law, could eventually develop in the public realm.[76]

Above all, legal relationships derived from the realm of *inter populum et privatum* remained distinct from the analogous relationships in the realm of *inter privatos*. The protection of the system of legal actions within private law was absent, and instead there appeared a purely administrative procedure whose basis was the decision of the community expressed through executive action.[77] In property law, the *populus* appeared everywhere as the sovereign totality transcending the rights of the individuals and nowhere as an individual on the same level with other individuals.[78] Beyond all positing of legal personality, the *populus* had the full constitutional powers derived from law - the same kind of legal ability ascribed to the individual. When the mutual legal relationships between the *populus* and the private individual became feasible, so that both parties were considered as legally entitled and obligated subjects, it did not follow that the

73 Mommsen, *Staatsr.* I, pp. 162 ff., 228 ff., 380; II, pp. 423 ff., 541; Pernice, I, p. 264. Thus the *adsignatio* (allotment), *occupatio*, and *possessio* of the *ager publicus* and the contracts of the *publicani* related to the *inter populum et privatos*. On the other hand, releases, sales, locations etc., when initiated by the state, resembled but were not identical with transactions among private parties (*inter privatos*). At an early stage, principles, originally alien to private law, were accepted. It was in the name *inter populum et privatum* that free business transactions, free representation, legitimate contracts between absentees, and direct transactions involving claims and debts were conducted.

74 Savigny, II, p. 305; Pernice, I, pp. 264-5; Mommsen, I, pp. 163, 230.

75 For the administration of state property in general cp. Mommsen, I, pp. 228 ff.; for the competence of the consul, censors, aedile, and quaestor, cp. II, pp. 123 ff., 419 ff., 494 ff., 531 ff. For the regulations under the Empire II, pp. 592 ff.

76 Cp. Mommsen, I, pp. 227 ff.; II, pp. 123, 423 ff., 500, 541, 952 ff.

77 Savigny, II, p. 246; Mommsen, I, pp. 162-82; II, pp. 102, 454-61, 542-43, 616, 979-80.

78 Savigny, II, p. 362; Mommsen, I, pp. 162, 171; Pernice, I, p. 281.

state was subordinated to the concept of person. Rather, Roman law retained, in this respect, the absolute distinction between single personality and universality that, in its own sphere, negated the concept of person.

This conception of the state's subjective ability to hold property was theoretically carried into the imperial period. Together with other republican institutions the *aerarium* was retained.[79] Side by side with it, the imperial treasury (*fiscus Caesaris*) represented the imperial property that grew in size and importance. It functioned, *de facto,* as the property of the state, but appeared, juridically, as the private property of the *princeps.*[80] Gradually the emperor became the representative of the state's legal subjectivity. Increasingly the *fiscus* was viewed as property legally belonging to the state.[81] This property was, on the one hand, legally separated from the emperor's private patrimony (*patrimonium principis*)[82] and, on the other hand, incorporated the old *aerarium* whose name it retained.[83] Despite this 'nationalization,' the *fiscus*, even though it came to occupy the privileged position of the people's *aerarium* which it had absorbed, remained in principle subordinated to the legal pronouncements, forms of transactions, and procedural means that had pertained to the private sphere.[84] The great step was taken: the state, in its relations to property law had entered the sphere of private law. At a time when the state *qua* state elevated itself above the law, the state as *fiscus* subordinated itself to the law and presented itself, void of its majesty, as a private individual among other private individuals.

Obviously, then, nothing barred the transference of the concept of person derived from the individual to the state as a subject of property relationships. There-

79 Cp. Mommsen, *Staatsr.*, II, pp. 952 ff., 970 ff.; Marquardt, II, pp. 293 ff. With regard to the *fiscus*, the *aerarium* was called *populus*; cp. Callistratus, *D.* 48.20.1; Tacitus, *Ann.* 13.31; Frontinus, *De Aquaeductu Urbis Romae* 118; Gaius, 2.150 and 286; Ulpian, 28.7 and 17.2. The theoretical survival of the old law did not prevent the emperor from obtaining the use of public land. Increasingly, the *aerarium* was moved from senatorial to imperial jurisdiction. Cp. Dio Cassius, 53.16 and 22. Therefore the special *aerarium militare* instituted by Augustus could be considered as a fund that belonged to the *patrimonium populi.* Only when the *fiscus* became the state treasury did it absorb the *aerarium*, while the *aerarium Saturni* survived as a city treasury.

80 Mommsen, *Staatsr.*, II, pp. 957 ff., 980 ff.; Seneca, *De Benef.* 4.39.3, 7.6.3; *D.* 43.8.2.4.

81 Cp. Mommsen, II, p. 958.

82 Originally, the separation between the *fiscus* and the *res privata principis* was an administrative measure. Mommsen, II, p. 962 note 2; for the later development cp. *Marquardt*, II, pp. 298 ff.

83 *D.* 49.14.13 and 1, 49.14.15, 48.13.9.6; *Cod.* 7.32.2 and 3; *Inst.* 2.6.14.

84 In this sense Trajan stated, 'the *fiscus* purchases whatever seems proper ... ' (Plin., *Panegyricus*, 29). Nerva established a *praetor* 'who gave judgment in cases involving private individuals and the *fiscus*' *D.* 1.2.2.32; *Cod.* 10.8.2 and 3, 4.12.2.

fore, in the later stages of Roman history, the *fiscus* does appear as a juristic person. However, reservations have to be made. First, the equation of the *fiscus* with a private party was carried out to an incomplete degree. There were exceptions to normal private procedures, such as the granting of special privileges[85] and the institution of special courts.[86] While in apparent accord with the principle of viewing the *fiscus* as a private party, these exceptions displayed the substantial contradiction between fiscal and private legal subjectivity.[87] Second, a theoretical construct was arrived at, although a clear formulation of the completed personification was not forthcoming. The *fiscus* endowed with rights and obligations was originally technically expressed in an objective sense as state treasure. It was, in many instances, referred to as owner, creditor, and debtor, as a contracting party to proceedings and as a willing and active being. But behind this apparently self-subsistent subject there stood the living personality of the *princeps* representing the abstract unity of the state as the true ruler of the fiscal legal sphere.[88] Thus the problem as to the real substratum and the substantial unity of the fiscal legal subjectivity remained in abeyance.[89] It was certain, however, that with the concept of the *fiscus* that part of the state which was capable of holding property divorced itself from its political identity and became personified. The state was not considered as an organically united whole endowed with a personality; rather it was assumed that some simple subject, comparable to the individual, had grown out of the state.

When finally Roman law came to consider the *fiscus* as a juristic person, it failed to develop this concept and to elaborate on it theoretically. The Roman jurists never specifically subsumed the *fiscus* under the generic concept of person. It remained inconsequential to Roman corporate theory that later on the *fiscus,* as a specially formulated case, approximated the older concept of the juristic person. Its direct descent from the all-encompassing state, its connection with the living personality of the emperor, and its unique position removed the *fiscus* from all such discussions because its legal status was considered to be special and self-explanatory. This uniqueness made questions with regard to its legal nature

85 For the *privilegia fisci* see Heimbach, *Rechtslexikon*, IV, pp. 302 ff.

86 For the development of judicature in the *inter fiscum et privatos* cp. Mommsen, II, pp. 968, 980-3.

87 Therefore the *privatus*, the *fiscus*, the *jus privati* and the *privilegium sive jus fisci* were contrasted frequently. Cp. e.g. *D.* 49.14.6, 49.14.35.

88 This point is made clear in *D.* 49.14 and *Cod.* 10.1. There is no explicit reference to the *fiscus* as a *persona.*

89 The impression gained from the sources is that the personification of the state treasury prevailed. But this conception always returned to the idea of the abstract unity of the state as represented by the *princeps*. Cp. e.g. *D.* 49.14.1; *Cod.* 11.5.1.

superfluous and made comparisons with related cases inadmissible. Despite the separation of the *fiscus*, one could hardly refer to a Roman theory of the juristic person because of a lack of continuous individual centres of law.

Roman law, however, could not entirely avoid the recognition of those associations that differed from the state and that could not be considered as mere contractual and communal relationships among individuals. In comparison to the role played by fellowships in the Germanic world, associations mediating between state and individual represented a relatively insignificant part and occupied a subordinate position in Roman law.[90] Nevertheless, secondary communal associations were not totally absent. Roman law focused on the exclusive sovereignty and the sole value of the centralized common will and upon the isolated individual will. Yet, somewhere a place had to be found for an intermediate sphere.

In accordance with the above argument, only the *jus publicum* could provide a basis for that legal realm that transcended the individual man.

The *jus sacrum* can be considered in this respect. According to the Roman conception, it was part of the *jus publicum*.[91] Thus the *jus sacrum* was unable to produce a theory according to which there could exist an independent religious association in the form of a corporate or institutional church. Rather, as part of the *jus publicum*, it belonged with the law that pertained to the Roman state and its centre of will was located in the state. The regulation of religious matters was the state's concern and the magistracy played a substantial role in these matters, while the priesthood was a special branch of the state's civil service.[92] Therefore, as far as the *jus sacrum* was concerned, the *populus* represented the original and the sole sovereign subject. In the realm of the *jus sacrum*, however, there developed a dual form of derivative and limited legal subjectivity. First, the *sacral collegia* gained recognition as associated unities in a corporative form. In this respect there was no substantial difference between the *jus sacrum* and the rest of the *jus publicum*. Second, in an institutional form, a temporal legal ability was ascribed to the deities of the community. This was and remained the peculiarity of the *jus sacrum*.

The ancient conception that the deities entered into the realm of human legal relationships as the representatives of law found in mature Roman jurisprudence a technical legal expression in the realm of property. Despite some earlier theo-

90 Cp. Bruns, *Enzykl.*, 3rd ed., pp. 80-1, 339, 359.

91 *D.* 1.1.1. Ulpian, 'public law is established for sacred things, priests and magistrates ... ' Cp. Mommsen, *Staatsr.*, II, pp. 52 ff.

92 For the relationship between magistracy and priesthood cp. Mommsen, II, pp. 17 ff.; for the *sacerdotes populi Romani* cp. Marquardt, III, pp. 211 ff.

cratic notions, the deities did not appear as subjects of an authority derived from the legal sphere.[93] Although the gods remained the owners of the sacral property,[94] in the realm of property law they were on the whole dispossessed by the state.[95] The large part of the public property that served the cult was considered the community's property. According to the ordinances of objective law, sacral property was distinguishable only in so far as it was administered specifically for religious purposes.[96] The ability of the deities to hold property was limited to a sphere that had been set apart from human activities.[97] Here, in fact, the deity was an independent legal subject distinct from the community.[98] Through his priestly representatives the deity could acquire and alienate property legally.[99] Finally, the deity could confront the community as well as the private individual as a legal party.[100] Besides the sphere occupied by the *populus* and the *privati*, the legal subjectivity of the deities appeared as a specific third institution. For that reason sacral law had special procedures that were distinct from those relat-

93 Constitutional law prescribed the seeking of divine agreement in important governmental actions. But no governmental act was carried out in the name of a god. The violation of the divine law by a sacral offence led to the *consecratio capitis et bonorum* (the religious condemnation of a person's life and property). This followed a priest's condemnation, *sacer esto* ('let him be accursed'). Thereby, however, a god's temporal power to punish was not acknowledged and thus no real legal action and sentencing could follow. In so far as the *consecratio* resulted from a violation of the *leges sanctae*, a formal punishment could result. The punishment was determined by the people and was executed by the tribune. Priestly participation and thereby the idea of a divine punitive justice receded into the background. Mommsen, I, pp. 150 ff., II, pp. 49 ff.; Marquardt, III, pp. 265 ff.

94 Pernice, I, pp. 255-63; Mommsen, II, pp. 57 ff.; Marquardt, III, pp. 142 ff.

95 Mommsen (*ibid.*) sees the introduction of the Republic as 'the community's quarrel with the gods.' In fact, the king represented divine and human delegation of powers, as well as priesthood and magistracy. Sacral and state property was not separated.

96 Mommsen, II, pp. 61-9; Marquardt, III, p. 217. The *servi publici* (public slaves), the *loca publica* (public places) the special funds of the temples, the *arca pontificum* (the pontifex's treasure) belong in this category. Therefore the collected fines, rents, and gifts were considered the income of the community. The inheritance of a vestal who died without a testament went to the *populus* (cp. Pernice, I, p. 182) and property designated as *Jovi Capitolino et populo Romano* was used as public property for sacral purposes.

97 Mommsen, II, pp. 58 ff.; Marquardt, III, pp. 142 ff.

98 The dedication of state property was considered a sale to the gods and it required popular assent. A vow made in the name of the community was an obligation towards the gods. Therefore such a vow could be made only with the consent of a magistrate and thereby with the consent of the people and the senate. Cp. Mommsen, I, pp. 233-6; II, pp. 601-6.

99 Mommsen, II, pp. 22 ff.; Marquardt, III, pp. 260 ff.; Pernice, I, p. 259.

100 For the treatment of the legal claims on part of the deities cp. Mommsen, II, pp. 47 ff.

ing to the state as well as to the individual.[101] But by no means did the deity become a third centre of legal authority in co-ordination with the universality and the individual. His temporal subjectivity was not the self-explanatory result of the deity's sacral personality but was attributed to him by the sovereign community's *jus publicum.*[102] Thereby the divine personality remained ultimately a separate part of the political communal sphere.[103]

Through the religious cult's ability to acquire property it could be connected to the 'command of the people,'[104] while the economic administration of the cult's property was transferred to the magistrates.[105] Through this free disposition, the sacral property could ultimately be utilized in accord with popular resolutions for non-religious uses.[106] Consequently, the cult's ability to participate in legal and other actions was severely limited. Specifically it lacked the right to trade (*commercium*) and the right to take under a testament (*testamenti factio*), even though the latter was eventually granted to specific deities.[107] Therefore, the fact that the deity was given a legal sphere of action meant not so much the granting of a positive authority but rather the negation of human rights in the field of divine law. It meant that certain issues, as far as human law was concerned, were considered a 'possession of no one' (*res nullius*).[108] Such a legal subjectivity was entirely *sui generis*. It could not be compared with the legal personality existing in private law, even though it coincided with it at a certain point, and it could not be subordinated to private law as a species. Nor could the position of sacral law be used as a model for institutional examples or for the purposes of foundations outside the religious realm. As faith in the deities waned, the place of a divine subject was not occupied by any temporal juristic person, but, instead, a vacuum developed.[109]

The concepts of the personified institution and of an independent foundation

101 Pernice, I, pp. 256-58; Mommsen, II, pp. 58 ff.; Marquardt, III, pp. 254 ff., 259 ff.

102 Marquardt, III, pp. 20 ff., 33 ff.

103 In a legal contest relating to property belonging to higher or lower deities (*sacrum* or *religiosum*), the state (*publicum*) or an individual citizen, the sentence *aut sacrum aut publicum esse* (it is either sacred or public) was pronounced in the event that the individual's case was dismissed. Doubts about whether something belonged to the *sacrum* or the *publicum* were rarely expressed in a legal contest. Rather they were looked upon as doubts arising out of the disposition of the *res publicae*. Cp. Mommsen, II, pp. 47-8.

104 Mommsen, II, p. 60, note 1.; Marquardt, III, p. 260 note 8; Cicero, *De Dom.* 53.134; *Ad Att.* 4.2; *D.* 1.8.6.3, 1.8.9.1. Gaius, 2.5.

105 Mommsen, II, p. 61, pp. 432-4.

106 Pernice, I, pp. 259-60.

107 Pernice, I, pp. 260-3; Mommsen, II, p. 60.

108 Gaius, 3.9 *Inst.* 2.1.7; *D.* 1.8.1, 1.8.6.2, 6.1.23.1.

109 E. Löning, *Geschichte des deutschen Kirchenrechts*, Leipzig, 1878, I, p. 218. The author assumes that an institutional property was created which later on led to the foundation of the bishopric.

remained alien to the Roman Empire of pagan times.[110] When Christianity developed such concepts, they did not emanate from the pagan conception of divine property or from the idea of setting aside some portions of public property for religious purposes; rather, Christian notions were derived from the concept of the church as a healing institution or as a divine foundation.[111] The legal order of Christian church property could be superficially connected with some of the features of ancient sacral law, but its innermost essence had to be altered dramatically.[112]

If we inquire about associations that did become corporative subjects under Roman law, we find that they are the products of the *jus publicum* and of that portion of the *jus sacrum* that could be classified as belonging to the *jus publicum*. No Roman corporation existed that had not at first been recognized by Roman constitutional law as a political unit and that was consequently an accessory to private legal subjectivity.[113] The relationships of constitutionally recognized groups were originally referred to by the terms *corpus, universitas,* and *collegium*.[114] This political character was ascribed, constitutionally, not only to political and religious corporations, the articulated citizenry, the collegial authorities, and the communities that had been subordinated to the state, but was also evident in the arbitrarily formed unions that were considered *corpora*. Originally, the Roman *collegia* were founded and shaped by a superior and external force rather than by the free will of their members. Their permanence and the independence of their existence, regardless of changes in membership, were the result

110 Cp. Pernice, I, p. 254.

111 Popular opinion endowed God and the saints with a legal subjectivity, but that was of no importance to Christian-Roman law.

112 The legal subjectivity of the ecclesiastical institutions referred to temporal as well as consecrated property. Therefore, it was a private legal personality with full *commercium. Dedicatio* and *consecratio* retained only their religious meaning so that consecrated objects could also become private possessions. *Codex Theodosianus* 16.2.33; *Cod.* 1.5.10.

113 Pernice, I, pp. 277 ff., 289 ff.

114 For the contentious terminology, cp. Pernice, I, p. 289. The expression *corpus* applied to all political associational unities. *Universitas* was nothing else but the 'totality.' In a legal sense it referred to a collectivity recognized as a unity and was thus synonymous with the expression *corpus*. (Cp. *D.* 3.4 and the use of the word *universitas* in paragraph 3.) The expression *corpus*, moreover, denoted primarily an association considered as an objective totality, while the expression *universitas* referred to the subjective unity belonging to this totality. *Collegium* denoted every union (or club) that was not a community. In order to gain legal recognition, the *collegium* had to be a *corpus*. *Corporatio* appeared only in *Nov. Severi* tit. 2a. 465, whereas *corporati* appeared also in *Cod.* 4.63.5 (alternating with *collegiati*) *Cod.* 11.1.8, 11.14 (15), 11.17 (18), 11.28 (29). Conversely, the term *societas* belonged exclusively to private law and was used in a non-technical sense similar to our current use of the word society.

of their having been formed for the purposes of constitutional goals beyond their own will.[115] This applied to the *collegia templorum* and to members of religious associations (*sodalitates*) who were in the service of the state religion,[116] to the class of subordinate officials,[117] and certainly to the older guilds of craftsmen.[118]

Later, as associational existence expanded and more initiative was ceded to the members, the newly formed groups followed the example of the older bodies. Like their predecessors, they came under the supervision of the *jus publicum*. Major examples of associations were the trade-guilds and the religious associations. In the first instance, the connection with sacral law was not absent. This connection was due partially to the utilization of the associations for state and communal purposes and partially to the official position of its members who retained a certain political status. The actual purpose of these associations consisted in mutual assistance, in the provisioning of members, and in other economic matters.[119] Similarly, religious organizations, even when not linked to the official state cult were, according to Roman understanding and by virtue of their political influence, considered as subjects that were of interest to the state. Therefore, the associations enjoyed a legal standing only in so far as they were classified as public bodies recognized by the state.[120] Their religious connotations were obviously derived from the burial associations.[121] Of all truly voluntary organizations, they were the only ones that enjoyed a greater distribution and independent development.[122]

115 Pernice, I, p. 290.

116 Mommsen, *de coll.*, paragraphs 1-3 and 12; Marquardt, II, pp. 131 ff.

117 Mommsen, *Staatsr.*, I, pp. 325-48, 353-4. The term *decuria* is significant.

118 Pernice, I, p. 290; Mommsen, *de coll.*, paragraph 4; Marquardt, III, pp 135-6. Tradition holds that they were instituted by the monarchs.

119 This was especially true of the *collegia* or *scholae* of the soldiers. They collected entrance fees and with these financed holiday trips, support in the case of promotion, compensation on dismissal, annual contributions for veterans, and funeral allowances. Marquardt, II, p. 544. These features also applied to the corporations of *publicani* when they were considered as acquisitive bodies.

120 For references to the *collegia* of foreign cults, cp. Marquardt, III, pp. 140 ff.

121 Cp. Mommsen, *de coll.*, paragraphs 14-16 and the laws of the *collegia* enumerated there. In the same way, other *collegia* concerned themselves with the funeral arrangements of members through *sepulcra communia collegii* (the common grave of the *collegium*) and *funeratica* (burial-guilds) (Marquardt, III, p. 139, note 4). The burial-guilds also supplied aid and support in other cases. They prevailed among the lower classes (even slaves could belong to them, *D.* 47.22.3.2) and were indeed the only form of association permitted to this stratum of society. The term *collegia tenuiorum* applied to them (*D.* 47.22.3.2).

122 According to Mommsen (*Staatsr.*, I, p. 326) the only associations permitted in Rome were the burial-guilds, the associations of *publicani*, and the associations of officials.

Besides these associations, there periodically appeared numerous other free private associations that manifested some collective, social, and political tendencies. By subordinating themselves to the provisions of sacral law, they attempted, in part, to fit themselves into the mould of the ancient associational practices.[123] But they lacked legal recognition, and their existence was tolerated only if they were considered harmless. But if they were assumed to represent a threat to the state, they were suppressed.[124] Moreover, the formation of those associations that determined their own goals belonged to the period of the late Republic. During this period the rule of the state was relaxed. But this was of such a passing nature that it did not leave lasting traces in Roman law.

First and above all, the Roman corporation denoted a political unity. As such, according to the conceptions of the *jus publicum*, it could derive its special existence only from the original and sovereign sphere of the public law. Therefore the corporation had to prove itself to be a self-determined part of the state, formed for a specific purpose. By reason of its political nature, each corporation was part of the whole of the state and appeared as having been formed by and for the whole.[125]

Within the intellectual framework of mature Roman law, it was irrelevant that there existed an articulation within the Roman citizenry that had, in times preceding the state, formulated itself into natural fellowships.[126] Clan and district communities that had, as autonomous societal associations, originally contributed to the legal existence of the state, were divested of their original meaning. Before the concept of corporations could be developed, the original corporate elements were absorbed by the state that had emancipated itself from its constituent parts. The remnants of the ancient clans and communities fitted themselves thoroughly into the legal order that recognized only the *populus* and the *paterfamilias* as the original centres of will. The Roman citizenry then viewed itself essentially as existing 'of and for the state.'[127]

123 This was especially true of the *collegia sodalicia* in the last century of the Republic. Mommsen, *de coll.*, paragraphs 5-9; cp. Marquardt, III, pp. 136-7. Also *D.* 47.11.2.

124 M. Cohn, *Zur Geschichte des römischen Vereinsrechts*, Berlin, 1873, pp. 35 ff.

125 In the state's constitution, the Romans saw the model for all associational and corporate arrangements.

126 For the original character of the *gens*, cp. Ihering, *Geist*, I, pp. 183 ff; Pernice, I, pp. 93 ff.; Marquardt, III, pp. 126 ff. The *tribus* and *curiae* were looked upon in historical times as categories of the citizenry. Originally they had been fellowship associations. The *plebs* was for some time considered a special community but it was eventually accepted as part of the state. The *plebs* did not attain its recognition as part of the *populus* on the basis of a free right to associate as Mommsen (II, pp. 269 ff.) assumes. Rather it attained its status through concessions by the state.

127 Cp. Mommsen, II, pp. 319 ff.

For the Roman citizenry this principle remained in force even after the territorial expansion took place. Therefore, the idea of a community acting as an organic intermediary between the individual and the state was never envisaged by the Romans. The Roman concept of community developed as a fragment of the concept of the state. Originally, as external communities came under the aegis of Roman power, two procedures were followed. According to one, the alien community's existence was retained. It remained a state in its own right that, as allied state, was bound to the Roman city-state according to the law of nations. Its sovereignty was limited by contractual clauses. Its citizenry was legally separated from the *populus Romanus* and, as such, remained alien to the Roman *jus publicum*.[128] According to the second procedure, an incorporation of the subjugated territory took place. The foreign community's essence ceased to exist and was transformed into a politically dependent part of the Roman city-state. The population of the former alien entity became, as far as the *jus publicum* was concerned, a merely locally separated part of the *populus Romanus* endowed with more or less complete civil rights.[129]

After the social war, the community of equal citizens was gradually extended over all of Italy. But the identification of the Roman city-community with the state was not carried out completely. Certainly the *populus Romanus* claimed the citizenship of the city of Rome. Every *civis Romanus*, even though a citizen of another city, claimed a simultaneous citizenship in Rome. After Roman citizenship became universal in the Empire, it was valid to make the claim, 'Rome is our fatherland.'[130] In numerous cases, however, some separate segments of the people, first in Italy and then in the provinces, even though becoming or remaining part of the *populus Romanus*, were constituted as special bodies and granted a measure of political autonomy. Municipal constitutions unknown to traditional law appeared, and their essence consisted of certain powers that represented part of the *populus Romanus*.[131] The Roman municipal communities were therefore members of the state that rendered themselves independent. Their special political status was derived from the state that had ceded to them the substance of sovereign rights. The municipal authorities did not specifically exercise the community's functions but rather the functions of the state. Their authority was derived from the state as a whole and had no independent legal basis. As former sovereign, the community, in numerous cases, continued to exercise more or less comprehensive sovereign rights as a result of constitutional protection and the indulgence of the state. But, juridically, from now on its political sphere did not ap-

128 Marquardt, I, pp. 44 ff., 344 ff.; *D.* 49.15.7.

129 Cp. Marquardt, I, pp. 26-44, 62; Mommsen, II, pp. 350-8.

130 Modestinus, *D.* 50.1.33; cp. 27.1.6.11, 50.5.9.

131 Marquardt, I, pp. 57 ff.; Mommsen, I, pp. 17 ff., II, p. 668.

pear as being based on an original but on a delegated right. With the subjugation of the community, its whole public and private law came under the rule of the Roman people. Part of its law was returned to it in the form of a gift.[132] The community, whether founded or newly organized by Rome as a *colonia* or a *municipium*, was always bound to the state by the delegated nature of its powers.[133]

For a part of the state to obtain such an independence, a formal *lex* was required. Thus, the communities that were recognized as independent, whether they were a Roman *municipium*, a Roman *colonia*, a Latin city, or an autonomous provincial city, had a *legis datio*. Through this law a *magistratus cum imperio*, empowered by the Roman people, issued a municipal charter (*lex civitatis* or *municipalis*) which served as the basis of and the matrix for all communal life.[134] Similarly, the municipal laws granted to numerous communities contained transfers of certain state powers by the sovereign.[135] Characteristically, the attempt was made to copy the basic features of the constitution of the Roman state on a smaller, local scale. Above all, following the example of the city-state of Rome, all communal life was centred on a city, so that politically independent communities could pass as urban city-communities. These urban communities came equipped with their own territories and politically dependent rural communities and other subsidiary districts.[136] The domestic arrangements of the city-communities, in so far as they were Roman, represented a copy of the state's institutions. They possessed a people's assembly, a senate, and a magistracy analogous to Roman practice.[137] In the provinces, on the other hand, non-Roman constitutions survived, and these were a sign of their incomplete absorption by Roman law. But as the latter expanded, the non-Roman constitutions came to approximate the Roman to an ever increasing degree.[138]

Under these circumstances the political and legal essence of the municipal

132 Marquardt, I, pp. 343 ff., 354 ff.; *D.* 11.7.36.

133 Marquardt, I, pp. 13 ff., 62 ff., 359 ff.; Mommsen, II, pp. 619 ff., 853 ff.

134 Surviving *leges coloniae* of municipalities are listed in C. Bruns, *fontes juris Romani antiqui*, Tübingen, 4th ed. See also the references to the *propriae leges* of the cities in *D.* 3.4.3. and 6, 43.24.3.4, 47.12.3.5, 50.1.21.7, 50.1.21.25, 50.3.1, 50.3.1.2, 50.4.18.27, 50.6.6.(5) 1, 50.9.6; *Cod.*8.49.1, 10.39.(40) 6, 11.29 (30) 4, 11.31.(32).1. During the Empire, the *princeps* supervised the promulgation of and changes in the municipal law. Thereby he exercised the rights of the Roman people. Cp. Marquardt, I, pp. 63 ff., 351; Mommsen, I, p. 619; II, pp. 853 ff.

135 Thus the *lex Rubria de Gallia cisalpina* and, above all, *lex Julia municipalis*.

136 Marquardt, I, pp. 13 ff., 341 ff.

137 *Ibid*, pp. 463-516.

138 *Ibid*, pp. 516-23.

communities became a copy and a result of the political and legal essence of the state. As a copy of the state, the community was a self-contained body,[139] whose life was regulated by the public legal order. This body incorporated, as special concepts, the citizens (*cives*) and the inhabitants (*incolae*) whose membership in the body was based upon and preserved by the firm rules of the *jus publicum*.[140] They were the subjects of local authority who were called upon to carry part of the communal obligations and honours.[141] The collectivity posited as a unity was the seat of the state's authority; as the substance of the *municipes* or *coloni*, it was, in short, the urban *universitas*. The whole considered as a unity expressed itself as an enfranchised citizenry in the constitutional assemblies and exercised its rights through appropriate majority decisions.[142]

If that was not the case, the city-community, following the example of Rome, came to be represented to an increasing degree by the municipal magistrate endowed with a certain legal competence and then increasingly by the senate of the city.[143] If in all these relations the community appeared as an image of the *populus*, its political unity remained, in the last instance, the result of the state's legal subjectivity. In its relationship to the state, the municipal *universitas* was not considered as either the source or the centre of its own political realm. Rather it was looked upon as having been endowed by the state with the delegated authority to administer its own affairs within a certain sphere. The municipal community did not have a special *jus publicum* but rather partook of the uniform *jus publicum* of the whole people. It was not recognized as an independent associated whole, as a group-person within its own sphere, but was considered as a part of the state that had attained autonomy. Therefore, the community's sphere of au-

139 Cp. E. Kuhn, *Die städtische und bürgerliche Verfassung des römischen Reichs*, Leipzig, 1864, I, pp. 1. ff.

140 The rules of Roman law, especially those of the *Cod Theod*. and the *Corpus Juris Civilis* with regard to the acquisition and the loss of municipal membership, are discussed by Kuhn, I, pp. 1-34; cp. also Savigny, VIII, pp. 39 ff.

141 For the extensive Roman statues with regard to *munera* and *honores*, the difference between the *munera personarum* and *patrimonii* and the real estate not sharply distinguished from the *patrimonii*, and the numerous grounds for exemptions, cp. Kuhn, I, pp. 35-226; also Savingy, VIII, pp. 69 ff.; Marquardt, I, p. 466.

142 Kuhn, I, pp. 229 ff.; Marquardt, I, pp. 467 ff.; Mommsen, I, p. 219.

143 Despite the fact that they represented it, the municipal magistrates were independent of the elective body of the municipalities. In this respect their position was identical with that of the Roman magistrates. Cp. Kuhn, I, pp. 233 ff.; Marquardt, I, pp. 475 ff. Like the Roman senate, the municipal senate was originally a council and, like the senate, acquired a representative character despite the fact that it was a non-elective body. A majority decision of two-thirds of the senate was assumed to be a decision made by the community. Kuhn, I, pp. 227 ff.; Marquardt, I, pp. 501 ff., 518 ff.

thority was not specifically delimited[144] and subordinated to the state's sovereignty and supervision.[145] But it was left to the state to determine whether and to what extent such a quasi-independent subordinate part should exist within the universal political whole. One can no more speak of a real right of the community pertaining to any public function, than one can refer to the rights of the single citizen.[146] The substantial independence that was available to communal life in the late stages of the Republic and the early period of the Empire denoted essentially, a decentralization of administration but not the separation of the community from the state.[147]

Precisely, therefore, the change in constitutional law under the Empire produced a necessary analogous change in community law. For the latter followed, in many instances, the example set by the former. The exercise of local political authority in the community continued for a longer time than in the state.[148] Ultimately, however, the last vestiges of the republican constitution disappeared also. The totality was relegated to the role of a ward without the ability to will and to act, while self-administration was changed into a tutelary administration by authorities and corporations.[149] Thereby, as in the state, the concept of the totality separated itself from the concept of assembly and instead assumed an institutional form. Increasing centralization and uniformity were reflected in the development of the imperial bureaucratic state. To a greater degree, the bureaucratic element assumed the public functions formerly ceded to the municipalities and played a substantial part in the supervision of communal life.[150] Ultimately this

144 Most important for subsequent times was the statement of Paulus that the *magistratus municipales* had *jurisdictio* but not *imperium* (*D.* 50.26). Cp. Mommsen, I, p. 183, note 3 and p. 217, note 1; Marquardt, I, pp. 66-7.

145 Marquardt, I, pp. 77 ff., 351 ff; Mommsen, II, p. 851.

146 A jurisdictional dispute between Rome and a dependent community was unthinkable. The idea of a mutual legal relationship between Rome and the dependent community was based on the *jus gentium*. Accordingly, the totality of the community was a *populus externus* and not a *pars populi* [of Rome].

147 Kuhn's argument (I, p. ix) comparing the Roman Empire to a federal state is disputable.

148 In the period of classical jurisprudence, the municipal magistrates were elected exclusively by the *curia* (Paulus, *D.* 50.2.7.2), and the decisive factor became the nomination of the predecessor in office (*D.* 50.1.11, 50.1.13, 50.1.15.1; *Cod.* 11.33 [34].1 and 2; *Cod.* 11.35 [36].3). Cp. Kuhn, I, pp. 236 ff.; Marquardt, I, pp. 469 ff.

149 The distinction between the municipal magistrate and the municipal senate gradually disappeared. All magistrates were members of the *curia* and all *decuriones* had to perform the official services. The *curia* became the representative association of administrators excluding the local associations. Cp. Kuhn, I, p. 242; Marquardt, I, p. 511.

150 For the gradual replacement of communal self-administration by the monarchy cp. Marquardt, I, pp. 76 ff., 355 ff., 483 ff., 511 ff; Mommsen, *Staatsr.*, II, pp. 1025-41.

culminated in that caricature of municipal institutions that was passed on to posterity by the late Empire. In fact, the real seat of local political power was represented by the imperial officials.[151] The communal administration as such was charged with defraying the cost and distributing the burdens of the state which had been passed on to the municipalities under the supervision of the court of a compulsory hereditary corporation. In turn, this corporation held the community together with the help of rigorous laws and it was burdened with unwanted offices and services.[152] A tutelary system concerned with the smallest details regulated all movements of the mutilated body of the municipality.[153]

These developments explain why the Romans failed to discover a constitutional personality in either the municipality or the state. The city-community, not unlike the state with respect to the relationships of its members, appeared as an all-inclusive associational whole.[154] But in its relationship with the state, the city-community was considered as void of its own political and legal subjectivity.[155] With the exception of the city-community, Roman law did not recognize an independent communal association. The territorial community did exercise, within its own district, a certain measure of self-administration.[156] But according to the prevailing political view, it appeared essentially as a subordinated and dependent part of the city-community.[157] The province, in keeping with its nature, remained at all times, subject to the state's central authority[158] even when with the estab-

The major aspect of these developments was the role played by the office of the *curatores reipublicae* and the increase in the authority of the governors.

151 The *defensor civitatis*, appointed by Valentian I, had the characteristics of an imperial administrator. Originally a representative of the *plebs urbana*, he became the municipal judge whose powers were enlarged by Justinian.

152 For the decline and the later form of the *curia*, cp. Kuhn, I, pp. 242 ff.; Marquardt, I, pp. 355 ff.

153 The *curator reipublicae* became the real administrator of the municipal treasury. Basically an imperial official, he was thus subject to higher supervision. Cp. Kuhn, pp. 37, 58-9; Marquardt, I, p. 335 ff., 483 ff.

154 The *civitas* claiming someone as its member and the individual without a city confronted one another before the *praeses provinciae* (Callistratus, *D.* 50.1.37). But membership in a community represented only a purely subjective relationship (Gaius, *D.* 50.1.29), according to which the totality and the individual related to one another like the whole to the part.

155 A different view was acceptable to the Romans only if the relationship was not viewed as a constitutional issue but as a matter belonging under the *jus gentium*. When permitted, the community's special interests and functions appeared in a representative form based upon the subjectivity of the *jus gentium*. This provision is evident in the institution of the *legati municipales*, *D.* 50.7; *Cod.* 10.63 (65).

156 Cp. Marquardt, I, pp. 8 ff., 12 ff.

157 *D.* 50.1.30. Cp. Kuhn, I, pp. 29-34; Marquardt, I, pp. 7, 12.

158 Kuhn, I, pp. 107 ff.; II p. 5; Marquardt, I, pp. 338 ff., 377 ff.

lishment of provincial assemblies there appeared a type of communal tie among the city-communities of the territory.[159]

As far as the Roman *jus publicum* was concerned, the concept of the community was a derivation and a copy of the concept of the state. The same applied to the concept of the *collegium*. This concept was originally derived from the association of officials and based upon the common origin of their technical relationship. The community of officials retained, according to custom, their common technical relationship after developing in two diametrically opposed branches. One of these consisted of the *collegium* of the magistracy which had been functioning in Rome since the conception of the Republic as well as in the municipalities. Although fellow officials were referred to as *collegae*, they did not form a *collegium* except accidentally,[160] because they did not receive the power of office as a totality but had it conferred upon them on an individual basis. Therefore an associational unity did not result. Rather a political group evolved that had its analogous counterpart in private law. Two or more holders of the same office were subject to an identical authority and each was confronted with identical limitations on their activities. Thus a member could be considered as occupying the position of a single official.[161]

Besides this body there existed from earlier times a second body of officials who administered the state's religious cult. This was considered the second form of a community of officials which exercised its authority as a collectivity.[162] Here the totality was considered a *collegium* and, as an associational whole, belonged under the *jus publicum*. Its political unity was derived essentially from the objective order of the state according to which a part of the body of the state was endowed with a permanent life. Its specific sphere of life was organized as a true copy of the collective body of the state. The totality constituted as a *collegium* had its divisions and its communal decision-making assembly which was supported by the senate in an advisory capacity in the same manner as the people's com-

159 Marquardt, I, pp. 365-77. The essential importance of the association was that it formed a society devoted to the cult of the emperor. For this reason the *concilium provinciale*, formed by the *legati* of the cities, annually elected a *sacerdos provincialis*, collected for the treasury of the temple, regulated the administration of the *arca* (money chest) and concerned itself with the erection of monuments. To this was added the political right to lodge complaints against the governor.

160 Normally, if there were only two *collegae*, the term *collegium* was inapplicable. Cp. Mommsen, *Staatsr.*, I, p. 31.

161 Ulpian, *D.* 50.1.25. Cp. Mommsen, I, pp. 27-59; II, pp. 1109 ff.

162 Marquardt, III, pp. 135, 230 ff., 333 ff., 364 ff., 400 ff., 422 ff., 427, 428 ff., 455 ff.; Mommsen, *Staatsr*, II, pp. 20 ff. Cp. also Mommsen, *ibid.*, pp. 1047-58 for the emperor's membership in the higher sacral colleges.

munity. The *collegium* appeared as the representative of the common interest only in a united form. It manifested itself visibly through majority-decisions in its assembly, and formed, despite possible changes in membership, a (permanent) identical *corpus*. The *collegium* of officials became and remained generally the model for Roman *collegia*. In the city of Rome a significant portion of corporate life took place within the framework of the corporation of officials.[163] Most of the other *collegia* appeared as analogous sacral or political institutions which had been founded directly by the state and which were entrusted with the functions of the state.[164] Similar bodies existed in the dependent city-communities where all *collegia* were incorporated in accordance with the municipal associational unit.[165] The originally arbitrarily formed associations were accepted as *collegia* by the *jus publicum* and were subject to an analogous conception. They received from the state a permanent political unity in order to execute certain public tasks. As such, they functioned as parts of the state that had been granted a measure of autonomy. All this took place according to the example set by the Roman city-state.[166]

Henceforth, every recognized *collegium* appeared as an exclusive, original, and sovereign associational subjectivity derived from the political unity of the group. Conversely, an association not recognized was considered illegitimate. It is a matter of dispute whether the free right of association existed in the Roman Republic.[167] It is certain, however, that the unsanctioned association did not receive

163 Cp. Mommsen, *Staatsr.*, I, pp. 325-54.

164 The *sodalitates* or *collegia templorum* that represented the public cult were modelled after the colleges of the priests. They were established by the state to replace the *gentes* or to introduce new cults and their state-directed rituals. E.g. the *collegium mercatorum*, Livius, 2.27.5, and the *collegium* for the *ludi Capitolini* (public games celebrated in the honour of the gods) Livius, 5.50.4 and 52.11. For other examples, cp. Marquardt, III, pp. 132 ff.

165 Mommsen, *Staatsr.*, II, p. 851.

166 This applied to all *collegia sacra* that had obtained a legal status even if they originally had been of private or foreign origin. The same was true in the case of the *collegia funeraticia* that represented a certain class of the *collegia sacra*. Finally it was applicable to those *collegia sodalicia* that pursued their political and other goals in the guise of sacral *collegia licitum*. Cp. Marquardt, III, pp. 136 ff., 156, 158, 205, 517, note 1.

167 In view of the absence of a free right of assembly it is hard indeed to speak of a free right of association. All assemblies and all resolutions and elections could be overruled by the magistrates. (Mommsen, *Staatsr.*, I, pp. 193 ff., 278 ff.). A *jus 'coeundi'* (right of assembly), as known to modern constitutionalism, was absent. The only justified question is whether the supreme power in Rome used its right to prohibit the formation of assemblies and associations.

legal protection.[168] Such an association was tolerated in practice but it could lose its status at a moment's notice.[169] It may have assumed *de facto* the form of a *collegium*, but *de jure* it was not considered as such. Therefore it remains dubious as to whether the voluntary formation of associations was ever permitted.[170] It was an unmistakable principle of late republican law that every association not specifically recognized as a *collegium legitimum* was classified as a *collegium illicitum*.[171] Stern laws were increasingly promulgated prohibiting the formation and utilization of associations for impermissible purposes, and similar laws were applied to free (freely formed) associations.[172]

From the time of the legislation passed by Caesar and Augustus, it became an uncontested principle of the Roman *jus publicum* that every association had to have the state's authorization.[173] No association was tolerated without this authorization.[174] But this did not, in any way, change the character of the group. The permission to form an association was never a case of a momentary suspension that prohibited the formation of such a group. Rather, the permission consisted of a legislative act that brought to life a unified *corpus* and placed it under the *jus publicum*.[175] This did not lead to the appearance of a class of legitimate private associations that had been incorporated into the political, organic bodies of the state and the municipality. Rather, every *collegium licitum* received in and through the grant a *corpus*, and each *corpus* was, in accordance with public order, a very subordinate political fragment of the unity of the state. Only the formation of associations useful to the state was permitted at all times. These associa-

168 Mommsen, *de coll.*, pp. 36 sq., 117 sq.

169 Cp. Pernice, I, p. 302; Cohn, p. 89.

170 Cohn, pp. 86, 93 ff., 153.

171 Cohn correctly distinguishes between the illegitimacy of prohibited associations and those that were permitted to exist until they exhibited illegal tendencies. The term '*collegium*' was used in the case of its *de facto* but not necessarily its *de jure* existence.

172 Cp. *D.* 48.4.1, 47.22.2. The arbitrary formation of an association was considered as an interference with the sovereign rights of the state.

173 Mommsen, *de coll.*, pp. 82 sq; Pernice, I, pp. 303 ff.; Cohn, pp. 80-9; Marquardt, III, p. 137. This sentence is pronounced in *D.* 3.4.1 and 47.22.3.1.

174 This common opinion is voiced by Pernice, I, pp. 303-6.

175 Therefore it is said that if by the authority of the senate or the emperor 'a *collegium* ... or such a body meets' (*D.* 47.22.3.1), the reference is directly to the establishment of a *collegium*. But a general distinction between associations formed by the state or the community and arbitrary *collegia* is not in evidence. Cp. also *D.* 50.6.6. (5).12.

tions did not exist for their own sake but merely for the purposes of the state.[176] A formal *lex specialis* was required for each individual *collegium.*[177]

The burial-guilds alone appeared to have been granted general privileges during the imperial rule. This is evident in a resolution of the senate under the rule of Septimius Severus which was extended to all the provinces. These guilds were, under the term *collegia tenuiorum*, fitted into the legally established matrix and were thus considered *collegia licita.* But they were subject to constant supervision, They were permitted only one monthly meeting and were administratively suspended in the event that they transcended their prescribed functions.[178]

Together with its right to exist, every association received its constitution from the state. Authorization by the state meant the recognition of the *lex collegii.* In a manner similar to the *lex municipalis*, the *lex collegii* supplied the basis for all corporative development.[179] The state did not sanction the statutes of the association drawn up by its members in such a manner as to give them an objective binding force. In so far as their influence was to extend beyond the law of contract, the statutes, through legislative sanction, became part of the public order. Thereby they emerged as the dominating norm superior to the collective will of the association.[180] The Romans therefore were unfamiliar with the concept

176 Pernice, I, p. 304; Cohn, p. 83. Cp. also Pliny's correspondence with Trajan concerning the formation of a *collegium fabrorum* (association of artisans) in Nikomedia (*Ad Traj.* 33 sq.). The authorizations to form associations were very cautious and rare: e.g., 'In a very few instances associations of this type are permitted ... ' (*D.* 3.4.1).

177 Mommsen, *de coll.*, p. 80; *Staatsr.*, II, p. 650; Pernice, I, p. 304; Cohn, pp. 80 ff. In Italy and the senatorial provinces the concessions were originally granted by the senate and in the imperial provinces by the emperor.

178 The *senatusconsultum* that is partially contained in the *tabula Lanuvina* reads, according to Mommsen's reconstruction, 'To whom permission has been granted to assemble, come together to form an association, in order to confer monthly on the matter of burial. Let them join together in a *collegium* and let them not meet more than once a month for the purpose of conferring with one another so that the dead may be buried.' With regard to the *collegia tenuiorum*, Marcianus repeats this statement almost verbatim, *D.* 47.22.1.

179 Cp. Pernice, I, pp. 292, 305. Of the *leges collegiorum* now available in Bruns, *fontes juris Romani antiqui*, only two can be considered as corporate constitutions. The first, the *lex* of a *collegium aquae*, and the second, the Lanuvian *lex collegii salutaris cultorum Dianae et Antinoi.*

180 The recognition of a *collegium* by a special *senatusconsultum* did not mean that its statutes were presented to or confirmed by the senate. But such a process would have been the logical one. The general concessions to the *collegia funeraticia* indicated the *a priori* legal recognition of their statutes as long as they were in accordance with the law. For this reason the *lex* of the Lanuvian guild members was considered *ab ipsis constituta* (a law established by themselves). Perhaps a certain constitution was normally granted to

of true autonomy.[181] The *collegium* had been [legally] enabled and empowered through its constitution that had received the state's recognition. It could independently exercise the substance of political rights to a certain degree. As a total unity, each *collegium* was granted the right to organize assemblies and to vote. It was permitted to accept or reject members, to determine entry-fees and contributions, to collect fines, to arrange for expulsions, and to endow the officials of the association with quasi-magisterial powers.[182] But the basis of all collegial rights involving the associational unity was derived from the authorization by the state.[183] The so-called 'inner corporate rights' were, according to Roman law, not

the burial guilds. The Lanuvian statute at least presupposes the rudiments of a constitution with a *populus, ordo, quinquennales*, etc. It specifies the entrance and membership fees, the right to burial, the arrangements for banquets, the payment of administrative officers and servants, the fines for disturbances and injuries during feasts etc. References to municipal authorities indicate a supervision from the outset of the constitutive assembly of the *collegia.*

181 The opposite view is maintained by many who refer to Gaius, *D.* 47.22.4 and his reference to the Twelve Tables: 'The members of this same association by virtue of the Twelve Tables have the power ... [to] make any agreement for themselves that they desire, provided public law is not thereby infringed.' These words were, following Mommsen (*de coll.*, pp. 35 sq.), interpreted as meaning that the *collegia* could be arbitrarily founded and that they could draw up their own constitutions. The inference is drawn from Mommsen's argument that the statutes of the free association were based on 'a law that granted to private persons the power conferred on an association' (*lex privata legi societatis omnino aequiparanda*). This, however, was not an indication of 'autonomy' but of a social contract. In reality, the Romans could not have interpreted the Twelve Tables in this manner; otherwise the incorporation of this section in the *Corpus Juris Civilis* would be incomprehensible. It is probably more correct to consider the *collegia* as they existed at the time of the Twelve Tables, as does Pernice, I, pp. 290 ff. These *collegia* were closely tied to the constitution of the state. But at the time it was certainly not the 'constitution' that was declared to be the subject of a free *pactio*. Rather, the organization of religious and political associations belonged to a realm that was free from the discretions of the *lex publica*. Within the framework of the corporate constitution, the *sodales* were granted the right to pass resolutions. But this process cannot be considered as a matter of establishing norms but rather as a matter of enumerating decrees and arrangements according to the tenets of private law. That is why it was called a *pactio*. It was concerned with those matters that subsequent associations could settle on their own, i.e. entry fees and contributions, the utilization of corporate property, the distribution of incomes and the granting of exemptions and privileges.

182 Cp. note 179 above.

183 Views are divided on this subject. In fact, it was constitutional law sanctioned by the government that represented the basis of all corporate power. This applied to rights of the majority over the minority and the rights of the officials of the association vis à vis its members. This constitutional law was part of the *jus publicum* and, like the *lex municipalis*, could not be considered a *lex privata.*

inherent rights but rather public functions. Therefore, in a political sense, neither the *collegium* nor the *municipium* had an inherent and true legal subjectivity *vis à vis* the state. In the final analysis, the association was considered by objective law as a special part of the state that had been organized for certain political and sacral purposes. It could not, in opposition to the whole, attribute to itself a subjective right derived from its communal functions. It did not even have a firm right to exist. Rather, the state could arbitrarily decide whether the association should be formed and could eliminate it at any time.[184] The same objective legal procedure applied both to the foundation and dissolution of an association.[185]

Each *collegium* represented an associational unity derived from the state. It was a true copy of the state's and even more of the city's communal being within the framework of its special existence. The *collegium* was, in the true sense, formulated according to the example set by the state (*ad exemplum reipublicae*). In its constitution and its administration the arrangements derived from the city-community were copied both in name and in practice. There was a *populus collegii* or a *plebs universa*, complete with assemblies and popular resolutions. There was a ruling body and a tablet containing the ordinances and the decrees governing the association. There were various kinds of magistrates who, in a manner analogous to the state and the municipal magistrates, administered the *collegium*. There were also the appropriate subordinate officials (*ministri*), etc.[186] Here also the assembly functioned according to the majority decisions emanating from all of its members. It was the representative of the collegial authority. Committees and functionaries represented the totality in accordance with the delegated powers ceded to them by the *lex collegii*. Here, as in the community, the associates appeared as individuals who had formed themselves into a totality. They appeared as a quasi-subject of the special political sphere.[187]

This close connection of the *collegia et corpora* with the state made it inevitable that in the first century of the Empire the corporations organized under the Republic provided a sphere for public life that had been by-passed by the state. However, they were gradually absorbed owing to the changes in the nature of the state in the imperial period. This change followed precisely the direction of that metamorphosis that took place in the realm of communal life. The efficacy of

184 Pernice, I, pp. 303, 309; Cohn, pp. 89 ff.

185 The association instituted by a *lex specialis* had to be abolished by law. The legislator had the highest jurisdiction in the affairs of the associations.

186 E.g. *populus collegii, ordo* and *plebs, magistri, quatuoviri* (board of chief magistrates), *curatores* or *quinquennales, quaestores* etc. (see note 179 above).

187 Hence the expression 'it was pleasing to everyone' (*placuit universis*) at the beginning of the resolutions of the *collegium Dianae et Antinoi* and the *collegium Aesculapii et Hygiae*.

the assembly of members was limited by the intervention of committees and authorities. The concept of the *universitas* was used in an increasingly abstract manner and the associational understanding of the collective unity was replaced by an administrative conception.[188] Moreover, the state intervened energetically in the corporations' affairs and gradually changed all *collegia et corpora* into institutions of public authority. This intervention was amply illustrated by the law promulgated by the *divi fratres** that prohibited simultaneous membership in other *collegia licita*.[189] Ultimately there could be no reference to the voluntary formation of an association in a centralized and bureaucratic state. Older corporations became hereditary compulsory associations, and their offices and obligations with regard to the community were determined by the state. This provided the public authority with the means to control the *collegiati* and the *corporati*.[190]

Thus the political essence of the associations adjusted itself to the basic Roman conception according to which each associational existence that was recognized by the law, and thereby placed above the individual as a higher unity, appeared as the result and a copy of the state's universality. As in the case of the state, a uniform sphere of property could now be joined to this political unity. Unlike the state, the close association's ability to hold property was not derived autonomously. Rather, it was present only and in so far as it was linked to a constitutional mandate which recognized it as a *corpus*. But many associations recognized by the *jus publicum* as *corpora* never attained a unity endowed with the ability to hold property. However, their political associational unity was retained.[191] The ability to hold property was granted to associations only on the grounds of special requirements. The application of this right of the *corpus* was

*Marcus Aurelius and Lucius Verus.

188 Significantly, in the early Empire when the associations were still tolerated, their resolutions were decreed by the *ordo* (the class of magistrates); e.g. *collegium Aesculapii et Hygiae*; cp. Mommsen, *de coll.*, p. 120, note 5.

189 *D.* 47.22.1.2.

190 For their hereditary character, cp. *Cod. Theod.* 12.19.1-2, 14.7.1-2; *Cod.* 11.17.1, 11.7.(8) 13, 11.9 (10) 5. The typical corporation in the *Corpus Juris Civilis* was the municipal *curia* that developed not only into a hereditary guild but into a penal institution (*Cod. Theod.* 12.1.66). The municipal *curia* was a corporation whose inner structure is described in Justinian's collection: cp. *D.* 50.2.3 and 9, *Cod.* 10.31-7.

191 This applied to the ancient *tribus, curiae,* and *gentes* (after the dissolution of their original communal properties), the *centuriae*, and other political and military segments of the population, the Roman senate and the colleges of higher officials and judges. Not even the colleges of priests had any property, only *possessio* in an *ager publicum* that had been assigned to them and in the case of some *servi publici* allotted to them. Marquardt, III, pp. 217 ff., 432.

gradually enlarged. Therefore, the question arose of how the essence of the association could be understood in terms of legal property-relationships.

Originally an understanding prevailed that was similar to the one applied to the state's property. Communal and corporate property, in so far as it did not come under private law, was not considered as being subject to the authority of private law. Rather it was seen as a part of that independent political sphere that had been set aside and made autonomous for the *corpus*. The result was that, through the equation of the property of the association with the property of individuals, a contradiction came into being. When property or right were considered as falling under the jurisdiction of private law, it meant that the property-relationships of the associations did not appear as private transactions. It appeared that they had transcended private law. It was assumed that the concepts of private law were inapplicable and that special concepts had to be developed. Actually, as far as private law was concerned, the property of the association belonged to 'no one.' Therefore, the processes of private law were supplanted by specially developed procedures that dealt with the property of associations.[192] Traces of this development could be found in late Roman times when the distinction between the property of the associations and the property of individuals was identified with the distinction between *publicum* and *privatum*.[193] It could be found in the comparison of the *res universitatis* with the *res singulorum*. The former, in so far as it served a common purpose, was classified as 'something that had no individual owner' or was exempt from the concept of property in private law.[194] These special procedures could even be seen as acting in favour of the *universitas*.[195]

At an early stage, however, the contrary tendency prevailed that treated the property of the association as belonging to private law. This treatment was made necessary by the practice of permitting an association to hold its own property while at the same time excluding it from the *jus publicum*. The political treatment of all associational property, if carried to its logical conclusion in the realm of property as well as in constitutional law, meant that it had been separated from all corporate and communal rights. All communal property that was not merely the common property of individuals could be viewed as an administra-

192 By stressing and utilizing these factors there developed the theory of a property for a common purpose (*Zweckvermögen*) without a subject.

193 Thus the term *res publica civitatis* that later became, in a technical sense, the 'treasury of the city' as distinct from the *fiscus*: e.g. *D.* 3.4.1.3, 3.4.2.7, *De V.S.* 16.17; *Cod.* 2.54. 4, 6.1.5, 6.49.3, 11.29 (30) 1-4, 11.30 (31).2, 11.31.32 (1-3), 11.32 (33) 1. Above all, Gaius, *D.* 1.8.1.

194 Cp. Gaius, *D.* 1.8.1; Marcianus, *D.* 1.8.2; *Inst.* 2.1.1 and 6.1 and 6.

195 For the *pollicitatio* (promise) in favour of a municipal community, cp. Pernice, I, pp. 279, 284.

tively independent segment of the state's property. The Romans had to retain the belief that the *jus publicum* was obliged to represent the uniform sphere of the power of the sovereign *populus* in order to avoid the consequences of this. But a middle ground between the *jus publicum* and the *jus privatum* was not imaginable. Therefore, nothing else remained but to co-ordinate the association with the individual in the sphere of property and to subordinate the association to the *jus privatum*.

This step was apparently taken by the Romans in their treatment of city-communities.[196] Since the development of the municipal constitution, the Romans considered the city's property as a closed and uniform associational property which belonged neither to the *populus Romanus* nor to the individual. They excluded it from all the privileges accruing to the property of the state which were a function of the sovereignty of its subject. Instead, it was argued that the city's property was independent of the state and of the citizens and that it was the property of the municipal *universitas* as such. From then on it was emphatically declared that the *res civitatis* did not qualify to bear the name *publicae*, and it was said that with respect to property states were legally considered of the same standing as private persons.[197] Otherwise it was maintained that in these matters it was the whole and not the individuals who possessed rights. In this manner, the *universitas* was made subject to private law. The new legal idea was extended from cities to other suitable collectivities. An analogous legal subjectivity could easily be ascribed to the *collegia licita* which had generally followed the pattern established by the city-communities.[198] The principle of equating the substance of the associations with that of a single being in legal property relationships was developed to the point that the state itself, in the form of the *fiscus,* entered into the realm of private law.

The development was applied gradually to various associational unities. Generally, the concept of property according to private law was made independent and was understood abstractly. This applied to communal property also. The derivation resulted from viewing both the concept of the family and of the association as essentially belonging to the category of the *singuli*.[199] Thereby the association was granted the ability to dispose of the special rights and obligations that were contained in the concept of property. The concepts of property, most of the real rights, and the active and passive *obligatio* were made applicable to the property of the association.[200] Other rights, such as that of usufruct, were modi-

196 This is correctly assumed by Savigny, II, pp. 246 ff.; Mommsen, *de coll.*, p. 121.

197 Gaius, *D.* 50.16.

198 *D.* 3.4.1. Cp. Mommsen, *de coll.*, pp. 117 sq.

199 Kuntze, *Kursus*, 1st ed., paragraph 122, p. 74.

200 Savigny, II, pp. 285 ff.; Pernice, I, pp. 263 ff., 277, 306.

fied in a special manner in order to make them applicable to the *universitas*.[201] Because the association was thus enabled to acquire property and to administer and use it, it also acquired the ability to participate in the *commercium* of the *singuli* and to carry out associational transactions. Ordinary procedures under private law were made available to associations as an adjunct to political transactions.[202] All of these procedures were originally instituted for the personal acts of individuals and were therefore not transferable to the *universitas*. One exception was derived from the provision that made possible the ownership of slaves as the result of purely acquisitive transactions.[203] But it appeared unthinkable to permit the representation of the *universitas* through legal forms which applied to children and other legally incapacitated persons.[204] The Roman principle that denied free representation remained relevant for associations in so far as they entered into the sphere of private law. However, the consequences of this principle frequently led to its being circumvented or rejected in the name of practical expedience.[205]

Thus, besides acquisitive transactions, numerous types of transactions of sale, as well as extraordinary transactions pertaining to property, offered a sphere in which the representatives of the *universitas* could be active.[206] Despite apparent theoretical doubts, the practice became indispensable for the acquisition of property for fully empowered representatives.[207] Through special laws, cities and ultimately all corporations were granted the right to manumit slaves. Thereby the associations were placed on the same level as the individual who had acquired all the rights inherent in such transactions.[208] Gradually, and obviously not without juristic considerations, the associations were enabled to enter the heretofore prohibited field of the law of succession. Ultimately, all types of corporations were granted the ability to act as legatees while most received permission to utilize the inheritance and to appoint heirs.[209]Above all, as soon as the associations received

201 *D.* 33.2.8; cp. Pernice, I, p. 282.

202 For the most complete enumeration and distinction of these issues see Brinz, *Pand.* pp. 1079-1100; cp. *ibid.*, pp. 992-5.

203 Savigny, II, p. 324; Brinz, p. 1080.

204 Savigny, II, p. 283 ff; Pernice, I, pp. 287 ff; Brinz, pp. 1080 ff.

205 Cp. especially Brinz, pp. 1080-4, 1118-20.

206 Savigny, II, pp. 283 ff.; Pernice, I, pp. 306-7; Brinz, pp. 1079-90, 1098-1100.

207 Savigny, II, pp. 289 ff.; Pernice, I, p. 282.

208 Savigny, II, pp. 286 ff.; Pernice, I, pp. 283, 306. Cp. *Cod.* 7.9.3.

209 Besides the Roman people, initially only the *singuli* were able to inherit. Municipalities received the right from Trajan and then, to a fuller degree, from Nerva to appoint legates and to hold *fideicommissum* (holding a legacy in trust): Ulpian, *fr.* 24.28; *D.* 30.117, 30.122). But the legal prohibition on accepting an inheritance remained. (Plinius, *Epist.*

their independence under private law, they were treated as *privati* by the courts. Consequently, the right to sue and to defend as an *actor* or *syndicus* and to participate in the required processes appeared as the real and decisive criterion of corporative legal subjectivity.[210]

Thus, through a number of property-relationships the *universitates* recognized as *corpora* became equated with the *singuli*. Certainly this trend remained incomplete and was applied in an unequal degree to various types of associations. Now the possible advantages of the association over the individual and the advantages of one association over another could be categorized as *privilegia*.[211] The incomplete legal ability of all associations as compared to that of the individual, as well as the difference between some associations and others, accounted for the fact that the subjectivity of private law was only partially transferred to the *universitas*. In many instances the special purpose of the collectivities further limited their sphere of activity.[212] Viewed in this light, the relativity of corporative legal subjectivity no longer presented an obstacle. In principle it was possible to grasp it in a manner analogous to the private legal subjectivity of the *singuli.*

Through this process Roman law arrived at the idea of the personality of the *universitas*. The association came to be considered as a subject capable of holding property. This ability was also partially ascribed to the individual through the *jus singulare*, reflecting the admittedly delimited value ascribed to him. But through this process the association came to be accepted as a person in Roman legal theory. A special terminology resulted from this, and the corporation was declared to be a *persona*, or rather it was stated that, within law, it acted as a person.[213]

The personification of the association did not go beyond the framework ascribed to it by the basic Roman idea. The concept of the personality was not enlarged upon so that it would include that side of human existence that was directed towards the life of the whole. The concept of personality remained identical

5.7; Ulpian, *fr.* 22.5.) Eventually, however, it became permissible to appoint cities as inheritors in the testament of free men (Ulpian, 1.c.1; *D.* 38.3.1). Finally, in the year 469, Leo granted them the full right to inherit (*Cod.* 6.24.12). Marcus Aurelius granted the *collegia* the right to appoint testators and to receive legacies from their free members (*D.* 34.5.20, 40.3.1). Otherwise, the right to inherit was bestowed upon individual colleges only as a special privilege (*Cod.* 6.24.8).

210 Cp. *D.* 3.4; Savigny, II, pp. 295 ff.; Brinz, pp. 1116 ff.; Pernice, I, pp. 293 ff.

211 Cp. Brinz, pp. 220, 1088, 1132-7.

212 The perspective changed gradually. Originally, any acquisition through inheritance was considered a privilege. Later, its limitation was considered an exceptional hindrance.

213 Florentinus, *D.* 46.1.22.

with that of legal subjectivity in the private realm.[214] As ever, the categories of *persona, privatus* and *singulus* were retained. By themselves, individuals were still persons, while human associations, as political entities, belonged to a higher impersonal order of existence. Some associations received, to a certain degree, the attribute of a person through positive law and they could therefore appear as a private individual.

The associated unity recognized in this manner as a person was, as we have seen, not the product of private law. Rather, private law received from the *jus publicum* those bodies that had constituted themselves into a unity. Therefore the juristic person of Roman law was, from its inception to its completion, constituted and determined by the norms of public law. Initially the view sufficed that the political associational unities as such played the role of a person in private law. But the principal accomplishment of the juristic development of Roman corporate theory was the attainment of independence for the personality of the association from its political substratum.

The formation of the juristic personality was always linked to a political act that posited and recognized the associations as a uniform *corpus*. But the grant of private legal ability to such an association appeared as a special constitutional enactment of the state. Roman thought did not distinguish between the granting of corporation rights and the political authorization of associations as it is known to contemporary jurisprudence.[215] The Romans did not perceive the role of the state in the foundation of corporations purely as an act of the public authority with the result that the legal ability of the association so recognized was independently derived from general legal principles, as had been argued recently.[216] Rather, Roman law considered the legal status of the corporation as emanating from the whole, from an act of concession on part of the state. While granting a public *corpus* to the association, it also granted the required ability to hold property that was embodied in a special law promulgated by the state.[217]

214 It cannot be argued that the expression '*persona publica*' was applicable. This expression did not refer to the political personality but to the private legal ability of a political unity. It is incorrect to assume that the Romans utilized the idea of personality in the realm of public law.

215 Following Savigny, the prevailing opinion assumes the opposite. In almost all countries, the relevant practices of the common law refer to the *Corpus Juris*. Cp. Savigny, II, paragraph 89.

216 This interpretation of the sources was common in the Middle Ages. Windscheid, paragraph 60; Böhlau, *Rechtssubjekt und Personenrolle*, Weimar, 1871, pp. 26 ff.

217 This was the prevalent interpretation of the sources in the older theories of common law. Cp. e.g. Thibaut, *Pandekten*, 7th ed., paragraph 219. Among the more recent commentators cp. Mommsen, *de coll.*, pp. 40, 119; Kuntze, *Kursus*, p. 267; Pernice, I, p. 303.

All corporate existence was derived from a legislative act (*senatus consultum* or imperial constitution) which transferred the *lex civitatis* or the *lex collegii* into objective law. Such an act was not a mere grant by the public authority in a political sense nor was it a mere 'constitution' or 'attestation' according to private law. Rather such an act was entirely constitutive not declarative. What was created by the act depended upon its content. Special rules determining the time and the extent of the cession of personality to a political body were not required. In so far as nothing unique resulted from the cession of a special right or privilege, the legal qualifications of the associations were derived from their names and from the forms they utilized. It is clear that the founding of a *municipium*, a *colonia*, a district (*vicus*), etc., represented the granting of a certain competence in private law. The concept of the *collegium licitum* also was increasingly identified with the conception of a certain ability to hold property within given boundaries. Thus the granting of a *corpus* to such an arbitrarily formed body was considered the equivalent of the grant of a juristic personality. In this sense Gaius states that 'Associations of this type are allowed to exist in very few cases. In these cases permission is granted for an association in the form of a *collegium* or a *societas* or some other body of this nature. It is a property of such an association, on the analogy of the state, to have joint property, a common treasure, and a common administrator or representative through whom the corporation's necessary business shall be conducted and exercised as if it were a state' (*D*.3.4.1). But it remained entirely possible to recognize an association and, concurrently, to deny it the ability to hold property.[218] In the case of arbitrarily formed groups the conceptual distinction inherent in the concession of the state was clearly observable. This distinction is illustrated by Gaius' reference to such term as *concedere, permittere,* or *confirmare* as they applied to the *corpus*. The ability to hold property and to enter into a legal process were implied by these terms.[219]

In an analogous manner the termination of a legal personality appeared as a consequence of a special case under the jurisdiction of private law. This procedure was relevant to each process that negated the real or legal existence of political associational unity.[220]

The whole development of the juristic personality remained linked to the development of the political *corpus*. While conceptually becoming increasingly

218 Cp. Mommsen, *de coll.*, p. 40; Brinz, pp. 1064-5.

219 It is unnecessary to stress that an association without a sanction had no rights in the realm of private law. It is generally agreed that no corporation could function without the state's co-operation.

220 Cp. 'Die Korporationstheorie des Corpus Juris Civilis,' in O. Gierke, *Das deutsche Genossenschaftsrecht*, III, section 6.

independent, the notion of juristic personality remained subordinated to the individualistic viewpoints of Roman law.

Every municipal or collegial constitution contained the political representation of the *universitas* through the officials of its ruling body that had a measurable influence upon its administrative and representative competence in the sphere of property. Representation, as derived from private law, was instituted at an early stage. The special relationship of representation to public law appeared therefore as the substratum of that representation which was ceded to a juristic person. Essentially, this representation was identical with that known to private law. It was expanded only in certain instances by the *jus singulare*. The categories of tutelary representation and mandate were applied unhesitatingly and became part of the political constitution in so far as civil law was concerned. These categories fitted into the matrix of Roman private law.[221]

Equally, the authority of the state rooted in the public order could be applied to the associations that resulted in the limitations upon the representatives of the corporations. It limited their will and action in the sphere of private law and could therefore be subsumed, in accordance with the state's tutelary position, under the concept of private law.[222]

Greater difficulties arose, however, when the position and the rights of the assembly of the association were taken into account. The political assumption was that the constitutional and legal requirements of the properly enfranchised assembly expressed its unified collective will through majority decisions. This had a far-reaching influence upon property matters as they related to the concept of the juristic person. The resultant view, as it existed not only *de facto* but also in jurisprudence, considered the political totality as a willing and active being in the sphere of private law. But a closer examination of the issue had shown that it was impossible for Roman jurisprudence to remain at that stage of development.

The rules of the *jus publicum* relating to the decisions of the associations indicated that a *universitas* was an element which had somehow gained independence within the universality of the state. It was assumed that it had been called upon to will and to act and that it was entrusted with expressing a portion of the public will. The *jus privatum*, however, required a subject that had at its disposal its own sphere of will according to its special and limited nature. Thus, despite some misgivings, the view emerged that the same collectively willing and acting entity, which, from a political standpoint, appeared as the direct representative of a common will, could be interpreted, in so far as private law was concerned, as a hidden

221 Cp. Notes 204 to 210 above.

222 Cp. Savigny, II, pp. 283, 325, 353; Brinz, pp. 1121-7. Significantly, the name *curator reipublicae* was applied to the imperial supervisor who ultimately ruled over the municipal financial administration.

individual will. Only in its representatives did this individual will really exist and it could therefore be considered as the ideal centre representing the source of activity in private law. The conception that the corporation as such was a subject incapable of exerting a will was a concomitant. It was analogous to the view that minors and the mentally retarded had to be legally represented in order to be able to exert an effectual will and to act.[223] This conception came to prevail as the activity of the corporate assemblies deteriorated.

In the political field, fellowship, that had been an element in promoting the unity of the assemblies, was replaced by the institutional conception of a theoretically conceived and represented collectivity. Later sources occasionally carried the political idea of an independently willing and acting *universitas* with its notion of representation into the sphere of private law. Basically, however, the contrary view prevailed and was expressed trenchantly in the sentence, 'Members of the association are unable to agree.' Numerous consequences resulted from that sentence.[224]

Ultimately, Roman jurisprudence had to adhere to this sole model of construction if it wanted to carry the essence of the juristic person to its logical conclusion.

The essence of the juristic person was consistently determined by the idea that it was a political *corpus* tied to a constituted totality. From this were derived its names *corpus* or, preferably, *universitas*. In the case of special generic corporations, the terms referred to the collectivity of members and to the customary pluralistic expressions such as the 'citizens of that municipality' (*municipes ejus municipii*) or 'members of that colony' (*coloni ejus coloniae*).[225] Numerous characteristics were derived from this that were transposed into the political concept of association and they were judged according to private law. In the sphere of all collective legal relationships, isolated rights eventually vanished and the *universitas* thereby subsumed the rights of individual members under its own collective right.[226] In theory, the popular view that equated the right of the *universitas* with the collective rights of all[227] was energetically opposed by jurisprudence and pre-

223 The comparison of communities with *infantes* (children) and *furiosi* (deranged) came about at an early stage. Certainly it still applied to the period when the civic community emerged as a willing and acting entity in the political realm and it was treated according to the tenets of private law. E.g. ' ... that the edict also pertains to mad persons, infants, and the state in the opinion of Labeo.' (*D.* 4.6.22.2) Cp. Pernice, I, p. 287.

224 Cp. Gierke, as in note 220.

225 Cp. Pernice, I, pp. 277-8.

226 Cp. Brinz, pp. 1029 ff.

227 For the idea of the communal sharing in the public property cp. Cicero, *Tuscul. Disp.* 3.20.48. The many decrees of the emperors opposing this concept show that in communities and corporations the idea prevailed that a slave of the *universitas* could not be

vented from influencing the formulation of laws.[228] It was strongly argued that even in the sphere of private law, the *universitas* was a collectivity entirely distinct from the sum total of the *singuli*.[229] It was maintained that this collectivity could function as a unity only within the organization ceded to it by public law.[230] Finally, it was contended that it was not the collectivity at any one point in time but only the permanent collectivity which retained its identity regardless of changes in membership that was to be taken into account.[231]

The more or less clearly developed view came to prevail that the unity organized as a collectivity represented the subject of corporate property. The consequences of this concept transcended Roman thought. Increasingly the principal contradiction between the *jus publicum* and the *jus privatum* came to the fore. This contradiction was reflected in the view that the indigenous totality conceived in public law was merely the substratum of private legal subjectivity and not a subject in itself. The essence of the juristic person was based upon the assumption that legally equated the *universitas* with the *singuli*. But it appeared impossible that this personality, whether as a part or as a result of political existence, could be taken as the direct and exclusive opposite of the individual's essence. Public law denied the association those characteristics that made the individual into a person. It constituted the association as a whole that transcended its members and subordinated it to the state as a constituent part. Thus it placed the association entirely within the impersonal order of legal communal life. If the association was granted a personality in order that it be organized according to the characteristics of its members, and in order that is be separated from the state, this personality could join the political essence of such an association only by an externally granted right.

The personality of the *universitas* had thus to be construed as a creation of private law bound to the political substratum. In no way could it be considered as an immanent unity of an associated group of persons, because all subjectivity in private law was equated with the concept of an independent single uniform essence. Owing to this, the associated *singuli* could not be considered the source of a distinct group-personality that had made itself independent. Such a view would

forced to testify against a citizen or a member of the corporation because they were co-owners of the slave. (*D.* 48.18.1.7, 1.8.6.1). A citizen could also refuse the summons of a person who had been manumitted by the community (*D.* 2.4.10.4) on the grounds that he had been a co-sponsor of the manumitted.

228 Cp. *D.* 48.18.1.7.

229 *D.* 3.4.7.1, 1.8.6.1, 2.4.10.4, 48.18.1.7 and 8; *Cod. Theod.* 13.5.18.

230 Cp. Pernice, I, pp. 266, 277-8.

231 Compare *D.* 3.4.7.2 with *D.* 5.1.76.

have stood for the negation of its independence. The *universitas* was not apprehended as a group-personality consisting of individuals because the Roman concept of the person lacked the important feature of an individual essence. The exclusive, indivisible, inflexible, and self-contained individual personality was unable to utilize one portion of its will in favour of a communal unity of wills, nor was it able to develop a unity of wills related to the subject of property. Thus it was unable to formulate itself into an organic composition of many wills. The juristic person could plainly be considered as a group of associated individuals to whom a new individuality had been ascribed by external sources. This individuality was alien to the members of the corporation and it confronted them as a third individual that neither detracted from nor added to their own personality.

The Romans were ultimately deprived of the opportunity to justify the real existence of the juristic person by virtue of this condition.[232] As a political being, the *universitas* was a real unity but it was not a person. As a subject of private law, it was a person but not a real unity. Only a human being was a real person because he alone possessed the individuality necessary to the concept of legal personality. If a *universitas*, even though it was not an individual according to its real substratum, was posited as a person and thereby as an individual, then this was the result of the juristic treatment of a condition that did not really exist but which was treated as if it did exist.[233]

Ultimately, therefore, Roman jurisprudence was forced to adopt the view that the personality of the *universitas* was a fiction. The Romans, however, did not formulate this idea as the result of one process or with any great clarity. They did not undertake theoretical speculations as to the nature and content of this fiction.[234] The entire edifice of Roman corporate law culminated in the assumption that as far as positive law was concerned, a non-person had been personified. Because of its acceptance of the actual subject's complete ability to will and to act in the corporate sphere of property, jurisprudence needed the fiction in order to create a relevant surrogate.[235] Necessity and legal logic produced the final step: private law postulated the person as a subject. But a real person was not to be

232 A certain similarity exists between the argument presented above and that of Böhlau, pp. 16-20.

233 The arguments of Kuntze (*Kursus*, paragraphs 408 ff.) and others stating that the Romans saw in the corporation a real natural unity is relevant only if the association is viewed, philosophically, as an organic body. They also refer to the political idea of a totality that had constituted itself into a unity. It is disregarded, however, that the Romans never utilized these notions in order to arrive at the concept of the personality of the association.

234 For this reason, the many nuances of the theory of 'personification' are not discussed here.

235 Even those commentators who deny the basic theory of fiction agree on this issue.

found and therefore they created, through a fiction, an imaginary artificial subject. In the absence of a natural individual and in view of the fact that they derived the individual entirely from the sphere of private law, the Roman jurists introduced into the world of legal concepts the legally created individual.[236]

That this assumption was familiar to Roman jurists is illustrated by the parallel drawn by Florentinus with the personification of the unclaimed inheritance (*hereditas jacens*).[237] The legal subjectivity of this unclaimed inheritance was mediated in such a manner that the deceased *persona* of the testator was fictitiously assumed to be alive.[238] Thus a *persona*, that had never existed, was fictitiously created.[239] The development of the fiction theory subsequently played an active role ih ascribing legal subjectivity to the *fiscus*. In keeping with this trend foundations in the Christian age were assumed to have a juristic personality, without the realization that this meant the establishment of a new category measurably different from the concept of corporations. To the real essence of an artificially conceived subject it was of fundamental irrelevance what real, factual conditions formed its substratum. As the fictitious person did not derive from, nor live in its substratum, its essence could not be determined by it.

The historical development of this theory by the Romans comes to an end with the adoption of the fictitious legal personality. From this point on, all manifestations of life that did not fit into the Roman principles of the subjectivity of the association and the individual could be treated according to a juristic formula that artfully circumvented the contradiction.

236 There is an agreement among the commentators on this point, regardless whether the Roman fiction is seen as an artificial 'creation' or a mere 'assumption' of a subject; e.g. Savigny, II, paragraph 87; Puchta, *Rechtslexikon*, III, pp. 65 ff.

237 *D*. 46.1.22.

238 This view is derived from connecting passages in the sources that either directly or indirectly personify the *hereditas*, *D*. 41.3.15, 28.5.31.1, 47.4.1.1, 9.2.13.2, 41.1.61, 43. 24.13.5; *Cod*. 4.34.9; *D*. 41.1.34 and 33.2, 28.5.31.1, 30.116.3; *Inst*. 2.14.2, 3.17.

239 Florentinus' remark (*D*. 30.116.3) precludes the possibility that the Romans arrived at the idea of a real collective personality that was inherent in the corporate organism.

III

Christianity and the Ancient Concept of Association

Christianity destroyed the foundations of ancient social theory by transferring man's conception of the ideal state from the temporal sphere to the Empire of God. The state no longer appeared as the universal expression of the human community. There was a higher and more thoroughly integrated society that encompassed both heaven and earth. As a living entity, society linked its members with the personality of God. The individual did not find his end merely as a part of the state who found his fulfilment in the life of the total community. Rather, by virtue of his immortal soul, man was endowed with an absolute value and a transcendental purpose.

These new ideas, deriving their logical formulation from theological speculation, displayed their imperishable power primarily in the realm of religious life. However, as long as the tenets of classical antiquity functioned, the new ideas were unable to alter the basis of legal life and these tenets remained juridically unchanged. Everywhere the seeds of a new type of legal thought of tremendous importance were planted. But it was left to the mediaeval spirit to develop these ideas fully and to form them into a complete Christian legal system. Even after they became Christianized, the legal values of classical antiquity remained within the matrix of conventional forms and customary concepts. Admittedly, the new institutions created by Christianity had to be absorbed into the existing legal system. But this process occurred almost exclusively by means of a mechanical addition to the body of already existing concepts that had been thoroughly systematized. The aging legal spirit of antiquity had lost the creative power necessary for the development of a new intellectual construct.

The significance of Christianity culminated, as far as the history of the corporate concept was concerned, in the introduction of the new idea of the church. Entirely new forms of associations were developed by the church and its articulated constituents. Precisely at this point it became evident that as early as late antiquity Christian thought had established the foundations of an association organism. Though the church was endowed with an adequate system of new and specific notions, it was subordinated to the established legal order from the beginning.

Christian theology bestowed upon the concept of the church, which had originally been of religious significance only, the image of an external legal association. During the first Christian centuries, the concept of the church passed through various phases of development. But all of these led to the notion of an externally organized and completely closed corporation. According to the formulation it received in patristic thought, the concept represented a new and specific legal phenomenon. Plainly, this idea was external to the framework of ancient legal thought. In fact, the concept of the church was already equipped with all those elements whose ultimate legal consequences necessarily culminated in the mediaeval idea of a universal spiritual state.

Originally, the community of the faithful was thought of as a spiritual and ethical unity. And with increasing frequency the expression of this unity was developed in its external organization. Everything that related to the origin, being, and purpose of the existing community with God that had been founded by Christ was transferred to the visible and emerging church. Increasingly, the external church-association appeared as at least the partial realization of the divine realm that had been contrasted with the temporal in Holy Scripture. Augustine's *De Civitate Dei*, which remained the cornerstone of mediaeval social philosophy, identified the visible church with the celestial one, or rather with those parts that were existent in this world. The state, on the other hand, was equated with the temporal realm. Thus the contradiction between the *civitas Dei* and *civitas terrena* nearly coincided with the hierarchical conception of the external relationship between state and church. Henceforth, the church, even in its external societal existence, was generally linked to its divine foundation. It was considered a living unity centred upon the personality of God and viewed as the carrier of a transcendental human purpose.

The church, within religious thought, was represented as the incorporation of a new and specific associative concept that, to an increasing degree, gained legal significance. In its origin, existence, and purpose, it was a transcendental associative unity that was called upon to act as a subject within the legal sphere. This role introduced a previously unknown element into the evolution of corporate theory. Increasingly, Christian consciousness viewed the church as a fully developed corporate being. It considered it as an association organized in the same way as the state. Owing to its nature, Christian consciousness endowed the church with an abundance of attributes that linked the divine and the temporal realms. This view was alien to and incompatible with the heretofore existing concept of association.

Ancient philosophy perceived the state as a living organism. Christian theology viewed the church in a similar manner, as an organism that was an independent and united whole. But the organic view now received a new religious and mystical content. Most significantly, it was held that the church constituted the mystical body of Christ, the *corpus mysticum Christi.* Later, this view became a stereotype and a central tenet in canon law. The basis of this mystical view was the profound Pauline allegory which in Holy Scripture envisaged mankind as united in Christ. The community of the faithful appeared as the united body of Christ and Christ Himself as the head of that body. According to the apostle, the community was a united whole ruled by the spirit of God:

'There are varieties of gifts, but the same Spirit. There are a varieties of service, but the same Lord. There are many forms of work, but all of them, in all men, are the work of the same God. In each of us the Spirit is manifested in one particular way, for some useful purpose.'

'But all these gifts are the work of one and the same Spirit, distributing them separately to each individual at will.'

'For Christ is like a single body with its many limbs and organs, which, many as they are, together make up one body. For indeed we are all brought into one body by baptism, in the one Spirit, whether we are Jews or Greeks, whether slaves or free men, and that one Holy Spirit was poured out for all of us to drink. A body is not one single organ, but many. Suppose the foot should say, "Because I am not a hand, I do not belong to the body"; it does belong to the body none the less.'

'God appointed each limb and organ to its own place in the body, as He chose. If the whole were one single organ, there would not be a body at all; in fact, however, there are many different organs, but one body. The eye cannot say to the hand, "I do not need you"; nor the head to the feet, "I do not need you." Quite the contrary: those organs of the body which seem to be more frail than others are indispensable, and those parts of the body which we regard as less honourable are treated with special honour. To our unseemly parts is given a more than ordinary seemliness, whereas our seemly parts need no adorning. But God has combined the various parts of the body, giving special honour to the humbler parts, so that there might be no sense of division in the body, but that all its organs might feel the same concern for one another. If one organ suffers, they all suffer together.'

'Now you are Christ's body, and each of you a limb or organ of it. Within our community God has appointed, in the first place apostles, in the second place prophets, thirdly teachers; then miracle-workers, then those who have gifts of healing, or ability to help others or power to guide them or the gift of ecstatic utterance of various kinds.'[1]

These and similar statements enunciated the idea that humanity, in its structure and purpose, was a united spiritual and ethical organism. At the same time, the image of the body endowed with a soul was transposed to a related and widely accepted concept of ancient philosophy. The totality, representing the transcendental centre, was endowed with a living spiritual unity having the highest personality. Moreover, its own value and a specific personality were given to each member. The relationships between the totality and its members and those among the members were perceived to be in a perfectly reciprocal condition. The principles of unity and multiplicity were seen as the real and necessary emanations of God. All of these ideas were initially directed towards the inner, spiritual side of communal life. Simultaneously they were also applied to an external legal association in so far as biblical sanction directly alluded towards the visible church. This interpretation was based upon the apostolic use of the term *ecclesia* as referring to the entire external concept of the church. The church, in its corporate form was, within the theological realm, identified with the body of Christ. The words of Paul (*Cor.* 1.10.16-17) alluding to the last supper refer to a community founded upon the body and blood of Christ. The statement 'we, many as we are, are one body,' establishes a union in the sense of an exclusive mediation between the members and the head, a mystery administered by the church. Thus the church appeared as a *corpus mysticum* that was endowed by God with a unified life, a soul, and a purpose. On the other hand, as a constituted 'body,' it formed an external associational subject with a claim over the temporal sphere.[2]

According to its internal structure the organism of the church was at all times considered from a dual point of view. It was the community of the faithful and the institution of the faith. But with the separation of the clergy from the laity and the emergence of the constitution of the bishopric, the old definition of the church as a *congregatio* or *coetus fidelium* came to express solely the passive side

1 Paul, *Corinthians* 1.12.4-28; *Ephesians* 1.22-3; 4.10 ff.; 5.23 and 30; *Romans* 12.4-6; *Colossians* 1.24.

2 Cp. Cyprian, *Ep.* 41, 44, 52; Jerome, *Ad Cor.* 12; Chrysostom, *Ep. ad Corinth. Homil.* 30-2; Augustine, *De Civitate Dei*, 21.25; 22.18. The dogmatic elaboration of the theory of the last supper became important for the conception of the 'mystical' unity of all Christians with the body of Christ. Augustine maintained that participation in the last supper meant the incorporation of the individual in the body of Christ. Thereby the individual was intimately linked with the idea of the church that spread over the whole world. Cp. A. Dorner, *Augustinus*, Berlin, 1873, pp. 102, 263 ff.

of the concept. Its active side was transferred to the healing task represented in its spiritual function.[3] The church as a whole still encompassed the totality of the faithful and unified them. But this subjective unity of the association, and its personality, survived and acted exclusively in the church's healing apparatus that was derived from its transcendental origin. The conception of the church, in so far as it appeared as a living legal entity, a fellowship, yielded entirely to the idea of a transcendental institutional church. Therefore, when it reached the stage where it became a subject to its own external sphere of power, the evolution of the church's constitution assumed a hierarchical character. The idea of a transcendental institutional church reached its completed form of legal incorporation when the unity of the church was concentrated in the hands of a temporal head. This head claimed full legal powers that were due to a direct divine delegation, and therefore he acted as the representative of Christ.

In its external manifestations, the church proceeded on the assumption that it had been granted, by its divine founder, a specific and independent right to fulfil its function within its own realm of activity. Unlike all other associations of the ancient world, it did not derive its existence, law, or purpose from the state. Therefore, as long as it was in opposition, the church appeared to contradict strongly the existing Roman view that accorded legal existence to all religious associations so long as they functioned in and for the state. Eventually Christianity was recognized by the state and allowed a preferential position that ultimately culminated in its acceptance as the state religion. It adjusted itself to those institutional measures that the emperors legislated for it according to the ancient laws of associations.

But within Christian thought there developed an energetic movement concerning the justification of resistance and its theological basis. In this regard Augustine summarized and systematically expounded the legal thought of western patristic literatures as well as eastern statements of similar nature. From the fifth century on, these views officially pitted the Roman bishop against the theoretical position of the emperor, disputing the emperor's sovereignty within the ecclesiastical realm. Indeed, the church was vindicated as having a significance that was entirely independent of the state. It was seen as representing an order of existence whose origin, content, and purpose made it the state's superior. Thus the basis of the mediaeval theory of the church was formulated by ascribing to it an independence and eminence that made it appear as a body similar to the state. Already the *imperium* was confronted by a *sacerdotium* that had become independent and that had turned into a real 'force' which represented a second, self-sufficient realm of power. Claims for the supremacy of the church over the state

3 This was clearly expressed by Cyprian, *Epist.* 33 and 66.8.

derived from the eminence of the ecclesiastical vocation. This attitude was reinforced by references to the rule of the soul over the body and that of heaven over earth.[4]

The development of these views about the nature of the church as a whole caused corresponding views about the nature of its members to evolve everywhere. All corporate creations with a religious content were considered, theologically, as parts of the single communal body of the church. The external as well as the internal living unity of these members represented an independent portion of the living unity of the entire totality. Therefore they all partook of the organic, mystical, and transcendental nature of the universal body. Its members owed it their lives and their opportunity for action, and as such they united the elements of the community and the institution. But, increasingly, the active unity was ascribed exclusively to the central church which received its authority from above. Everywhere the original, living, local ecclesiastical communities became constituent elements of the special personality of the church. Accordingly, the constituent organs derived their entire existence, and the external legal subjectivity required for fulfilling their tasks, exclusively from the communal church and thereby from God. The state's recognition of this legal sphere was indispensable, as was the state's competence in determining their limitations and purposes.

It was on the basis of these fundamental tenets that the church began to build its own positive law of associations. In doing so, it utilized Roman law to a substantial degree. It was precisely this transference into church law that brought about the uninterrupted, though at times latent, survival of Roman legal concepts that were to be of service in later centuries. However, all these elements of Roman law underwent a substantial change. This development made it possible

4 These statements are collected and discussed in E. Löning, *Die Haftung des Staats*, I, pp. 70-94; J. Hergenröther, *Katholische Kirche und christlicher Staat*, Freiburg, 1872, I, pp. 375 ff., 384 note 1; Molitor, *Die Dekretale per venerabilem*, Münster, 1876, pp. 213 ff. The following ideas were of importance to the development of mediaeval thought: the comparison of the church and the state with the soul and the body (Chrysostom, *Ep.* II *ad. Cor. Hom.* 15.4-5; *De Sacer.* 3.1; Greg. Naz. *Orat.* 17; Isidore Pelus. 3. *Ep.* 249); or heaven and earth, as well as the consequences deduced by Chrysostom. Also the sentence of Ambrose, 'The emperor is within the church, not above it' and the reference to the emperor as *filius ecclesiae* (*Sermo ad Auxentium* 36). Equally important were Augustine's pronouncements that the *civitas Dei* or *coelestis* coincided with the church speaking and acting through its clergy. Like the body of Christ, it was relevant to the whole world. The *civitas terrena* could only be freed from its sins by serving the *civitas Dei*, Augustine maintained (*De Civitate Dei*; cp. *De Unitate Ecclesiae* 49 and *Ep.* 141). He also put forth the dogma that temporal laws which violated ecclesiastical ones were not binding (*Ep.* 105 c. 6-7; *Sermo* 62). Finally, among the lasting ideas conveyed to the Middle Ages, there was the theory of Pope Gelasius I about the two powers.

to fit them into the system of Christian-Germanic thought as homogeneous parts. The process became particularly relevant to those parts of Roman corporate theory that played a role in the development of the corporate law of the church.

While the Roman state remained in existence, all evolution took place within the theological sphere. The legal order remained essentially untouched until the collapse of the ancient world. The outlines of canon law had already been proclaimed but canon law as such did not yet exist. Temporal law remained the sole law. With regard to the church it adhered to those fundamental principles that dealt with the essence of associations.

The concept of the church remained obviously meaningless to Roman law until the advent of Constantine. Individual Christian communities were subject to the established law of associations. They were *collegia illicita* and as such were not endowed with any rights but were subject to severe penalties.[5] When tolerated at all they were, in the guise of a *collegia tenuiorum*, able to lead an admittedly precarious existence,* although they were permitted to hold corporate property.[6]

Constantine absorbed the Christian church into law. Henceforth the laws of associations recognized by the state applied to it.

As a recognized associative unity the church became a corporate unity under the Roman *jus publicum*. In its uniform communal existence, the church was, first and foremost, a representative of the political authorities. Like other public institutions, the church was considered a part of the state that had organized itself for its own purposes. In keeping with the state-theory of the late Empire, this segment of the state was judged according to a strictly institutional principle. It is known that in the ancient Roman system the *jus sacrum* was subordinated to the *jus publicum*. This approach was also applied to the Christian church. The emperor was the representative of the total legal subjectivity of the *jus publicum*. Simultaneously, he was the living source and active representative of the unity of the church. He could assemble the ecumenical council that was dependent upon

* This theory is discredited by L. Duchesne, *Early History of the Christian Church*, London, 1909, I, pp. 278-9 and by W.H.C. Frend, *Martyrdom and Persecution in the Early Church*, London, 1965, pp. 325-6.

5 Paul, *Sent. Rec.* 5.21 paragraph 2; *D.* 48.19.30; Plinius, *Ep.* 10.97-8; Tertullian, *Apol.* 10-36.

6 Cp. Löning, I, pp. 195-211. Tertullian (*Apologeticum* 38-9) claimed that the Christian communities had a corporate life based upon the existing law. He saw them as associations for mutual support and as burial guilds with monthly contributions and meetings. Hence Cyprian's reference (*Ep.* 50 and 52) to the property of the church and especially the wording of the Edict of Milan of 313 (Lactantius *De Morte Persec.* 48).

him. Only under his rule and with his collaboration could the church give the impression of unity. Consequently, the emperor *qua* emperor could rule over its dogma and its constitution.[7]

All member associations were bound to follow the example set by the entire church and act as institutions of the state. But it remained true that despite the total incorporation of the church into public law, its constituents remained primarily church organs and its members parts of the church. Even though organized for their own purposes, they remained, as members of the church, subject to the complex of the norms of the state. Therefore, the special legal existence of the religious associations was confirmed by the state. It granted them recognition, erected limitations for them, determined their sphere of activity, ruled upon clauses in their constitutions, supervised their management, and controlled their activities. All this was done with the co-operation or through the mediation of the authority of the church and was in keeping with the specific coherence of the church.[8]

Similarly, the associations of the church that had been incorporated in the state were moved into the realm of private law. They were also granted the ability to hold property. The church as a communal body, however, was never granted its own legal subjectivity.[9] But individual churches were immediately accorded a juristic personality to the fullest extent,[10] and an increasing number of special privileges were conferred upon them.[11] The church as an associative unity under the bishop formed the primary substratum of this personality. This associative unity was subordinated to the corporate concept as it had been developed in classical Roman law. The property of the united totality was ascribed to a *concilium*, *conventiculum* (assembly), or *corpus* of the faithful.[12] But actually, in the course

7 Cp. Löning, I, pp. 39 ff., 64 ff., 500 ff.

8 It follows that in the Justinian sources the church appeared as an organism composed of many members. In this organism the emperor could be replaced by the pope and the image of a hierarchic spiritual state emerged in juxtaposition to the bureaucratically articulated temporal state. This enabled mediaeval jurisprudence to utilize the *Corpus Juris Civilis*.

9 Cp. Hübler, *Die Eigenthümer des Kirchenguts*, pp. 88 ff., Löning, I, p. 221, note 3.

10 They were endowed by Constantine with the full ability to inherit. *Cod. Theod.* 16.2.4; *Cod.* 1.2.1. Cp. Löning, I, pp. 220 ff.

11 *Tit. Cod. Just.* 1.2; *Nov.* 131; *Cod.* 1.3.20 and 42; *Nov.* 5.5; *Cod.* 1.2.23; *Nov.* 9, 131.6; *Cod.* 8.54.34, 1.2.19, 1.2.22; *Nov.* 131.4; *Cod.* 1.2.15, 1.2.22; *Nov.* 131.10-12; *Cod.* 1.2.5; *Nov.* 131.85; *Cod.* 1.2.12 and 16; *Nov.* 131.4.

12 Cp. wording in Lactantius with regard to the Edict of 313, 'With respect to their corporation, you will order to be restored to the corporation and assemblies ... '; and

of receiving recognition by the state, the alleged corporation had become an ecclesiastical institution. According to the law of property, it henceforth appeared as the institution of the state church. As a subject capable of holding property, the associative unity was represented exclusively by the bishop who received, symbolically, his authority to administer and represent ecclesiastical property not from the community but from his spiritual office. The bishop, in utilizing property, was bound by the purpose of the church. This purpose was external and superior to the association. Since the prohibition on ecclesiastical sales and on the sales on state holdings had been lifted, the disposition of real property was limited only by external pressures.[13]

Actually, both *de facto* and *de jure*, a conception came to prevail according to which the church, founded by God and represented by the bishop, appeared as a subject that had been endowed by the state with the ability to hold property.[14] Such a personified institution assumed, generally, the name *ecclesia*. In a technical sense it denoted the ecclesiastical legal subject.[15] Similarly, the growth of specific properties within the holding of the diocese was regularly linked to a

'That at last they should be Christians and form their assemblies'; Eusebius, *Hist. Eccl.* 9.c.10, 'That all things should be established according to the ancient right and ownership of the Christians'; especially Constantine's edict of 321, 'Let each man have the freedom at his death to leave to the most holy, universal, and venerable council those of his goods that he desires to.' (*Cod.* 1.2.1).

13 For the bishop's administration of church property, cp. Löning, I, pp. 213 ff., for its utilization, cp. pp. 240 ff.; for its limited rights of sale, cp. pp. 236 ff. Justinian exempted the sale of ecclesiastical property to the state by proclaiming, 'Neither does the priestly or imperial power differ greatly between themselves nor sacred matters from public ones, since all status and wealth are provided for the most holy church by the munificence of the emperor'. (*Nov.* 7.2)

14 Cp. Brinz, pp. 1053.; Hübler, p. 85.; Löning, I, p. 214.

15 A glance at the *Codex* and the *Novellae* shows that the term *ecclesiae* was the proper technical term for the totality of ecclesiastical legal subjects, while *ecclesia* referred to individual subject. Cp. Löning, I, p. 215. Generally, attributes such as *sacrosancta, sacratissima, venerabilis, religiosa, beata* were added. It follows that the term *ecclesia* was not to be interpreted in the traditional meaning as assembly or community. It can be shown that the idea of the rightful and dutiful church was linked, on an institutional level, with the newer concept of *ecclesia* as the house of God. This follows from the parallel use of the words *domus, locus, aedes,* also *martyrium, templum, oratorium* etc. Besides statements with regard to the *ecclesiae*, references were also made to *venerabiles domus* (*Cod.* 1.2.17, 1.3.49 [48]; *Nov.* 7.120, 123, 131,); to the *divina domus* (*Cod.* 1.2.7.) or *pia domus* (*Cod.* 1.2.20); and to *venerabilis locus* (*Nov.* 7.1, 7.3, 7.5, 120.6, 120.7, 120.11, 131.6). All these were considered as legally empowered and obligated, earning and owning manifestations of the *ecclesia.*

single *ecclesia* that appeared as a local institution.[16] This link made the abstract concept of the institution more accessible to popular understanding in so far as it approximated the actual church building to the spatial centre of the property. This practice also represented the continuation of the pagan assumption that considered Christ and the saints as the owners of such property.[17] Despite all this, jurisprudence continued to subsume the *ecclesia* under the existing concept of the corporation.[18] Not even the slightest attempt was made to formulate a special institutional concept for it. No need for doing so was felt since the concept of the corporation itself had essentially a purely institutional aspect.[19] The *ecclesia*, however, possessed characteristics which were entirely contrary to that concept of the corporation that had rejected the aspects of fellowship. Nevertheless, jurisprudence contented itself with an ordering according to the norms of positive law as derived from traditional classifications. This decaying legal science lacked the spiritual power to produce an adequate legal concept to cope with the new manifestation. In dealing with it, jurisprudence relied on notions developed by its classical predecessors and did not examine the inner legal nature of the new institutions.

After having been recognized as a form of church organization and thereby as a state institution, the monastic fellowships were categorized under the generic term of *ecclesia.*[20] They were granted a legally ordered sphere of activity and the

16 In this respect, Justinian's decision in *Cod.* 1.2.26 (25) and *Nov.* 131.9 is significant. Cp. also *Cod.* 1.2.13 and 23, 1.3.20 and 42 (41).

17 Cp. *Cod.* 1.2; *Nov.* 131.9; *Cod.* 1.2.2, 1.2.15.

18 Therefore the reference to the term *concilio* (*Cod.* 1.2.1) could be retained without difficulty. Justinian himself used the words *consortium, collegium,* and *corpus* as a generic concept that encompassed all churches and ecclesiastical institutions. *Cod.* 1.2.22, 1.3.57 (55), 1.3.46 (45); *Nov.* 7.2, 7.9 and 12, 7.1; *Cod.* 1.3.57 (55), 1.2.23, 1.2.19.

19 The use of the words *concilium, collegium, consortium* in the above-quoted passages indicates the predominance, in the late Roman mind, of the institutional aspects of the corporate concept. Elements were added to the developing bishoprics that were derived from the corporations. These elements, however, were not borrowed from the community, as Savigny and others claim, but came from the rudimentary foundations of a clerical *collegium* that represented the institutional church. One may consider the attempts of the bishops to establish controls over the diocese through the clergy, the position of the *oeconomus* who was appointed from among the clergy of the diocese, but above all one can consider the requirement that all sales required the consent of the clergy (*Cod.* 1.2.14 and 17; *Nov.* 120.6).

20 For the gradual change of the monasteries from free fellowships to clerical institutions cp. Löning, I, pp. 332-61.

ability to hold property as well as a series of privileges.[21] Their classification as corporations did not present any difficulty. Despite their corporate constitutions however, the monastic orders were considered as ecclesiastical establishments. They were viewed, in every respect, as associative subjects fully equal to those churches that lacked a corporate constitution.[22]

Ecclesiastical welfare institutions entered into late Roman law as charitable foundations and only as such did they become legal subjects.[23] Legally, the foundations were envisaged as having an assigned purpose with a limited application relevant to the existing temporal and ecclesiastical corporation or institution.[24] An independent personality within the ecclesiastical whole could be ascribed to a subordinated institution that was devoted to a *pia causa*.[25] Such an institution received the indispensible ecclesiastic authorization that was necessary for its existence. This also equipped it with the required power to act in private law. The institution received its personality from the church and indirectly from the state, and it was the interaction of both that produced its status.[26]

21 Cp. *Cod.* 1.2.13, 1.2.16, 1.2.17, 1.2.20, 1.2.22, 1.2.23, 1.3.20, 1.3.47 (46), 1.3.54 (53), 1.3.57 (55); *Nov.* 5, 7.11, 76, 79, 120.7, 123.23 and 37-8, 131. In private law the monasteries were generally placed on an equal footing with the *ecclesia*. The right to inherit (*Cod. Theod.* 5.3.1) was granted to them provided members had not disposed of their property before entering the orders (*Nov.* 5.5, 123.23 and 38). The monasteries attained a juristic personality without a special concession from the state, and their organization was dependent upon authorization by the bishop. (*Nov.* 67, 131.7).

22 In the above quoted passages the monasteries were ranked with the *ecclesia*. These legally enabled and obligated subjects were referred to as *monasterium, monachium, asceterium* etc. but not as *collegium, conventus, congregatio* etc. But they always coincided with the churches under the rubrics '*domus*' or '*loci venerabiles*'.

23 Cp. Pfeifer, *Jur. Pers.*, paragraphs 42 ff.; Kuntze, *Kursus*, paragraph 963; Löning, I, pp. 250 ff.

24 Special regulations existed according to which *captivi* or *pauperes* could be appointed as direct inheritors even though their status was that of *incertitudo personarum*. These measures were obviously to be interpreted as appointments to inherit *sub modo* (in such a manner) or as bequeathals of special, existing ecclesiastical legal subjects. The bishopric of a specific location was the legal subject in the case of the purchase of captives (*Cod.* 1.3.28 and 49; *Nov.* 131.11). In case of numerous almshouses, those that stood in greatest need received the inheritance (*Cod.* 1.3.24 and 49; *Nov.* 131.11). As long as the purpose was a pious one, charitable donations carried with them the privilege of *ad pias causas*. Under such circumstances bequeathals to independent institutional foundations were possible, cp. *Cod.* 1.2.19, 8.54.34 and 36; *Nov.* 131.6 and 12. Donations for purchasing the freedom of captives enjoyed special privileges.

25 But only for a *pia causa* and only in the case of the founding of an ecclesiastical institution.

26 There is a dispute in contemporary common law whether charitable foundations require the permission of the state. Both contending parties refer to Roman law. Quoting

Institutions thus personified were, in a wider sense, considered as members of the church. They were endowed with the privileges of the churches and were consistently viewed and treated as members of the church that had become independent in the sphere of private law.[27] Therefore monastic fellowships were classified under the generic concept of corporation and subsumed under the term of *collegium, consortium,* or *corpus*.[28] In reality, however, they were formed and viewed as institutions. In their constitutions and administrations, the monastic fellowships followed the purely institutional order of the bishop's church.[29] There was a specific building and a director who represented an institutional unity. These features formed the substratum of the [monastic] personality. In this respect, the sources refer to the legal subject by using expressions that denote local institutions. They are called orphan asylums (*orphanotrophia*), orphanages (*brephotrophia*), poorhouses (*ptochotrophia*), public buildings for the reception of strangers (*xenodochia*), almshouses for the aid of aged destitutes (*gerontocomia*), hospitals (*nosocomia*). Besides the *ecclesia* and the *monasteria*, these appear as owners, creditors, and debtors. All of these institutions are referred to, most fre-

sources, one party maintains that foundations can exist without references to the granting of their personality by the state. They are recognized as legal subjects merely on the basis of their existence. Cp. Puchta, *Pandekten*, paragraph 28, *Krit. Jahrb.*, VIII, pp. 705 ff.; Arndts, *Pandekten*, paragraph 46; *Rechtslex*, III, pp. 915 ff.; Brinz, pp. 1096 ff.; Windscheid, paragraph 60, note 3. The other commentators maintain that in the absence of specific pronouncements endowing the foundation with a personality, recognition by the state is presupposed in all cases. Savigny, II, pp. 276 ff.; Pfeifer, paragraph 44. In reality the case is identical with that of the corporations. Roman law did not recognize any independent foundations other than ecclesiastical institutions that attained legal existence through the co-operation of the leaders of the church (*Nov.* 67, 131.7 and 10). The organizing of such institutions created a political associational unity. It endowed this unity with a special right relevant to a special personality.

27 Cp. *Cod.* 1.2.13, 1.2.15, 1.2.17, 1.2.22; 1.2.23, 1.3.42.6-9, 1.3.46 (45), 1.3.49 (48), 1.3.57 (55); *Nov.* 7.120, 123, 131.

28 Cp. references in note 18 above.

29 According to the sources, the organization of the institutions was left to the judgment of the founders (*Cod.* 1.2.15), but the administration and representation was always in the hands of *ordinatores, administratores, curatores, rectores* etc. They supervised orphanages and acted as overseers of the poor, heads of guest houses, heads of homes for the aged, heads of hospitals, and watchmen etc. The sources give details about the appointment and powers of the administrators (esp. *Cod.* 1.3.32 (31), 1.3. 35 (34), 1.3.46 (45); *Nov.* 131.10 and 15) and they refer to the bishops' supervision of these matters. There were also regulations with regard to the sale of ecclesiastical property. But they fail to establish any connection between possible corporate or collegial elements contained in the constitution of these institutions and their legal position (cp. e.g. *Cod.* 1.2.17, 1.2.22; *Nov.* 7).

quently, as *venerabiles domus* or *loci.*[30] Christian charitable institutions profusely multiplied. But Roman jurisprudence did not utilize them as a substitute for its partially extinct corporate life, nor did it develop the concept of the foundation in a manner analogous to that of modern jurisprudence.[31]

The appearance of the church and its members did not bring about a process of rejuvenation and change in Roman law. The theory of associations in Roman jurisprudence was in no way connected with the new concept of community that had been produced by Christianity.

A similar divergence appeared between the influence of Christianity upon the concept of the state and the nature of temporal associations. This divergence was most notable in the separation of the emerging theology and late jurisprudence.

The bases of the Christian state and the legal philosophy that was a universal system to the mediaeval mind were already established in antiquity.

Christian religious consciousness, however, as long as it was confronted by a pagan state, did not interfere in a positive manner with the existing concepts of the law and the state.[32] Rather, by concentrating exclusively upon the inner life of the individual and the ecclesiastical community, Christianity accepted the external communal order as a matter of indifference. In accordance with Scripture,[33] it envisaged the existing authority, regardless of its origin, as ordained by God. Temporally, even Christ owed obedience to this authority. The development of new, positive views about the nature and the purpose of the state was, initially, alien to Christianity. Such was obviously the case during the religious persecutions when the tendency of the church consisted of a total negation of temporal life. This tendency survived even when Christians were accepted as citizens. The spirit of the new religion had to prevail, as far as the individual Christian was concerned, in both political and all other activities. No thought was given to a reformulation and a renewal of the existing order of both state and society.

Christian principles contained basic negations of ancient views of the state and the law. They deprived the state-association of a large part of its content in favour of the religious community and the individual. The belief was unanimously accepted that the inner life of the individual and his religious and ethical asso-

30 Cp. sources in note 27; cp. also note 15 above.

31 In the *Codex* and the *Novellae* the expression *pia causa* was never used in the subjective sense, rather it always denoted a pious intention. It may be accidental that the expression *pium corpus* is not to be found in the *Corpus Juris Civilis*. It would have suited the ideas of the age.

32 For the relationship of the Christians with the pagan Roman state, cp. Löning, I, pp. 27 ff., 35 ff.

33 Paul: 'Every person must submit to the supreme authorities. There is no authority but by act of God, and the existing authorities are instituted by him ... ' (*Romans* 13.1); Matthew: 'Then pay Caesar what is due to Caesar, and pay God what is due to God' (22.21).

ciations were subject to no temporal power. They were indeed above the order of political existence. Thereby the state's universal significance disappeared. Man's existence was not exhausted in his citizenship nor was the community identical with the state. The influential idea that obedience was due to God rather than to men began its victorious career. The pagan state's omnipotence vanished before it. The idea of an inherent limitation of the powers of the state and of the duties of all subjects gained ascendancy. The right and duty to resist the coercion of the state were sealed with the martyrs' blood.

Eventually Christianity conquered the state. Then the speculative theology of the fathers of the church developed new positive thoughts about the nature and aims of society. Demands were made that the state partake of the spirit of Christianity in a manner similar to the church. This would result in a rejuvenated and sanctified power devoted to the service of the religious idea. A specific ecclesiastical theory of the state emerged. This was most clearly enunciated in St. Augustine's *De Civitate Dei*.

The patristic theory of the state was built upon intellectual elements derived primarily from Holy Scripture and from interpretations of it. But it also combined a multitude of other elements derived from Graeco-Roman theories of the state and the law. This reproduction in patristic literature of numerous theories about the origin, nature, and purpose of human associations accounted for the fact that they survived the collapse of the ancient world. Thus, these theories were never entirely lost to European civilization. They became an integral part of the Christian-Germanic view of the world.[34] In the course of being absorbed by a system based upon Christianity, the fragments of classical theories about the

34 This influence applies to the idea of natural law, the determination of the purpose of the state, the organic view of state and society, the differentiation between the various forms of the state and to a certain extent, the idea of popular sovereignty. Until the nineteenth century, some passages of Cicero's *De Re Publica* that were of great importance to the Middle Ages were known only through the writing of Lactantius and Augustine. Lactantius preserved the idea of a natural law that was applicable to all people in perpetuity and from whose rule neither the senate nor the people were exempted (*Inst. Div.* 6.8). Similarly he retained the idea of the foundation of the state as being due to the natural sociability of man (*Inst. Div.* 6.10). Augustine, in turn, compared the state to an organism and the *imperium* to the soul (*De Civ. Dei* 14.23; *Contra Julian. Pelag.* 4.12); he defined the state as a *societas* and as a 'multitude of men assembled in some bond of concord'; he exposed the *res populi* as the essence of the *respublica* and examined the good and perverse forms of state derived from it (*Ep.* 13.10; *De Civ. Dei* 2.21, 19.21, 15.8). Augustine also considered the longevity of the state and maintained that its end was not due to natural law but rather its own mistakes (*De Civ. Dei* 22.6).

state were assigned a different place and significance. The impetus of the thought of the ancient philosophers and jurists was preserved by the church, but these thinkers remained latent until the first signs of the Renaissance* when they again emerged as a potent influence.[35]

The new ecclesiastical theory of the state produced a system that combined biblical and classical elements. It produced, fundamentally, a theocratic society. In its formulation by St. Augustine, the theory recognized the church as the universal and uniform factor. It was an association whose founder and ruler was God. 'The state whose king is Christ' was an expression denoting the ethical order of the world. The temporal state with its articulation and institutions was valid only in so far as it subordinated itself to the divine state and by that was meant a state that recognized the church as the source and the purpose of its existence. The temporal order was denied by justification in so far as it was a mere human and natural construct that had been founded and developed for its own ends.[36] The origins of the temporal power contradicted the transcendental origins of the church. The basis of the state was derived from a worldly and sinful source. The important axiom was developed that the rule of men over men was the result of the sinful deterioration of human nature. It was the fall [from grace] that brought into the world political rule and property. In contrast, pure divine and natural law sanctioned freedom and collective ownership of goods.[37] Accordingly, the foundation of the state was the result of the activities of human forces, and its purposes were carried out by these same forces. Above all, injustice and force were the characteristics of this worldly realm, especially of the Roman Empire.[38] Hence the subsequent demand that the state eliminate the stain of its illegitimate

*Gierke is referring to the intellectual consequences of the 'reintroduction' of classical works into twelfth- and thirteenth-century Europe.

35 Referred to here are those theories that became the bases for the idea of the sovereignty of the state's power and its transcendence of positive law, and theories with regard to contracts between states and the sovereignty of the people etc.

36 Cp. esp. Augustine, *De Civ. Dei* 14.28, 15.2, 15.22, 18.54, 19.24.

37 Cp. *Ibid.* 19.15; 15.4; *De Correctione Donatistarum Epist.* 185.9; *Tract.* 6. n. 25-6, *Ad c. 1 Joann.* 32-3. Other patristic statements of similar content are mentioned by Hergenröther, p. 461.

38 Augustine, *De Civ. Dei* 11.1, 14.28, 15.5, 15.17, 16.3-4, 17.6, 18.2. Of importance here are the references to the foundation of the state through fratricide by Cain and Romulus, also the introduction of kingship among the Jews as an act of rebellion against God and the foundation of world monarchies through wars of conquest. At the same time Augustine recognizes the natural social inclinations of man as the cause for civil society, cp. *ibid.* 19.12, 'How much more strongly is a human being drawn by the laws of nature, so to speak, to enter upon a fellowship with all his fellow-men and to keep peace with them, as far as lies in him.' [H. Bettenson transl., Harmondsworth, 1972, p. 868].

origin. It was argued that the temporal order received divine sanction only through the church and that it thus became a recipient of the full divine power.[39]

In a similar vein, strict ecclesiastical theory held that the nature of the state was, by necessity, sinful and unjust. It did not have the means to develop into a realm of virtue and justice and to partake of the true nature of that state which had been founded by the Empire of God.[40] Only through the mediation of the church could such a condition be attained. Primarily, the new theory saw the state, in its preoccupation with temporal happiness, to be entirely objectionable and lacking in a justification for its existence.[41] It was generally maintained that the worldly state attained a legitimate purpose only by serving as a means to the higher transcendental aims of the church. The state's concern for temporal welfare had to be subordinated to the church's concern for eternal welfare.[42] The essential conclusion was that the irrefutable and sole important task of the state consisted of the external defence of the true faith and church. Moreover, it followed that the state's task and aim was to consist of utilizing its power in the service of religion by fighting infidels, schismatics, and heretics.[43] Only when it established this close connection with the church was the state granted any value and considered to be a qualified member of the divinely ordained human association. The church required external peace, and the state received its legitimate sphere of activity and authority by acting as the custodian of the ecclesiastical organization.[44] In this capacity, the state served as the protector of the eternal

39 Augustine considered the formation and fate of the pagan states, the granting of rule to evil as well as to good rulers, and the attainment of a world empire by the Romans owing to their civic virtues as manifestations of the divine will. (*ibid.* 4.3, 4.31, 4.33, 5.15). The acts of divine rule and judgment, however, are not seen as a justification for endowing the temporal ruler with divine powers.

40 According to Augustine, states without justice are nothing but great robberies (*ibid.* 4.4). Rather, 'True justice is found only in that commonwealth whose founder and ruler is Christ' (*ibid.* 2.21). In itself, the worldly state is sinful and, together with the devil, is subject to eternal judgment (15.1, 15.4, 19.21, 19.23). 'There can be no true virtues where true religion is absent' 19.25). Where there is no justice according to God's rule and where neither the totality nor the individual obey Him in faith and love, 'There is certainly no association of men united by a common sense of right and by a community of interest,' 19.23). Neither for the individual nor the state is there another way to salvation. (*Ep.* 155; cp. *De Civ. Dei* 5.24-6).

41 Cp. *ibid.* 4.23, 19.21, 19.23.

42 For the relationship between the two ends cp. *ibid.* 19.14.

43 For an exposition of Augustine's theory with regard to this point see Dorner, pp. 302 sq. For similar views by Jerome and other fathers of the church, cp. Hergenröther, pp. 547 ff.

44 *De Civ. Dei* 15.4, 19.17.

treasure (*dona Dei*). The state could, within its legitimate sphere, bind the church and could demand its attention and obedience,[45] but it always remained a subordinate and serving member of the mystical body whose head was represented by Christ. The state, by virtue of its origin, essence, and purpose, was related to the church as was the body to the soul.[46]

The conception of law was changed in order that it correspond to this idea of the state. It was altered by the new ecclesiastical philosophy in accordance with theocratic thought. The ancient antithesis between natural and positive law was retained by the fathers of the church and was transmitted to the Middle Ages. But henceforth natural law was plainly identified with the law expounded by Holy Scripture. Positive law was equated with human law. All ecclesiastical law was derived from divine law, all temporal law was the product of human statutes.[47] Consequently, it was inevitable that the state received its norms and limits from the church. Its own legal development remained confined to the area that was untouched by ecclesiastical law.

No further elaboration is required to point out that these views of the state and the law, as developed by Christianity, did not influence the valid legal order of the Roman Empire, nor did they change, to any substantial degree, the intellectual content of jurisprudence. The concepts of the state and of the temporal associations that emerged in the sources of the Empire were essentially identical with those of pagan times. Certainly the emperors accepted the thesis that their power was derived from God, but they devoted little thought to the ecclesiastical mediation of their divinely ordained powers. Rather, the emperors thought that the office bestowed upon them by God meant the authority to rule over both the ecclesiastical and the religious sphere. For this reason, they took upon themselves the task of protecting the true faith and of combatting heresy and schism. They had the support of the church in doing so. The emperors did not vindicate their actions by referring to ecclesiastical authority but rather spoke of their own divine right. This idea too was rooted in ecclesiastical thought.[48] At the termina-

45 *Ibid*. 19.17, 19.19, 19.26.

46 Cp. note 4 above. Augustine attributes no divine meaning to the Christian state. In comparison to the eternal and universal empire instituted here on earth and ruled by Christ, the wordly state is beset by its temporal conditions (*De Civ. Dei* 15.17) and it is therefore of a transitory and particularistic nature (15.4, 19.7). The state's only task and sole essence is the protection of the higher order of the church. Basically, the church is the only true state and it utilizes the temporal power as a tool for its own higher ends.

47 Augustine, *Tract*. 6 n. 25; *Ad c. 1 Joann*. 32. Thomas Aquinas was the first to separate divine from natural law.

48 Cp. *Cod. Theod*. 16.5; *Cod*. 1.1.1, 1.5; *Nov*. 115.3, 132. Hergenröther, pp. 543 ff.; Löning, I, pp. 95 ff.

tion of the classical era, theology thus created an absolute monarchical state-power with a new title and an enlarged sphere of activity. But it left its real inner core untouched. Not even in the sections dating from the period of the early church, did the *Corpus Juris Civilis* transmit a specific body of Christian doctrine of the state and the law. Rather it remained with a Roman and pagan conception of political and legal theory that was overlaid with Christian elements.

Index